READINGS IN LANGUAGE STUDIES

VOLUME 7

INTERSECTIONS OF PEACE AND LANGUAGE STUDIES

INTERNATIONAL SOCIETY FOR LANGUAGE STUDIES

READINGS IN LANGUAGE STUDIES

VOLUME 7

INTERSECTIONS OF PEACE
AND LANGUAGE STUDIES

EDITED BY

ERIN A. MIKULEC
SAI BHATAWADEKAR
CUHULLAN TSUYOSHI MCGIVERN
PAUL CHAMNESS IIDA

A PUBLICATION OF THE
INTERNATIONAL SOCIETY FOR LANGUAGE STUDIES, INC.

Copyright © 2018

International Society for Language Studies, Inc.
1968 S. Coast Hwy #142
Laguna Beach, CA, 92651, USA

All rights reserved.

ISBN 978-0-9964820-2-8 HARDCOVER
Library of Congress Control Number: 2008927091

ISBN 978-0-9964820-3-5 PAPERBACK
Library of Congress Control Number: 2008927091

Text design by One On One Book Production, West Hills, California

Cover art comes from the original painting of Fuente de Paz, by Hector Rolando Garza. Cover art reproduction of the painting used with permission from the artist. Those interested in his work may reach him at hgarza26@gmail.com.

This book was printed on acid-free paper.

Printed in the United States of America.

This volume is dedicated to all of those
who are struggling to live a life of peace,
and to those who speak out
to bring more peace to the world.

CONTENTS

Introduction		ix
1	Foreign Popular Media: Boon or Bane for Peaceful Educational Outcomes in Japanese University EFL Learning Contexts? *Brian G. Rubrecht*	1
2	For the Peace of Mind of Language Learners: Understanding Constraints on Learners in an EFL Environment *Chieko Mimura*	23
3	Identifying and Identifying With: A Critical Look into Student Interaction with Peace, Activism, Altruism, and Love in a Japanese University Setting *Kirk R. Johnson and Tim M. Murphey*	45
4	Peacebuilding and Social Justice in English as a Foreign Language: Classroom Experiences from a Colombian High School *Yecid Ortega*	63
5	Incorporating Peace Education into EFL *Maki Taniguchi*	91
6	Critical Foreign Language Pedagogy: Peace Education & Confronting and Negotiating Aggressive Situations *Gerrard Mugford*	111
7	Social Dispositions Against Women in Bangledesh: Using Critical Media Literacy to Promote Social Justice *Sabiha Sultana and K. C. Nat Turner*	133
8	Bilingual Teacher Candidates Speak of Peace, Language, and Identity: Reflecting on the Era of Restrictive Language Policies in California *Ana M. Hernández*	151
9	The Tattooed Body Speaks Peace: Centering the Male Brown Body as Language of Rebellion, Resilience, and Emancipation *Mia Angélica Sosa-Provencio and Tamara Anatska*	173

10	Pragmatic Acts of the Talking Drum in Pre-Colonial Yoruba Warfare and Peace Initiative *Waheed A. Bamigbade*	195
11	The Roles of Language Use in the Elusive Peace of the Nigerian Social and Political Landscapes *Babatunji Adepoju*	223
12	Investigating Language Politics Before and After the 2016 U. S. Election *Nicole King, Jackie Ridley, and Esther Yoon*	241
13	The Role of Language in the Western Sahara Conflict Between Algeria and Morocco *Kamal Belmihoub*	271
14	Waging War in the Language of Peace: The Use of Esperanto as the "Aggressor Language" by the U.S. Army *Timothy Reagan*	291
Index		315
About the Editors		319
About the Authors		323

INTRODUCTION

The International Society for Language Studies has its origins in a grassroots effort to bring together multiple disciplines around issues of language, power, and identity. In 2002, a group of international scholars began planning a conference that would eventually grow to forty papers, representing such diverse fields as medicine, law, education, and linguistics, presented the following year in St. Thomas, U.S. Virgin Islands. This fledging "society" was further advanced through its incorporation as a 501c(6) non-profit with the vision of founding a volunteer-based organization of scholars and practitioners committed to critical, interdisciplinary, and emergent approaches to language studies. Fast forward to 2018, we are well into our second decade as an organization, as well as wrapping up the fifteenth volume of the society's official journal, *Critical Inquiry in Language Studies*, published by Routledge/Taylor and Francis. Our first conference in Asia was successfully organized in 2014 in Akita, Japan, and we are currently planning our twelfth conference, our second in Asia, to be held at The Open University of Hong Kong in 2019. We have also been experimenting with recruiting universities to host our conferences in an effort to involve more local scholars in the planning process, as well as to offer greater savings to presenters and attendees facing ever-decreasing travel budgets. We are also delighted to have a formal travel grant competition available to support scholars who would otherwise be unable to afford conference participation.

International membership continues to grow, and throughout this period of growth the society has remained committed to disseminating the important scholarship of its members. This seventh volume of the *Readings in Language Studies* series, focusing on intersections of peace and language studies, represents ISLS's continued efforts to provide peer-reviewed fora as a reflection of its mission.

Readings in Language Studies, Volume 7: Intersections of Peace and Language Studies features international contributions that represent state-of-the-field reviews, multi-disciplinary perspectives, theory-driven syntheses of current scholarship, reports of new empirical research, reflections on pedagogical practices, and critical discussions of major topics centered on the intersection of language studies and peace. Consistent with the mission of ISLS, the collection of 13 chapters in this volume seeks to "bridge these arbitrary disciplinary territories and provide a forum for both theoretical and empirical research, from existing and emergent research methodologies, for exploring the relationships among language, power, discourses, and social practices."

Language and peace are in themselves incredibly complex concepts. They are simultaneously interpersonal in their function and effect as well as intimately personal in their experience. From everyday communication to the pragmatics of world diplomacy, from embracing a foreign culture to embarking upon a journey of self-awareness, language and peace are inseparably intertwined. To reveal their myriad interconnections, in local and global contexts, is a limitless task; nevertheless, we attempt to bring you a few glimpses from far corners of the world. It is also a linguistic and postcolonial mission of this society and the book series to publish the voices of non-native speakers of English. Decolonizing the academic enterprise is part of our commitment to diversity.

In Chapter 1, Brian Rubrecht explores the contradiction between the inherent peace that has been, at least in part, at the root of language learning and the many authentic materials such as music and movies that may have underlying themes of violence. In particular, his empirical study examines if foreign popular media, especially when such media contains violence, has an impact on Japanese learners of English in terms of their educational goals, their motivation to learn English, and "the mismatch in the nature and content experienced by learners of English and English-language culture" (Chap. 1, p. 7). One of the key findings from Rubrecht's study is that including foreign popular media with violent content may provide a venue for discussing conflict, as well as conflict resolution.

Through the lens of Bourdieu's notion of habitus and cultural capital, Chieko Mimura explores in Chapter 2 how students learning English view English education in Japan, and the inequality that exists among leaners. Mimura focuses on understanding how her students perceive the struggles that may impede language learning. One revelation from her students is that the inequality that comes with language learning may be perceived as symbolic violence. Finally, she addresses a critical finding in that it is important to avoid viewing English as the only cultural capital that learners bring to the classroom.

Kirk Johnson and Tim Murphey describe in Chapter 3 how they move beyond content-teaching to bringing students to recognize their agency. They address this topic in their English language classroom by considering abstract concepts that are often not openly discussed and by engaging their students in peace, activism, altruism, and love. The key questions Johnson and Murphey answer are, "To what extent would they *identify* these concepts as important in their own lives, and to what extent would they *identify* with these concepts as major guiding points in their lives?"

In an action research project, Yecid Ortega details in Chapter 4 what took place in an urban school in Bogota. In collaboration with an EFL teacher, she engaged her students in discussions related to bullying, intolerance, and violence at school. With a peacebuilding approach, Ortega reveals how students developed an awareness of the violence that is prevalent in the school setting.

In Chapter 5, Maki Taniguchi brings us into her classroom. Incorporating peace studies in EFL and weaving them both into each individual student's major is a model that should be implemented across the world in liberal arts education. The most striking aspect of Taniguchi's own pedagogy is encouraging her students to fearlessly connect with people across continents who have experienced terrorism first hand. This connection proved to be life-changing for her sensitive and motivated students, who will only go on to become agents of social change.

Gerrard Mugford offers the reader, in Chapter 6, an analysis of a peace education activity in Chapter 6 in which he engaged pre-service EFL teachers. He explores with his teacher trainees various approaches to address conflict that may arise in cross-cultural communication. By critically examining several real-life scenarios, Mugford develops a critical pedagogical framework for language educators to employ when faced with rejection, racial insults, and linguistic discrimination.

A very important moment of self-awareness in this volume comes from South Asia. Sabiha Sultana and K. C. Nat Turner's chapter (Chapter 7) reflects upon Sultana's childhood in Bangladesh and uses that reflection to raise her voice against the unequal and violent treatment of girls and women across the globe, against the stifling of their creativity and critical thinking. It is an excellent example, especially within gender studies, how the personal at once is and should be political.

Ana Hernández provides an important collection of voices of teacher candidates in Chapter 8. The candidates reveal their experiences during California's infamous ban on bilingual education – Proposition 227. They reflect on their struggle with their bilingual identity, the loss of language and its preservation. Hernández describes how the candidates garnered linguistic peace with their heritage language by seeking support from family, religious communities, the media, and other activities. Despite the ban having been lifted, bilingual teacher candidates continue to deal with language erosion, resulting in a struggle with Spanish academic language.

In Chapter 9, Mia Sosa-Provencio and Tamara Anatska present their ethnographic study on how tattoo artistry is used by Mexican/Mexican-American struggling class male tattoo artists as a representation of the language of peace, rebellion, resilience, and emancipation. This significant work offers the reader a deeper understanding of how Latino/Mexican-American males, living in an oppressive society, respond through the language of body art. Sosa-Provencio and Anatska aim at illustrating one way language can be used to promote peace.

Waheed Bamigbade's words take us beyond language in Chapter 10, or rather shows us how language itself is far beyond what we conventionally understand under that label. Pragmatically analyzing the Yoruba talking drum, Bamigbade examines how it quite literally "plays" a strategic sociocultural role in war and peace negotiations. The chapter is a rhythmic exploration into the Southwestern Nigerian region, where language, music, and peace merge in fascinating patterns.

Chapter 11 transports us in the middle of Nigeria's ethnic and political verbal wars. In addition to giving an informative sketch to those of us unfamiliar with the African context, Adepoju Babatunji, with his pragmatic linguistic analysis, encourages us to make cross cultural parallels, in order for all of us to be conscientious and compassionate citizens of multiethnic, multilingual societies.

In light of the political climate after the 2016 presidential election in the US, Nicole King, Jackie Ridley, and Esther Yoon explore in Chapter 12 how language choices of multilingual students are influenced by politics. Their qualitative study investigates multilingual students across languages and grade levels and the perceptions they had about their language rights in the United States before and after the 2016 presidential election. Their illuminating findings reveal a number of factors that have an impact on learners' perceptions of their linguistic rights.

Turning to politics in Northern Africa, in Chapter 13 Kamal Belmihoub presents an analysis of the language used by journalists in online French and English news sources. He offers the reader an eye-opening illustration of how language choice and the words used in reporting stories can marginalize, show bias, and favor one political view over another.

This volume of *Readings in Language Studies* closes with Chapter 14 where Timothy Reagan discusses the shocking history of Esperanto, a language that was created to promote harmony and community. Despite the purpose of peace as the goal of this language, the US Army used Esperanto for training exercises, and was used as the "aggressor language." Reagan reveals this as an example of how something created to promote peace and social justice can be subverted to do quite the opposite.

Since its inception, ISLS has had as its mission the bridging of disciplines around language studies with a particular emphasis on critical theory. With few venues, the Society, with its conference, journal, and publications initiative, now stands as a major advocate for this paradigm. *Readings in Language Studies, Volume 7,* represents contemporary issues, theory, and practices in language studies around issues of language and peace. Volume 8, scheduled for publication in 2019 will continue to focus on emergent international perspectives on the intersection of language and activism. This forthcoming volume, as well as future volumes, will further the Society's core mission and the work of its members.

CHAPTER 1

FOREIGN POPULAR MEDIA:
Boon or Bane for Peaceful Educational Outcomes in Japanese University EFL Learning Contexts?

Brian G. Rubrecht

Worldwide, students are required to learn English as a second or foreign language (ESL or EFL, respectively) at pre-tertiary education levels. In Japan, students receive eight years of compulsory English education prior to university matriculation (Fukuda, 2010). This means that after taking a year or two of English classes at university, the typical Japanese student will have ultimately been exposed to roughly a decade's worth of what may be termed filtered language and cultural content (FLCC).

This content is considered filtered because, much the same as in other institutional second or foreign language (L2/FL) teaching and learning situations, the students' English classes present them with formal aspects of English and English language culture (EELC) that are pre-selected because they are deemed appropriate for promoting educational goals (e.g., increasing students' knowledge and language abilities). Language classes, therefore, become sheltered havens from undesirable aspects extant in the target language and culture (e.g., expressions of violence, vulgar language) that run contrary to underlying institutional and educator goals of establishing and maintaining peace and harmony with others, and as such, are not incorporated into curricula.

Outside of the language classroom, though, ESL/EFL students are exposed to various forms of unfiltered linguistic input. This unfiltered language and cultural content (ULCC), being undidactic, has not been tailored to fit predetermined pedagogical goals. It may seem to many instructors that this "authentic" material is *prima facie* superior to anything created explicitly for classroom use because, being meant to be consumed by native language speakers/target culture individuals, it supposedly shows "more real" language as it is used in culturally-bound settings. However, such material, which includes Western movies and music, may not be unproblematic. Being unfiltered, such material may espouse that which didacticized material does not, such as violence and vulgar language, behavior that is unacceptable in the classroom. Thus, such material may contradict and impede the implicit goals of peace ensconced in the notion of democratic institutional learning by running contrary to what instructors teach, endorse, or permit in their classrooms.

Generally speaking, FLCC is intentionally positive, as it is purposefully designed or selected to further the educator's or institution's goals in regard to the students' learning and development. ULCC, on the other hand, is at best random in nature and at worst counterproductive to such goals, making its contributions to the aforementioned sought outcomes suspect. Due to its pervasive and unregulated nature, it is thought that ULCC nevertheless influences student perceptions of the target language and culture, particularly regarding English native speakers and their cultural attitudes, the result of which impacts institutional EELC learning goals. Whether or not these perceptions promote or hinder these goals has yet to be determined.

The current chapter aims to increase our understanding of ULCC's influence on learner perceptions of the English language and its speakers through a mixed-methods research study conducted with Japanese EFL university students. The study also aims to determine ULCC's influence on student perceptions of English native speakers, English language culture, and their overall purpose for learning. After relating information about authenticity, peace education, and foreign popular media, the chapter will present the specifics of the study, the research results and their analyses, and the conclusions drawn. The chapter will end with a discussion of the implications derived from the research and future research directions.

The Literature
The "Here" and "There" Dichotomy

Schmidt (1994) remarked that the main goal of modern language teaching is to enable learners to function in the target language/culture once they step outside of the language classroom. However, a long-recognized problem in L2/FL education circles is the clear demarcation that separates the "here" of the classroom from the "there" of the outside world. For many, this demarcation is metaphorical rather than simply the visible line in the classroom doorway separating the "here" of the classroom from the "there" of the hallway and all that lies beyond. As the job and desire of the L2/FL educator is to educate students so that they gain the necessary skills that will allow them to function in the specific target language/culture under study, language educators want their students to traverse that metaphorical chasm separating where the language is taught and learned from where the language can be used for meaningful unscripted and unsupervised communication. Put simply, the chasm is traversed when students utilize the skills and knowledge accrued from purposeful "here" classroom study.

Second and foreign language educators have traditionally sought to bridge this chasm by developing students' language skills that are ultimately transferable for communication purposes in the "there" (e.g., by teaching students grammar, vocabulary, and communication strategies). Many do this by incorporating pre-selected target language and culture aspects found in the "there" for use in the classroom. These aspects, commonly referred to as "authentic materials," are sought after and used because it is believed that such material will help students become more familiar with and accustomed to the target language and culture in ways and for purposes akin to those experienced by native speakers of that language.

Authentic Materials

Due to demands for "real life" language in the classroom, the need for authenticity in L2/FL teaching situations is clear and strong (Nikitina, 2011). Even so, there is little consensus regarding how to define material as being authentic (see Adams [1995] for a review of the popular early attempts at a definition, and Al-Surmi [2012], for later ones). It would appear *prima facie* that material constructed by native speakers of a language for other native speakers should not only be considered "authentic" but should also provide better examples (generally speaking) of how language is used in the "there" space. Although it fails to address language learning appropriateness or suitability in the "here" of the L2/FL classroom, Morrow's (1977, as cited in Gilmore, 2007) definition of authentic text comes as close as any to clearly delineating what "authentic" is typically understood or expected to mean: *language produced by a native speaker of the language for a native speaker audience, the purpose of which is to convey a message with meaning.* Instructors turn to various forms of target language and culture media as a means to span the "here" and "there" chasm because, being considered "authentic," they are meant to indicate to learners what language exists in the "there" space and how such language is used by native speakers/target culture persons.

Foreign Popular Media
Language instructors have long incorporated various forms of target language and culture media, otherwise termed "foreign popular media"[1] (hereafter, FPM), into their lessons. This FPM is usually viewed by all parties concerned to be both "authentic" (particularly when viewed through the lens of Morrow's previously-cited definition) and rich in providing benefits to the language acquisition process. Indeed, research from the 1990s (see Mejia & O'Connor, 1994; Numrich, 1990) through to the present (Al-Surmi, 2012; Ashcroft, 2015) has documented such benefits, which include increased proficiency stemming from increased target language input exposure (Lin, 2014), exposure to and experience of the dynamics of native speaker communication in cultural contexts (Stempleski, 1992; Telatnik & Kruse, 1992), and familiarity with cultural, historical, and political issues of the culture under study (Ashcroft, 2015). Wang's (2012) review of the literature indicates that the incorporating of audio and visual aids (i.e., FPM) into language lessons results in vocabulary retention (see specifically Canning-Wilson, 2000; see also Alipour, Gorjian, & Zafari, 2012; Medina, 2002) and increased and more efficient information processing by the brain (Oxford & Crookall, 1990).

More specific to the current study is the examination of "learning in informal settings" (Hung, Lee, & Lim, 2012). Foreign popular media consumption "there" is frequent (Sargsyan & Kurghinyan, 2016), especially with music used for English language learning (see especially the edited volume by Berns, de Bot, & Hasebrink, 2007; see also Baoan, 2008; Domoney & Harris, 1993; Grau, 2009). Music has been found to be pivotal in indicating English's importance in students' lives (Ranta, 2010). In Japan, English music is both consumed and constructed, for example, in J-pop (Takahashi & Calica, 2015).

Peace Education
Peace education, while not fully the focus of the current study, shares many aims and goals with underlying institutional and classroom policies. Like authentic material, there is a lack of consensus behind its definition (Trifonas & Wright, 2011), but put simply, peace education is directly concerned with the topics of peace and violence and their effects on society. Education in typical institutional settings functions on the same tenets that peace education proposes to instill in students and what peace education supporters envision for society as a whole. Peacemaking means accepting oneself and others, communicating effectively, resolving conflicts, and understanding intercultural differences (Nair & Nath, 2009).

However, in typical classroom situations, the default stance in creating peaceful and "ethical" classrooms is often a covert rather than an overt one involving "negative peace" or "the cessation or temporary prevention of overt violence" (Bickmore, 2011, p. 89). By simply blocking that which is negative, schools turn to the use of monitoring, which simultaneously influences the selection and incorporation of "authentic" material for classroom use (as previously explained) and functions as a gatekeeper for FPM (see the following).

Ban and Cummings' (1999) exhaustive content analysis of the curricula of Japanese and U.S. schools has revealed educational institutions in both countries attempt to instill in their respective student bodies the core values of compassion, cooperation, democracy, fairness, and tolerance, among others. Their findings are important, for they indicate that Japanese university EFL students are likely to be both accustomed to peaceful classroom displays (their own and others') and share with Westerners as well as their own peers the same concept of what constitutes peaceful behavior in the classroom.

Peace, Language Learners, and FPM
Gallagher-Brett (2005) explains that one reason for studying languages is "for citizenship." Because "citizenship is essentially about belonging, about feeling secure and being in a position to exercise one's rights and responsibilities" (Osler, 2005, p. 4), language learners would likely find the task of acquiring linguistic skills and cultural knowledge daunting, if not meaningless, if they were to perceive their language learning endeavors as opening them up to hostility, either physical or otherwise, either real or perceived. Language learners are those who, by virtue of engaging in the learning of the language and culture of others, are making attempts to become "citizens" of a different linguistic and cultural community. Should the target language or culture evince harmful terminology, attitudes, or physical demonstrations, be they to others in general or to the learners specifically, it is speculated that learners might be reluctant to engage in target language communication, or indeed, in general language learning endeavors overall.

Although L2/FL instructors have viewed FPM as authentic and thus beneficial language learning material (Ashcroft, 2015; Herron, York, Corrie, & Cole, 2006; Schoepp, 2001; Waldman, 2010), authenticity alone is insufficient justification for FPM inclusion into language lessons, as not all FPM evinces notions of peace. There is no shortage of Western movies or music presenting or expressing violent themes (Cardiner, 2015; Drexler, 2013). Because schools and the classrooms within them are meant to provide students a setting where peace may be both lived and experienced (Johnson & Johnson, 2005), FPM that depicts, describes, or promotes violence or that presents vulgar language, no matter how "authentic," would be deemed non-peaceful and would, barring special circumstances[2], be excluded by default from classroom-based language learning activities.

FPM in Japan

Media consumers in Japan are no strangers to violent film imagery or vulgar song lyrics, respectively, especially from foreign sources. For example, of the top 50 box office films of 2015 in Japan, 18 (36%) were of foreign origin (BoxOfficeMojo.com). Of these, 14 can be classified as action (read: violent) movies (e.g., *Avengers: The Age of Ultron*, *American Sniper*, *Mad Max: Fury Road*). These action movies accounted for 78% of the top foreign films that year.

Although violent FPM is neither all pervasive in Japan nor fully indicative of Western culture (for instance, Pixar's family-friendly *Inside Out* made the 2015 list), such media nevertheless is consumed in great quantity by the Japanese and present more or less realistic elements of Western language and culture. As such, one may suspect that such media can influence Japanese people's perceptions of Westerners and Western culture, potentially making FPM a form of "cultural violence" (Galtung, 1990), that is, making it a cultural form that furthers the legitimization of either structural violence or direct violence, particularly as it (a) acts as a representative of Western people and culture, and, in certain instances, (b) indicates that violence is acceptable and justified in the West, especially when expressing the ideology that violence is acceptable for general conflict resolution, escapes to or in the pursuit of freedom, or demonstrating personal growth[3].

The Research

The Research Impetus

It is at present unknown how and to what extent FPM, with its potential themes of violence, influences the perceptions of Japanese university English language learners regarding the English language and the target culture of English-speaking countries. Specifically, the present research study aimed to determine if FPM influences their perceived goals for education, if it promotes or hinders their motivation to learn English (especially when the FPM contains violent images or language), and if the mismatch in the nature and content experienced by learners of English and English-language culture via FPM "here" and "there" influences learners' language learning endeavors.

The Participants and Classes
The participants ($n = 170$, 80 males, 90 females) were Japanese university non-English majors from 11 classes at four different universities located in Tokyo, Japan. They were a mix of freshmen, sophomores, and juniors. All participants were students of the researcher, and all had given their consent to participate in the research. Several students (19) were excluded from the study (e.g., they were not native Japanese or they had lived many years abroad). Three students declined to participate in the research.

The Questionnaire
The questionnaire, which was written in Japanese, contained six sections. Section I asked the students to provide their background information (e.g., age, nationality). Section II asked the students to rate how strongly they agreed with a range of statements (see below) on a Likert scale between 1 ("strongly disagree") and 7 ("strongly agree") pertaining to their beliefs regarding the purpose of education and to indicate which they viewed as most important. Additional space was provided so that students could include additional beliefs and explain their answers. Sections III and IV asked about Western (i.e., English language) movies[4] and why Japanese would and would not watch such movies. The students were then asked to rate the influence of Western movies using the previously provided education statements and Likert scale and answer a series of questions about Western movies in their own lives. Sections V and VI closely mirrored Sections III and IV in asking similar questions about Western music, its influence, and the students' perception of it. At the end of the questionnaire, space was allotted for students to provide additional information not specifically asked for on the questionnaire.

Method
All students were informed of the purpose and voluntary nature of the study. Questionnaire administration was conducted for the various classes in a manner and at a time that was least disruptive to the classes and students. Questionnaire analyses were conducted by placing all student questionnaire responses into an Excel spreadsheet. The answers to the open-ended

questions were translated and categorized in order to look for patterns in the students' responses.

Focus Group Discussions
One class engaged in a focus group session whereby the students were split into three groups consisting of four to five students each. Each group was provided a digital audio recorder so that the researcher could later listen to, transcribe, and analyze what the students discussed. This class engaged in the focus group discussions because they were advanced-level English learners and had been specifically taught data-gathering methods (e.g., surveys, interviews, focus groups) as a part of their regular class lessons. The students were allowed to speak in either English or Japanese during the discussions, and they were instructed to take notes (to be handed in to the instructor later) if they wished. Discussions lasted less than 20 minutes.

Results
General
Before discussing the data results, it should first be noted that not all students answered all the questionnaire questions. This was not unexpected, as (a) most students were not particularly concerned with English language studies, and (b) there were multiple open-ended questions. Second, some data calculations did not add up to the total number of student participants, as (a) some students claimed to not consume foreign media, leading them to leave some questionnaire questions unanswered, and (b) some students provided multiple answers to some of the open-ended questions. Third, in order to avoid accidentally priming the students, the questionnaire made no explicit mention of the themes of peace or violence. Thus, any statements made by the students about peace or violence in regard to FPM came solely from the perceptions of the students themselves. Finally, students' responses regarding why they specifically did not view FPM as violent or vulgar were also taken into consideration for data analysis purposes.

Section I: Background Information

The average age of the participants was 19. Only 47 students (28%) provided TOEIC or TOEFL scores, but being students of the researcher, a majority of the students could be classified as low- to high-intermediate-level English language learners. Around 20 or so students could be classified as high beginners, with a similar number labeled as advanced learners, as some students (i.e., some focus group students) had TOEIC scores surpassing 800.

Section II: The Purpose of Education

To understand students' views of the purpose of public education in general (i.e., the education they had received/currently receive in the Japanese education system), the students were presented with the following nine categories and were asked to rate them via the previously-mentioned 1-to-7 Likert scale:

1. To gain new knowledge (e.g., about math, science, other cultures, the world)
2. To learn new skills (e.g., math skills, language skills, science skills)
3. To learn to work well with others (e.g., to cooperate, to listen to others' opinions)
4. To learn about who you are as a person, as an individual (e.g., find out what you enjoy, how you want to live your life)
5. To allow you more employment opportunities (e.g., to get a higher paying job)
6. To learn how to be a responsible member of society (e.g., to be a morally proper person)
7. To learn how to be a peaceful world citizen (e.g., to understand and accept people from other cultures, to promote peace toward others)
8. To learn how to be independent from your parents (e.g., to support yourself financially)
9. To learn how to make Japan prosperous (e.g., economically strong)

For brevity, these categories will henceforth be referred to as Category 1, Category 2, and so on (or C1, C2, etc., for short), respectively. Also for brevity, when reporting responses, only the top three most common responses (hereafter called R1, R2, and R3) will be listed.

When rating the nine categories, the students responded in the following manner, with the number of responses in parentheses:

Table 1.1
*Top Three Most Prevalent Ratings for
Participants' Views on the Purpose of Education*

	R1	R2	R3
C1	5 (50)	6 (42)	4 (38)
C2	6 (49)	5 (45)	4 (37)
C3	6 (50)	5 (47)	4 (35)
C4	4 (47)	5 (43)	6 (33)
C5	6 (56)	7 (48)	5 (34)
C6	6 (58)	5 (43)	4 (29)
C7	4 (56)	3 (34)	5 (32)
C8	4 (42)	5 (36)	6 (33)
C9	4 (51)	3 (37)	5 (28)

As Table 1.1 shows, most ratings are in the 4-to-6 range, indicating overall moderate to slightly strong agreement with the provided categories. Thus, the participants overall appeared accepting of the purposes for education listed to them. Several students (30) proffered their own differing categories and gave them ratings mostly between 5 and 7. These categories focused largely on reasons related to opening one's world to get different points of view, making friends in society, and gaining experiences.

When asked to ascertain which three categories were most pertinent to education, Categories 5, 1, and 3 received the most responses (93, 77, and 67 responses, respectively), indicating that the participants generally believed education is primarily meant to help learners gain employment opportunities, acquire knowledge, and learn to cooperate and work well with others, respectively. These responses made sense, as university matriculation is traditionally the last step before entering the job market, university is ostensibly for learning knew information and gaining knowledge, and Japan is a collectivistic society that ingrains group mentality and a focus on others from a young age (see Dien, 1999; Nishiyama, 2000).

Section III: Western Movie Background
In this section the students were asked if they watched Western (i.e., English language) movies, to which 121 students (71%) answered affirmatively. It was

found that the FPM-consuming students both overwhelmingly normally watch (96 students) and prefer to watch (70 students) English language movies with the aid of Japanese subtitles. Of the 45 students who answered that they did not watch Western movies, only 13 explained why they did not, with the two most common reasons being that they either do not watch movies much in general or that they watch Japanese movies only.

When asked why Japanese people in general would watch Western movies, the five most common responses were: better quality than Japanese movies (i.e., larger scale, more action; 69 students), stories are good/interesting (51), a means to learn English (14), admiration of/desire to be in contact with Western culture (13), and movies are movies (i.e., all are entertainment; 12 students). As for why they would not watch such movies: language-related reasons (e.g., do not like/poor at English, prefer Japanese; 34 students), dislike Western movies (e.g., not interesting; 18 students), nothing lost if not watched (e.g., watch Japanese movies, pursuing other interests; 14 students), dislike of subtitles/dubbed voices (7), and find expressions of Western culture to be too different (7). These answers reveal that the students are cognizant of large Hollywood movie budgets and the reason for them being *omoshiroi* ("interesting") and *sukeeru wa ookii* ("they are large scale"). Also of note here is that the reasons why the students believed Japanese people might not watch Western movies are largely source language (i.e., English) related and have little to do with movie content.

All but five participants provided open-ended question responses here. The objectively negative aspects of the English language and Western culture were mentioned only three times and centered on depressing Western movie themes (e.g., the destruction or near-annihilation of the human race, as in *The Day After Tomorrow*) or Western movies being too forceful with an overall *kowai* ("scary") image (e.g., *The Cabin in the Woods*).

Section IV: Western Movie Influence
To determine students' beliefs regarding Western movie influence on their educational goals, they again rated the previous nine categories with this new criterion in mind. The results are in Table 1.2 as follows:

Table 1.2
Top Three Most Prevalent Ratings for Participants' Views on the Impact of Western Movies on the Purpose of Education

	R1	R2	R3
C1	4 (58)	5 (46)	6 (30)
C2	4 (45)	5 (40)	3 (30)
C3	4 (44)	3 (39)	5 (36)
C4	4 (52)	5 (39)	3 (29)
C5	4 (43)	3 (42)	2 (41)
C6	4 (56)	2 (31)	3 (29)
C7	4 (48)	5 (34)	2 (25)
C8	2 (40)	4 (39)	3 (37)
C9	4 (43)	2 (42)	3 (32)

These responses were considerably more moderate, with ratings of the median "4" being the most common first-choice rating. Thus, overall, the students found Western movies to not be directly related to their educational goals, the only exception to this being how the students somewhat believed that Western movies can provide new knowledge. This latter finding was supported by the open-ended responses, which included students remarking that Western movies allow them to (a) learn about others' opinions, (b) gain new perspectives about the world (especially without having to travel), and (c) experience and examine cultural differences between East and West. High-level students gave a few language-related responses here (e.g., English language movies provide English listening opportunities, English language movies boost their language learning motivation). One student mentioned that if the purpose of watching a movie is for language study, then any foul language used in the movie is really of little concern. Although only eight students provided additional categories here, they indicated how students generally believed that movies are an easily accessible route for them to come into contact with Western culture and English pronunciation. Again, these responses were written by the high-level students.

At this point, the students were asked directly about Western movies presenting a positive or negative image of Western culture and people to the typical Japanese person and to themselves specifically:

Table 1.3
*Views of Western Movies Presenting
Positive or Negative Images of Western Culture/People*

	For Japanese		For students	
	Positive	Negative	Positive	Negative
Image of Western culture	143	23	149	15
Image of Western people	134	28	136	23

As seen in Table 1.3, responses were overall indicative of positive impressions. If any students found on-screen violence or vulgar language usage to be positive, none mentioned as much. The students who found Western movies to present negative images of Western culture and people often explained that violence was specifically the reason: "They sometimes use pistols, and that makes Japanese people scared." "There are many Western movies which features [sic] war, battle. This might present a negative image." "Sometimes there is violence [sic] situation. Some Japanese might think the country in movie is scary."

The open-ended responses here included several comments regarding Western movies often portraying gangs, casual drug use, racial discrimination, and general scenes of fighting, war, cruelty, and death. The negative views offered here were often used in conjunction with the word "*osoroshii*" ("frightening"). Thus, the potentially negative aspects shown in Western movies such as guns, drugs, and fighting with others are precisely what students, Japanese or otherwise, are taught to avoid when learning in the public education system.

Of particular importance here is that Table 1.3 reveals relatively few instances of negative responses. While the students generally find Western movies to be large in scale, interesting, and at times beneficial English-learning material (at least for the high-level students), they note their drawbacks, for they bring with them images of Western life and people that are at times at odds with Japanese life and Japanese people's sensibilities. Based on the negative responses (or more importantly, the overall lack thereof), these images do not appear sufficient to negatively influence the ways in which the students relate to each other or to the world around them or have an undesirable bearing on their language learning endeavors.

Section V: Western Music Background

In this section, the students were asked if they listened to Western music, with 123 (72%) reporting that they did, but 80 students (65%) reported listening to such music half the time or less when listening to music. Self-reporting about their music listening habits indicated that while the students were generally aware of or listened to Western music, most only listened to such music passively (e.g., as background music in coffee shops or via television commercials).

When asked why Japanese people might not listen to Western music, the most common responses were that listeners (a) do not understand the lyrics, (b) prefer other types of music, or (c) have no interest in music. There was no mention whatsoever of violent themes or vulgar language in Western music.

Section VI: Western Music Influence

For this final section, the nine categories were again presented, and the students rated the influence of Western music on their educational goals:

Table 1.4
Top Three Most Prevalent Ratings for Participants' Views on the Impact of Western Music on the Purpose of Education

	R1	R2	R3
C1	5 (43)	4 (43)	2 (26)
C2	5 (41)	4 (32)	6 (28)
C3	4 (48)	3 (37)	2 (36)
C4	4 (46)	5 (29)	3 (28)
C5	2 (43)	4 (42)	1 (36)
C6	2 (42)	4 (38)	3 (37)
C7	4 (45)	3 (32)	2 (30)
C8	2 (45)	1 (42)	3 (39)
C9	3 (43)	1 (40)	2 (39)

Comparisons between the results in Table 1.4 with those of Table 1.2 reveal that the students overall find Western music to present less of an impact on their education than Western movies. The open-ended responses strengthened this stance, as several students specifically wrote that there is no relation between Western music and educational goals. Additionally, only 5 students added their own categories here, which were related only to learning English (e.g., pronunciation, rhyming words) and to feeling a foreign atmosphere. These responses were, again, provided only by the high-level students.

When asked their views regarding positive or negative images that Western music presents of Western culture and people to Japanese people in general and to the students themselves specifically, the following results were revealed:

Table 1.5
*Views of Western Music Presenting
Positive or Negative Images of Western Culture/People*

	For Japanese		For students	
	Positive	Negative	Positive	Negative
Image of Western culture	148	12	142	17
Image of Western people	140	13	138	12

The results of Table 1.5 are only slightly different from those found in Table 1.3 (*Views of Western movies presenting positive or negative images of Western culture/people*). Of the negative responses, several included comments about how the rhythm of Western music is too loud or forceful compared to Japanese music, and only one directly mentioned violence: "There are many songs about war and race" (translated from Japanese). One other written response was vague but could be interpreted as concern over offensive language or themes found in Western music: "Some people do not like what is contained in the lyrics" (translated from Japanese).

Focus Group Results
Because the focus group discussions occurred after questionnaire analyses, which had revealed few responses related to FPM violence or vulgar language, the students were instructed to specifically discuss their views on violence in such media. In the focus group discussions, all three groups (a) mentioned violent Western movie titles (e.g., the *Biohazard* franchise), (b) attributed Western movie violence to large production budgets, and (c) found movie violence an often-necessary film element, as films become deeper and more meaningful if there is a hero protecting others (i.e., "the guy saves the girl").

The students in all three groups unequivocally indicated disdain for violence. However, several mentioned that the world is a better place because of violent movies, for they are just "dynamic" entertainment. Two groups equated FPM to forms of art. Being art, it need not be appreciated or even experienced by all people. People will consume FPM because "if people like it, they will enjoy it, and if they do not, they won't. It is up to the individual" (translated from Japanese).

Western music discussions were less clear. Several students were unsure how such music could be considered violent, while several others mentioned genres that were either typically loud (e.g., heavy metal) or that contained dirty words (e.g., rap music). One group mentioned how lyrics explaining drug use must necessarily make such music violent and how vulgar language is the reason why some genres of music sell so well in the West. In general, however, much like for movies, the students in the focus groups generally believed that people will listen to the music that they are interested in and, like the movies they consume if they are inclined to do so, can present things to be learned.

Discussion

Although the students in the present study expressed a clear awareness of FPM, they did not appear to be great consumers of such media, which, given the pervasiveness of FPM in Japan, went against expectations. Low FPM consumption came from personal preferences, and as such, the content of such media – be it violent, vulgar, or otherwise – was of little concern to them. Thus, in answer to the research questions regarding FPM's influence on Japanese university English language learners' perceptions of the English language, the target culture of English-speaking countries, and their motivation to learn English, it appears that outside of exceptional cases the influence on these areas is minimal.

For the students in this study, questionnaire results suggest that the occasional displays of violence or instances of vulgar language in FPM acts as neither a draw for nor a deterrent to FPM consumption. While the students were cognizant of the differences between Western and Japanese popular media, they rarely characterized FPM as violent or vulgar. Rather than categorize FPM on good/bad or positive/negative dichotomies, the students' take was to just say that such media is artistic expression and that, being different from Japanese media, liking, disliking, interest in, or effects from such media ultimately rests on individual tastes and preferences.

Consequently, given that the students rarely characterized FPM as being harmful or detrimental to their learning by being either violent or vulgar and because they did not find a direct relationship between FPM and their learning, the conclusion drawn from the current research study is that FPM cannot specifically be considered an obstruction for English language university students to the notions and ideals of peace on their educational goals and on their perceptions of English speakers and English target language culture. FPM violence (e.g., guns, drug use) was attributed to differences in culture, but such violent themes were balanced out by FPM's perceived positive aspects (e.g., inexpensive and easy access to the West, language learning opportunities).

Although care should always be taken concerning the generalizing of research results to larger populations, several implications can be drawn from the current research. First, if the study participants are indicative of typical Japanese university students, such students find FPM largely unrelated to education or to their learning endeavors, the exception being high-level students or students who have a specific interest in the English language or in Western culture. Additionally, FPM consumption is attributed mainly to individual preferences and tastes. Given these findings, it is recommended that educators not automatically assume that FPM will necessarily be a draw for students in the "here" of the classroom, particularly for low-level students. The takeaway from the current study is that there should ideally be an initial sound pedagogical rationale for the inclusion of FPM, as well as sound reasoning for the type and amount of FPM to be included. Claims of authenticity, however cogent, are insufficient for FPM inclusion in all educational contexts.

Second, educator apprehension regarding the use of FPM that includes violent themes or vulgar language may not necessarily be justified. As "a culture presented as uniform and without complexity is likely to be stereotyped to the point of absurdity" (Starkey, 2005, p. 30), educators need not avoid at all costs FPM that contain violent themes or vulgar language. Any FPM utilized for learning purposes should ultimately pass a "fitness to the learning purpose" test (Hutchinson & Waters, 1987, as cited in Gilmore, 2007). If there are cogent pedagogical reasons for its inclusion in a lesson, violent/vulgar FPM may actually provide educators opportunities to discuss cultural differences, conflict, and conflict resolution with students. Future research could therefore center on determining if and how utilizing violent/vulgar FPM in the "here" of the classroom can spur and nurture students to become global citizens with concerns for creating and maintaining peace in "here" spaces in the short term and in "there" spaces for the rest of their lives.

References

Adams, T. W. (1995). *What makes materials authentic.* (ERIC Document Reproduction Service No. ED391389)

Al-Surmi, M. (2012). Authenticity and TV shows: A multidimensional analysis perspective. *TESOL Quarterly, 46*(4), 671-694. doi:10.1002/tesq.33

Alipour, M., Gorjian, B., & Zafari, I. (2012). The effects of songs on EFL learners' vocabulary recall and retention: The case of gender. *Advances in Digital Multimedia, 1*(3), 140-143.

Ashcroft, R. J. (2015). Exploiting movies effectively. In P. Clements, A. Krause, & H. Brown (Eds.), *JALT2014 Conference Proceedings* (pp. 596-604). Tokyo, Japan: JALT.

Ban, T., & Cummings, W. K. (1999). Moral orientations of schoolchildren in the United States and Japan. *Comparative Education Review, 43*(1), 64-85.

Baoan, W. (2008). Application of popular English songs in EFL classroom teaching. *Humanising Language Teaching, 10*(3). Retrieved from http://www.hltmag.co.uk/jun08/less03.htm

Berns, M., de Bot, K., & Hasebrink, U. (2007). *In the presence of English: Media and European youth.* New York, NY: Springer.

Bickmore, K. (2011). Education for "peace" in urban Canadian schools: Gender, culture, conflict, and opportunities to learn. In P. P. Trifonas & B. Wright (Eds.), *Critical issues in peace and education* (pp. 88-103). Abingdon Oxon, UK: Routledge.

Box Office Mojo. (2018). *Japan yearly box office.* Retrieved from http://www.boxofficemojo.com/intl/japan/yearly/?yr=2015&p=.htm

Canning-Wilson, C. (2000). Practical aspects of using video in the foreign language classroom. *The Internet TESL Journal, 6*(11). Retrieved from http://iteslj.org/Articles/Canning-Video.html

Cardiner, B. (2015). #HSTBT: The first hip-hop album to carry a "Parental Advisory" sticker. Retrieved from http://www.highsnobiety.com/2015/08/13/ice-t-rhyme-pays-first-hip-hop-album-parental-advisory/

Dien, D. S.-f. (1999). Chinese authority-directed orientation and Japanese peer-group orientation: Questioning the notion of collectivism. *Review of General Psychology, 3*(4), 372-385. doi:10.1037//1089-2680.3.4.372

Domoney, L., & Harris, S. (1993). Justified and ancient: Pop music in EFL classrooms. *ELT Journal, 47*(3), 234-241. doi:10.1093/elt/47.3.234

Drexler, P. (2013). Violence in movies: More, bigger–worse. *Psychology Today.* Retrieved from https://www.psychologytoday.com/blog/our-gender-ourselves/201311/violence-in-movies-more-bigger-worse

Fukuda, T. (2010). Elementary schools to get English. *The Japan Times.* Retrieved from http://www.japantimes.co.jp/news/2010/06/29/news/elementary-schools-to-get-english/#.Vun2fkatSbd

Gallagher-Brett, A. (2005). Seven hundred reasons for studying languages. *The Higher Education Academy.* Retrieved from https://www.llas.ac.uk/resourcedownloads/6063/700_reasons.pdf

Galtung, J. (1990). Cultural violence. *Journal of Peace Research, 27*(3), 291-305. doi:10.1177/0022343390027003005

Gilmore, A. (2007). Authentic materials and authenticity in foreign language learning. *Language Teaching, 40*(2), 97-118. doi:10.1017/S0261444807004144

Grau, M. (2009). Worlds apart? English in German youth cultures and in educational settings. *World Englishes, 28*(2), 160-174. doi:10.1111/j.1467-971X.2009.01581.x

Herron, C., York, H., Corrie, C., & Cole, S. P. (2006). A comparison study of the effects of a story-based video instructional package versus a text-based instructional package in the intermediate-level foreign language classroom. *CALICO Journal, 23*(2), 281-307. doi:10.1.1.333.5082

Hung, D., Lee, S.-S., & Lim, K. Y. T. (2012). Authenticity in learning for the twenty-first century: Bridging the formal and the informal. *Educational Technology Research and Development, 60*(6), 1071-1091. doi:10.1007/s11423-012-9272-3

Hutchinson, T., & Waters, A. (1987). *English for specific purposes: A learning-centered approach.* Cambridge, UK: Cambridge University Press.

Johnson, D. W., & Johnson, R. T. (2005). Essential components of peace education. *Theory Into Practice, 44*(4), 280-292. doi:10.1207/s15430421tip4404_2

Lin, P. M. S. (2014). Investigating the validity of internet television as a resource for acquiring L2 formulaic sequences. *System, 42*, 164-176. http://dx.doi.org/10.1016/j.system.2013.11.010

Medina, S. L. (2002). Using music to enhance second language acquisition: From theory to practice. Retrieved from https://www.scribd.com/document/125157425/Using-Music-to-Enhance-Second-Language-Acquisition-From-Theory-to-Practice

Mejia, E. A., & O'Connor, F. H. (1994). *Five star films: An intermediate listening/speaking text.* Englewood Cliffs, NJ: Prentice Hall Regents.

Morrow, K. (1977). Authentic texts and ESP. In S. Holden (Ed.), *English for specific purposes* (pp. 13-17). London, UK: Modern English Publications.

Nair, S. S., & Nath, B. K. (2009). Integrating principles of peace through effective transaction. (ERIC Document Reproduction Service No. ED507654)

Nikitina, L. (2011). Creating an authentic learning environment in the foreign language classroom. *International Journal of Instruction, 4*(1), 33-46.

Nishiyama, K. (2000). *Doing business with Japan: Successful strategies for intercultural communication.* Honolulu, HI: University of Hawai'i Press.

Numrich, C. (1990). *Face the issues: Intermediate listening and critical thinking skills.* White Plains, NY: Longman.

Osler, A. (2005). Education for democratic citizenship: New challenges in a globalised world. In A. Osler & H. Starkey (Eds.), *Citizenship and language learning: International perspectives* (pp. 3-22). Stoke on Trent, UK: Trentham Books.

Oxford, R., & Crookall, D. (1990). Vocabulary learning: A critical analysis of techniques. *TESL Canada Journal, 7*(2), 9-30. https://doi.org/10.18806/tesl.v7i2.566

Ranta, E. (2010). English in a real world vs. English at school: Finnish English teachers' and students' views. *International Journal of Applied Linguistics, 20*(2), 156-177. doi:10.1111/j.1473-4192.2009.00235.x

Sargsyan, M., & Kurghinyan, A. (2016). The use of English language outside the classroom. *Journal of Language and Cultural Education, 4*(1), 29-47. doi:10.1515/jolace-2016-0003

Schmidt, T. Y. (1994). *Authenticity in ESL: A study of requests* (Master's thesis). (ERIC Document Reproduction Service No. ED415686)

Schoepp, K. (2001). Reasons for using songs in the ESL/EFL classroom. *The Internet TESL Journal, 7*(2). Retrieved from http://iteslj.org/Articles/Schoepp-Songs.html

Starkey, H. (2005). Language teaching for democratic citizenship. In A. Osler & H. Starkey (Eds.), *Citizenship and language learning: International perspectives* (pp. 23-39). Stoke on Trent, UK: Trentham Books.

Stempleski, S. (1992). Teaching communication skills with authentic video. In S. Stempleski & P. Arcario (Eds.), *Video in second language teaching: Using, selecting, and producing video for the classroom* (pp. 7-24). Alexandria, VA: TESOL.

Takahashi, M., & Calica, D. (2015). *The significance of English in Japanese popular music: English as a means of message, play, and character.* Proceedings from the 21st Meeting of the Association for Natural Language Processing (pp. 869-871).

Telatnik, M. A., & Kruse, W. D. (1992). Cultural videotapes for the ESL classroom. In M. Geddes & G. Sturtridge (Eds.), *Video in second language teaching: Using, selecting, and producing video for the classroom* (pp. 171-181). London, UK: Heinemann Educational Books.

Trifonas, P. P., & Wright, B. (2011). Introduction. In P. P. Trifonas & B. Wright (Eds.), *Critical issues in peace and education* (pp. 1-7). Abingdon Oxon, UK: Routledge.

Waldman, E. (2010). Teaching and learning through music in the contact zones. *The Language Teacher, 34*(6), 70-73.

Wang, Y.-C. (2012). Learning L2 vocabulary with American TV drama. *English Language Teaching, 5*(8), 217-225. doi: http://dx.doi.org/10.5539/elt.v5n8p217

Notes
1. In this chapter the term "media" is used as a collective noun and is therefore treated as being singular rather than plural.
2. For example, video clips of "The Three Stooges," a decidedly violent American comedy trio, may be used to illustrate Western slapstick comedy.
3. Examples, respectively, are the endings of any of the *Die Hard* movies, *Escape Plan*, and *Back to the Future* (i.e., when George McFly knocks out Biff in the parking lot).
4. The questionnaire only asked students' opinions about Western movies and not other video media (e.g., Western television shows). This was done primarily to simplify the questionnaire but also because it was speculated that if the students consumed foreign visual media it would most likely be in the form of movies (e.g., either at movie theaters, through video rental establishments, or via online sources).

CHAPTER 2

FOR THE PEACE OF MIND OF LANGUAGE LEARNERS:
Understanding Constraints on Learners in an EFL Environment

Chieko Mimura

In a globalized world, it is considered essential to be able to communicate in a shared language, and proficiency in English is believed to be key to success in global business, education, information technology, communication, and various other areas of human society. World Englishes and English as a *lingua franca* are concepts of global English that promote equality and connectedness of people in the world by means of English. However, globalization and English also have the potential to cause inequality. English as a *lingua franca* may be a false assumption in that it supposes English as "neutral, free of cultural ties, and serves all equally well" (Phillipson, 2009, p. 338). However, a widely-discussed issue is linguistic imperialism (Phillipson, 1992), and the suppression of minority languages, mother tongues, indigenous languages, and varieties is even described as "genocide" (Skutnabb-Kangas, 2009, p. 340), therefore suggesting that English learning can be counterproductive when considering issues of equality and peace.

Issues of linguistic imperialism aside, however, globalization creates discourse that English is a symbolic form of capital. According to Bourdieu (1986), capital is presented in three forms: economic capital, cultural capital, and social capital, all of which can shift into one another to some degree (p. 243). A "strong" language such as English is considered to have symbolic power (i.e., symbolic capital), and therefore also offers cultural/

linguistic capital (i.e., "knowledge, skills, and other cultural acquisitions, as exemplified by educational or technical qualifications;" Thompson, 1991, p. 4), which can be translated into economic capital (i.e., job opportunities) as well as social capital (i.e., networking; Bourdieu, 1986). It is understood that by learning a second language (e.g., English), learners are investing in their future and expect to acquire a wider range of symbolic and material resources (e.g., Norton, 2000).

However, opportunities for learning a second language are not equal across learners. According to cross-cultural studies, access to resources and speakers of English and the resulting efficiency in learning the language is affected by various social identities, such as race, ethnicity, and gender (e.g., Kanno & Varghese, 2010; McKay & Wong, 1996; Morita, 2004; Norton, 2000; Shin, 2014). In addition to these factors, underexplored preconditions also affect language learning, such as social class, social status, life conditions, and social practices (Darvin & Norton, 2014; Vandrick, 2011). From my years of teaching experience, I have noticed that social factors have a crucial impact on language learning in a country like Japan, which belongs to the expanding circle in Kachru's (1985) global English model.

This chapter is part of my ongoing investigation into gaps and inequality in English education in Japan that can be attributed to globalization. Specifically, by describing individual English learners and their social conditions and practices, I will identify various preconditions that may hinder English language learning and those preconditions coming from habitus (Bourdieu, 1991). I also describe the symbolic power of English in Japan and how this causes language learners to sway between feelings of limitation and feelings of freedom. Finally, I link the empirical side of my study back to the theoretical investigation of habitus and symbolic power. The implications and suggestions of this study include possibilities for a peaceful alternative to the often-criticized language education system that creates inequality.

Gaps and Inequality in English Education in Japan
English as a *lingua franca* for wider communication was mentioned in education policy in Japan as early as the 1980s (The Provisional Council of Education Reform, 1986), and in the year 2000 the Japanese government

issued a strong statement about making English a second official language as a strategic imperative in the 21st century Japan (The Prime Minister's Commission on Japan's Goals in the 21st Century, 2000). More recently, "nurturing global human resources" has been a popular slogan, not only in education but also in business and other areas. For the past 20 years, the government, as well as business sectors, have issued a succession of policies and recommendations aimed at all Japanese people developing English skills. In addition, the focus of policies in recent years has shifted to favor supporting elite education with profuse subsidies and increasing opportunities to a limited number of elite universities and individuals (e.g., the top global university project in 2014; Ministry of Education, Culture, Sports, Science and Technology, 2013). This has created a huge gap between the elite and non-elite, as well as between government policies and reality. Under these policies, which give preferential treatment to the elite, the average high school student will find it difficult to develop the English skills the government recommends, let alone enjoy studying English. A prime example of this is that the majority of public high school students dislike English and almost 90 percent of them are at the A1 level (Breakthrough Beginner) of the Common European Framework of Reference for Languages (CEFR; Ministry of Education, Culture, Sports, Science and Technology, 2014).

In addition, a number of government plans do not seem to be working well for non-elite high school students. For example, contrary to the government belief that native speakers are a necessity in order to provide a better environment for English learning, as illustrated by the government policy of hiring native speakers, my interviews and informal talks with my students indicate that they did not necessarily feel comfortable interacting with English native speaker teachers. Additionally, starting English education at an early age has been promoted since the year 2000 (Japan Federation of Economic Organizations, 2000), despite having been met with criticism (e.g., Otsu, 2005), and despite poor results in achievements in English learning. The government will finally make teaching English in primary school mandatory in 2018. The gap between the elite/government and the non-elite/unsuccessful English learners looks set to continue and even widen in the future.

The government, as well as educators, should be aware of this gap and not ignore the students who are not on the "right" track in terms of globalization. In other words, even though some students might not develop into the government's ideal of English-speaking global citizens, it is not appropriate to blame those students for lack of effort in language learning. Rather, I would argue that some aspects of the students' backgrounds, such as their educational background, family background, and/or economic background, may hinder their academic success, and therefore language study, and that more focus should be given to these students. As Block (2014) states, "'who language learners are' is surely a factor that needs to be taken into account" (p. 162).

Looking beyond the backgrounds of individual learners, Japan's English education system has faced criticism for a long time. This criticism includes, but is not limited to, the fact that English is dominating in Japan, creating "English imperialism" (e.g., Torikai, 2010), English is not used as a *lingua franca* in multicultural communication settings in Japan (Kubota, 2011; Kubota & McKay, 2009), English as symbolic capital stratifies society and people (Kubota, 2011; Okado, 2015; Saito, 2004), simply learning English alone does not serve to nurture global human resources (Naruke, 2013; Torikai, 2010), and early English education in Japan faces many obstacles, ranging from children's cognitive development to limitations in infrastructure and teacher resources (Ichikawa, 2004; Otsu, 2005). Despite such criticisms, the government, as well as the economic sector, is still vehemently promoting English. It is time to shift from criticism to finding solutions for the students who may never in their lives need English for interpersonal communication. This shift means considering solutions which involve the possibility of not teaching or learning English, instead of only considering how to teach and learn the language.

Bourdieu's Habitus to Explain Individual Language Learners
Bourdieu's concepts of habitus, cultural capital, and social reproduction have been applied to social research, especially in the analysis of power, domination, and cultural superiority/inferiority. In second language research, a common understanding of these concepts is that habitus, as defined as "dispositions"

(Bourdieu, 1991), is the social conditions of language learners, such as their social class, family background, and educational background, and that these conditions affect the acquisition of cultural capital, that is English. As English is cultural capital, which can be turned into economic capital (i.e., job opportunities), as well as social capital (i.e., networking; Bourdieu, 1991), it serves to reproduce social inequality (e.g., Shin, 2014), otherwise known as the "English divide" (Shin, 2014; Terasawa, 2015).

According to Bourdieu, education plays a crucial role in the ability to accumulate cultural capital and convert it into economic and academic achievements, thus embodying habitus and reproducing power relations in society. Educational institutions also impose mainstream values. In terms of the English education system, imposing English on those who do not need it and those who do not have equal access to language resources is an act of "symbolic violence" (Bourdieu & Passeron, 1990).

In this way, Bourdieu's concepts are easily applied to explain the education system. However, as Reay (2004) argues, there is an increasing tendency for habitus to be "sprayed…without doing any theoretical work" (p. 432). One of the issues is related to the criticism of the concept of habitus as deterministic without any allowance for individual agency. Kanno and Verghese (2010) explain habitus as "students' acceptance of the status quo" (p. 313), which is "ESL habitus" (p. 321). On the other hand, the common notion of investment (Norton, 2000) is based on the language learners' agency and ability to break the habitus; and similarly, as Menard-Warwick (2005) states, a "thorough-going process of counter training, involving repeated exercises, can durably transform habitus" (p. 255). I would argue that habitus may not be at the level of being breakable; it is another dimension, which I will return to later in this chapter.

My Project: Hearing Students' Voices

My focus is a detailed description of each language learner and her or his experiences of learning English. Beyond that, I do not intend to draw any generalizations or patterns, but I do attempt to understand the shared values, behaviors, and feelings of the English learners.

I set the scene in Sugino Fashion College (hereafter, Sugino), where I have been teaching since 2002. In terms of English, I have felt the lower end of the stratification that I discussed in the beginning of this paper: the government's policies of globalization sound irrelevant to the school, most students' English skills are far from the level required for global communication, and many students seem almost distressed about studying English even before entering the school. However, the students are talented in a different area, in art and fashion. Sugino is a private, bachelor-degree-based college, where students major in fashion design or fashion business. The school requires students to study a foreign language, choosing from English, French, or Chinese, with the majority of students enrolling in English classes.

The selection process of choosing participants for my study was carried out in an unsystematic fashion; I randomly talked to individual students and asked if they would be willing to participate in my study and come to my office to talk about English. In addition, I recruited participants from my once-off lecture on globalization for freshmen. I asked students to write down their contact information if they would like to participate in the study. Fifteen students in total agreed to participate in my study between 2014 and 2017, one male and 14 females, aged between 18 and 25 years old. I conducted a semi-structured interview with each of them, asking about their experiences with studying English, their feelings about English, as well as their thoughts on globalization, the opportunities they had in using English, their daily lives, and their future dreams. The interviews were transcribed and coded (Holstein & Gubrium, 1995) and I let the analytic categories emerge from the interview data, rather than predetermining them (Hammersley & Atkinson, 1995). Specifically, for the purpose of this chapter, I selected themes that had emerged which are related to the students' habitus and hindrance of their language learning; thus, not all of the 15 participants appear in this chapter, but only those relevant to the themes. The names of the participants are all pseudonyms.

Findings
Family Background and Educational Experience Affect Students' Learning/Acquisition of English

Non is a rare case in Sugino in that she has an international family background. She was born in Japan to a Japanese father and Israeli mother, and moved to Israel at age 13 and started to study English and Hebrew there as her second and third languages. She wanted to become more fluent in English, however, and thought it would be better to live in a county where English is spoken as the main language, and thereafter moved to Australia at age 20. In her words:

> My English level was very low and I felt regrettable, and so I decided to go to Australia.... I didn't go to a language school, but I communicated with my friends there, and I became able to speak English more and more. I may not be able to do business in English, but I have acquired English with which I have no problem with every day conversation. (Non, interview in 2016)

Non did not study English in the Japanese education system, and unlike most other Japanese students who went through this education system, she is confident in communicating in English. She hopes to go to the Fashion Institute of Technology in New York after she graduates from Sugino. I did not ask in detail about her family as I felt it was not appropriate, but her international family background allows her to travel and stay in different countries, and promotes a positive attitude toward English.

English Not Taught as a Tool for Communication
Miyoshi was the only male participant in my study. He wants to be a high school home economics teacher, which is the only reason why he entered Sugino since it has a teacher-training program, and his current motivation to study English stems only from his desire to pass the teacher-qualifying exam. However, since high school, he seems to have been urged to study English, and at the same time, has been disappointed about having not been successful, even though he has also made an effort by attending a cram school. He showed me meticulously written notes he took while in cram school, which showed many structurally-complicated English sentences written one after another without any context and which had been mechanically analyzed. However, when I asked him if he could say anything in English, he couldn't say anything, not even a simple sentence such as "I'm majoring in fashion." He said:

> I was taught by a famous cram school teacher, and tried many different ways to study English, only in vain. All of them failed, and honestly, I have no idea now what I should do…. (Miyoshi, interview in 2016)

I thought that he was not taught English as a tool for communication; rather, he was taught English as a subject to study. I suggested he practice conversational expressions such as the ones he would use at his part-time job at a supermarket, where he often had chances to speak with non-Japanese people. We started weekly short conversation lessons to practice customer-clerk exchanges, but he stopped coming. After a while, he came to my office again, saying that he decided to take an English proficiency exam, and showed me a notebook again with the mechanical analysis of English grammar. I realized that for him it would be perfectly reasonable to understand English as a series of grammar structures, not necessarily as a tool for communication, because that was the way of studying he was familiar with. I realized that if he does not need to communicate, communication does not have to be the sole purpose of language learning.

Students' Resistance to Teachers and Power
Shoko was from a wealthy Christian family. She went to an international kindergarten and started going to private English lessons from the second grade. She also traveled to many countries for vacation with her father, who works in international business. Therefore, she is able to speak English. However, in her private high school, she refused to study English because she did not like the teacher. She said:

> I didn't want to understand what my teacher said. I was completely rebellious. Nothing came into my ears. I hated the way my teacher spoke, and everything passed through my head. I didn't like the teacher imposing her way, like, "I did this, so you should do the same way." I had some teachers who'd had overseas experience. They boasted about their experience, which I didn't like, and I came to dislike English too. (Shoko, interview in 2016)

It is quite natural for a teacher to think it may be inspiring to talk about her or his international experience in the classroom. However, in Shoko's case, the teacher's way of teaching, checking homework, and talking to students discouraged her from listening. It is disappointing that the good intentions of the teacher can sometimes fail and even hinder student learning.

The manner of teaching can frequently cause negative feelings among the students. Another interview-participant, Mina, also said that she always disliked English because of her teacher in high school. She said:

> The teacher didn't teach me anything but gave me pressure.... I was like, "Oh no, I can't make it." Then the teacher ridiculed me, "Don't you understand such an easy thing?" (Mina, interview in 2014)

Some students I interviewed said they did not like English native speakers. Sato, another participant, went to a private high school where the curriculum placed great emphasis on English learning. She enjoyed speaking English and the overseas school trip, but she disliked English classes in Japan. She said:

> Sometimes a foreigner came. They came like they were doing volunteer work. But we [the students] were only speaking Japanese because we couldn't speak English.... (Sato, interview in 2014)

Another student, Mami made a similar comment. She said:

> The class I hated most was the kind in junior high school where a native speaker teacher came and played games and so on.... (Mami, interview in 2014)

This suggests that the government recommendation to hire English native speakers does not always have favorable results among the students.

Students' Social Practices Limit Their Willingness to Study and the Time They Have Available

Shio and Fu are good friends and I rarely see them separately. They came to talk to me together, so I interviewed them at the same time. They are always smiling and appear happy, but in fact, the interview revealed that they feel insecure and are not confident. Despite the fact that they are full-time students, their priority in life was working and making money. We had the following conversation:

> *Fu:* My mind is too busy to think about something like a big dream. I have no time or mind space.
> *Shio:* But it's better to be busy,
> *Fu:* Yes, otherwise I tend to think about unnecessary worries. As the reason for being busy is because I'm working, I feel better because I'm making money.
> *Shio:* I feel good to think that I'm making money.
> *Chieko (me):* Study or work…is work more important?
> *Shio:* It may be so.
> *Fu:* Making money.
> *Shio:* We are always saying that we wish we could be paid for going to school. We go to school from morning 'til night, and then go to work, and have no time for ourselves. So, even cheaply paid, if we made money by going to school, that would be great.

Neither Fu nor Shio came from families with a low income, and they received scholarships to pay their tuition. However, they are focused on making money.

Low Self Confidence
Shio and Fu have a positive attitude about English and intercultural communication. However, they are not confident when it comes to studying English, other subjects, and in various skills. Their lack of confidence may be demotivating them from making an effort to learn. Fu said:

> I wanna speak to famous people overseas. It should be really fun! But I will never be able to understand what they say, …. English is absolutely necessary. But I don't think I can speak English for my whole life, even if I study it. English is difficult, isn't it? I don't have good writing skills, I can't use the computer so well. As I study here, I have come to feel I can't do anything. (Fu and Shio, interview in 2017)

Shio was disappointed after entering the fashion college. She said, "Studying at a fashion college does not automatically lead to my future dream of getting a job in the fashion industry coming true" (Fu and Shio, interview in 2017). One of the reasons for their lack of confidence may be that they do not have a concrete picture of their future. In terms of English, they vaguely understand that English will be necessary in the future, but they do not have a clear idea of why. From our conversation:

> *Chieko*: Do you think you will use English in your work in the future?
> *Shio*: Yes!
> *Fu*: Yes! There will be more foreigners in Japan and also in the workplace.
> *Shio*: You will definitely meet foreigners in fashion business, in fashion brands, in meetings.
> *Chieko*: What do you want to do in the future?
> *Fu*: Well.....uh.... (Fu and Shio, interview 2017)

Another participant, Kana, talked about her unhappy high school experience because she did not get high grades in English. She was actually a good student, and the number one basketball player in her school. But she believed that English was more important than anything else. She said, "If only the English grade is high, we don't have to study (any other subject), do we?" (Kana, interview in 2014).

She also jokingly talked about her dream:

> I don't want my future child to have a big problem like me being poor at English...So I would like to get married to a man who can use English, and then I will become able to use English and I want my kids to be bilingual. If we use English in my family... they will become able to use English. (Kana, interview in 2014)

Traditional Japanese Society as an Obstacle
Berdy was an international student from Indonesia. Having graduated from a 2-year fashion school in Indonesia, she transferred to Sugino as a junior and graduated in 2015. She was very fluent in English and wanted to get a job in Japan. In our interview, she shared her experiences about job-hunting.

I thought her English ability must have been a big advantage when she was looking for a job. And I believed she thought so, too. However, she had a difficult time finding employment and came to the conclusion that English would never be an advantage in finding a job in Japan.

As Berdy commented, it is a Japanese norm that one's outstanding skills should not be ostentatiously shown or mentioned when looking for a job. She said:

> Maybe it's because Japanese culture, and with job-hunting, it's really a difficulty–Japanese culture. You don't literally put things.... You put your TOEIC score in your resume, but you won't say, I'm confident in English. I think in case of Japanese people–they don't really want you to brag about your skill or something.... (Berdy, interview, 2015)

In another conversation, Berdy again mentioned English as a hidden skill.

> *Chieko*: So for job-hunting, do you think university students need English?
> *Berdy*: It should be necessary at this time, as a matter of fact.
> *Chieko*: But the fact that it is necessary is hidden?
> *Berdy*: Yes, it seems hidden. (Berdy, interview in 2015)

At the same time, Berdy also commented that English is also a status symbol, which would cause gaps or differences among people.

> Everything is really equal in Japan. But in terms of English, it costs money [to study English] a bit. So, it seems that only upper, middle [class] people can speak English, and people in the lower class cannot. In job ads, it seems Japanese companies don't put English as a requirement so as not to hurt those people [who can't use English] (Berdy, interview 2015)

In the end, her job-hunting did not go as she had imagined; her English skill was not advantageous for employment. She was employed in a uniform factory in the southern part of Japan. After a year of working there, disappointed and unsatisfied, she moved to Vancouver, Canada, where her sister is living. She was employed at a doll factory.

Thus far, I have shown some of the themes I extracted from my interviews with the students in Sugino Fashion College. One case, that of Non, showed successful language learning, while another, Berdy, showed the unsuccessful pursuit of a future dream. The other students all displayed various forms of unsuccessful language learning. Except for the rare cases of Non and Berdy, the students are at the non-elite end of the spectrum of inequality that I described in the beginning of this chapter. They are also a part of groups that do not fit neatly into the government policies and subsidies aimed at nurturing global human resources. Teachers may tend to consider these students as having not made an effort to learn English, but the students themselves are not solely to blame. There are some internal, as well as external, preconditions that promote or hinder language learning, and these preconditions are greatly affected by habitus.

Discussion: Bourdieu Revisited – Habitus and Cultural Capital

Habitus and Field

I have focused on aspects of habitus that cause limitations. However, habitus is not a negative notion, but is a human condition. Under any normal situation in modern life, every human being is living naturally in their own "fields" (Bourdieu, 1991) with attitudes and values without feeling excessive oppression and inconvenience. In the life of my participants in this study, the fields are families, schools, and other various social places where they belong. In these fields, individuals are given their subject positions (i.e., habitus or "dispositions;" Bourdieu, 1991, p. 12) that constitute what they are (i.e., identities) and how they live. To better understand the concept of habitus, I turn to the words of Bourdieu (1977) himself, who explains habitus as follows:

> The structures constitutive of a particular type of environment produce habitus, systems of durable, transposable dispositions, structured structures predisposed to function as structuring structures, that is, as principles of the generation and structuring of practices and representations which can be objectively "regulated" and "regular" without in any way being the product of obedience to rules, objectively adapted to their goals without presupposing a conscious aiming at end of an express mastery of the operations necessary to attain them, and being all time, collectively orchestrated without being the product of the orchestrating action of a conductor. (p. 72)

In this study, Non was born and raised in an international family, and traveling and studying other languages was a way of life. Therefore, English comes naturally to her. On the other hand, for the Japanese students Miyoshi, Fu, and Shio, their fields, in Japan, do not require English, except in school where English is a mandatory subject. Especially for Fu and Shio, financial independence is a great priority. For these Japanese students, English is alien, and how much it is accepted depends on habitus, which is "a socially constituted cognitive capacity" (Bourdieu, 1986, p. 255), and linked to an individual's background (Bourdieu, 1990).

Habitus is Internalized, Causing Limitation
Habitus is a "complex internalized core" (Reay, 2004, p. 435), where there are various factors intertwined, sometimes clashing with each other. In the case of Shio and Fu, their urge for financial independence clashes with their obligation to go to college, and their current habitus does not allow them to break through the clashing values. In addition, globalization discourse urges them to master English, but they have no concrete plan or idea about a future in which to use English, which has inadvertently and unfortunately led to their having lower self-esteem towards English and other subjects as a whole.

Miyoshi also has the globalization discourse internalized; although nobody told him to study English, he continued to study it believing that English is necessary for the profession of a high school teacher. He continued his way of studying it, even though he had never been successful, only to repeatedly feel that he would never be successful at English.

In the case of Berdy, an external habitus clashes with her internalized one; the Japanese norm that "the nail that sticks out gets hammered in" was incompatible with the globalization discourse; that is, outstanding English skills are useful for employment. Despite her international background and her educational and family background that allowed her a high-level of English education from a young age, Berdy was confused and disappointed in Japan's job market.

Unfortunately, as I have seen above, my participants struggled among conflicting habitus, but were unable to take agentive actions. This is related to my question that I posed earlier in this chapter, whether one can go beyond habitus through effort. Bourdieu (as cited in Menard-Warwick, 2005) describes habitus as "neither mechanical nor inevitable" (p. 255), rather the "art of inventing" (Bourdieu, 1990, p. 55), which develops and changes through the clashing of identities and experiences, a situation that my participants encountered. However, invention of self may be limited by habitus, as "choices inscribed in the habitus are limited" (Reay, 2004, p. 435).

Here I would like to note that there is a similarity between habitus and discourse (Foucault, 1977) in that both give humans subject positions. Discourses are also conflicting and inconsistent, and accordingly "provide the possibilities of refashioning them" (Hackman, 1990, p. 187). However, discourses/habitus always bind individuals, and if not externally bound, individual self-creation is bound by subjection to one's own knowledge and conscience, led by discourse/habitus (internally bound; Foucault, 1983).

English Education as Symbolic Violence?
Violence is a strong word, but as observable in the Japanese government's policy of nurturing global human resources, only a limited number of elites are given educational and financial favor, and the mainstream value of globalization and the capital of English are promoted and reproduced through education, thus producing inequality.

Some of the participants expressed their displeasure about the classes taught by English native speakers, saying they did not understand what the English native speaker teachers said (Sato). The learners who have benefited from the government policy of hiring English native speakers are those who already have some basic conversation skills, and those students developed their skills further, while the students who did not have the basic skills never had the chance to improve their situation.

In addition to the above, the participants also disliked the high school teachers whose expectations they were never able to meet. The students were scolded and ridiculed and they felt that they never learned anything (Mina). Shoko was rebellious towards her teacher who she felt imposed her ideas too much, and felt she never learned anything and even lost some English skills that she developed from her early education. Miyoshi was taught English in a way that did not present the language as a tool for human communication.

In these situations where students never learn, it is regrettable to say that education violates the students' right to learn, which is a major failure of education at the most basic level.

In general, school education in itself is a failure as it only promotes mainstream social values and behaviors, indifferent to various social backgrounds and practices, and favors a limited number of elites and thus reproduces social inequality (e.g., Bourdieu, 1986). In addition, my interviews revealed the ignorance of teachers who, in the name of teaching English for a globalized world, squashed students' motivation to learn. As Bourdieu and Passeron (1990) state, "All pedagogic action is, objectively, symbolic violence insofar as it is the imposition of a cultural arbitrary by an arbitrary power" (p. 5).

English May not Be a Type of Cultural Capital
In ESL research, English as cultural capital is often described as being attained through investment and effort (e.g., Norton, 2000). However, according to Bourdieu (1986), it is limited by habitus.

> Cultural capital can be acquired to a varying extent, depending on the period, the society, and the social class, in the absence of any deliberate inculcation, and therefore quite unconsciously.... It cannot be accumulated beyond the appropriating capacities of an individual agent.... (p. 245)

Following Bourdieu's argument, English in Japan cannot be cultural capital if it is imposed by society or the education system, and if it is beyond the cognitive capacities of individual agencies based on their own individual history and experience. In addition, the concrete economic and social benefit of having English skills in Japan is not proven. However, English does have symbolic power, which is created through the discourse of globalization.

Berdy recognizes this when she describes English as prestigious in Japan. She said, "[If you can use English,] you become a really prestigious person. Wow, you can speak English! It's a little embarrassing, though" (Berdy, interview in 2015). The symbolic power of English was also expressed by other participants. Shio, Fu, Miyoshi, and Kana all had the ungrounded belief that English would be absolutely necessary in their future, or English would be a panacea for academic achievement.

On the other hand, however, symbolic power can be illusory; Sato, whose high school had an intensive English program, was disenchanted about the fictitious power of English. She said, "I don't care (about English)" (Sato, interview in 2014).

Thus, English is symbolic capital that is recognized as "legitimate competence" (Bourdieu, 1986, p. 245) and "accumulated prestige or honor" (Thompson, 1991, p. 4), although this symbolic capital may be elusive. There is no concrete benefit from this symbol recognized by the learners as described above.

Conclusion, Limitations, Implications, and Future Study
In this study of non-elite English learners who are not on track in terms of the government policy of nurturing global human resources, various preconditions that may hinder language learning have been presented. These preconditions included: family background and economic conditions, the education system and the schools' pressure that may discourage students from studying, resistance to power, low self-esteem, and traditional Japanese norms. Also discussed was the idea that habitus limits the choices of human beings, and cannot be overcome by investment and effort. Another conclusion is that English in Japan does not equate to cultural capital; rather, it is symbolic capital with no concrete benefits recognized.

A drawback of this study is that the data is not longitudinal; in order to understand individual learners, especially their habitus, which are related to their background, it would have been better to have repeat interviews to further reveal the narratives of the learners. In addition, it may be necessary to ask more about family background, particularly social status and economic background to investigate more deeply about various aspects of habitus. However, these are sensitive issues to ask participants (Darvin & Norton, 2014). Even though social status is represented in various ways, such as behavior, clothing, manner of speaking, word choice, and other attributes (Kelly, 2012), I would not feel comfortable describing my participants from these points of view. Another limitation of this study is that I was not able to find agentive aspects within my participants. It could be better to focus on habitus' relation to the various personal identities intertwined within an individual person, clashing with each other, and creating the possibility for agency; however, this process is still largely only in theory.

Despite the limitations of my study, some implications for language educators are drawn. It is always important to try to listen to each individual learner's voice, which is often unheard; it is crucial to understand that the cause of learners' inability to learn a language may be the educators themselves and the education system that imposes only one value on the learners, specifically the value of English as cultural capital. It is crucial to understand the learners' inner struggles from the clashing habitus that may hinder language learning.

Another implication is more personal as a researcher and educator, and offers insight for my own future teaching and research. As I mentioned earlier, it is meaningless to only continue to focus on criticisms against the government's policies for globalization and against inequality in education. For the peace of mind of learners, as well as teachers, an alternative language curriculum may include not teaching or learning English, but trying other ways of interpersonal and intercultural communication, for example, by communicating in Japanese with non-Japanese people, or communicating in mixed languages. I came across this idea during my conversation with Shio.

> *Chieko*: For you, it doesn't matter whether it's Japanese or English (to communicate)?
>
> *Shio*: Either Japanese or English, it doesn't matter. It's like, Ohayo [Good morning]! It's really fun to talk to foreigners. (Interview with Shio in 2014)

Not only for Shio, but other young students have also often shown no barrier between the different languages they use in interpersonal communication. In terms of mixed language, I would like to refer a scene that I witnessed at an annual fashion contest organized by Sugino in October 2017. A Filipino contest-participant and a Japanese fitter perfectly communicated in their own languages to explain how the garment should be fitted to a model. Through this experience I thought I might be able to promote various forms of intercultural communication without English.

In the same vein, it is reasonable, especially for fashion major students, to have other kinds of cultural/symbolic capital other than English. Even in a language class, it would be reasonable to focus on the content areas, such as art and professional skills, as alternative forms of capital.

References
Block, D. (2014). *Social class in applied linguistics*. New York, NY: Routledge.
Bourdieu, P. (1977). *Outline of a theory of practice*. Cambridge, UK: Cambridge University Press.
Bourdieu, P. (1986). The forms of capital. In J. G. Richardson (Ed.), *Handbook of theory and research for the sociology of education* (pp. 241-258). Westport, CT: Greenwood.
Bourdieu, P. (1990). *The logic of practice*. Cambridge, UK: Polity.
Bourdieu, P. (1991). *Language and symbolic power*. Cambridge, MA: Harvard University Press.
Bourdieu, P., & Passeron, J.-C. (1990). *Reproduction in education, society and culture*. (R. Nice, Trans., 2nd ed.). London, UK: Sage.
Darvin, R., & Norton, B. (2014). Social class, identity, and migrant students. *Journal of Language, Identity, and Education, 13*, 111-117. doi:10.1080/15348458.2014.901823
Foucault, M. (1977). *The archaeology of knowledge and the discourse on language*. New York, NY: Pantheon.
Foucault, M. (1983). The subject and power. In H. L. Dreyfus & P. Rabinow (Eds.), *Michel Foucault: Beyond structuralism and hermeneutics* (pp. 208-226). Chicago, IL: University of Chicago Press.
Hammersley, M., & Atkinson, P. (1995). *Ethnography: Principles in practice* (2nd ed.). New York, NY: Routledge.
Holstein, J. A., & Gubrium, J. F. (1995). *The active interview*. Thousand Oaks, CA: Sage.
Ichikawa, C. (2004). *Eigo wo kodomo ni oshieruna* [Don't teach English to children]. Tokyo, Japan: Chuko Shinsho.
Japan Federation of Economic Organizations. (2000). *On developing human resources in the era of globalization*. Retrieved from http://www.keidanren.or.jp/japanese/policy/2000/013/
Kachru, B. B. (1985) Standards, codification and sociolinguistic realism: The English language in the outer circle. In R. Quirk & H. G. Widdowson (Eds.), *English in the world: Teaching and learning the language and literatures* (pp. 11-30). Cambridge, UK: Cambridge University Press.

Kanno, Y., & Varghese, M. M. (2010). Immigrant and refugee ESL students' challenges to accessing four-year college education: From language policy to educational policy. *Journal of Language, Identity, & Education, 9*(5), 310-328. doi:10.1080/15348458.2010.517693

Kelly, P. (2012). Migration, transnationalism, and the spaces of class identity. *Philippine Studies: Historical and Ethnographic Viewpoint, 60*(2), 153-186. doi:10.1353/phs.2012.0017

Kubota, R. (2011). Immigration, diversity, and language education in Japan: Toward a glocal approach to teaching English. In P. Seargeant (Ed.), *English in Japan in the era of globalization* (pp. 101-122). New York, NY: Palgrave Macmillan.

Kubota, R., & McKay, S. L. (2009). Globalization and language learning in rural Japan: The role of English in the local linguistic ecology. *TESOL Quarterly, 43*(4), 593-619. doi:10.1002/j.1545-7249.2009.tb00188.x

McKay, S. L., & Wong, S. C. (1996). Multiple discourses, multiple identities: Investment and agency in second-language learning among Chinese adolescent immigrant students. *Harvard Educational Review, 66*, 577-608. doi:10.17763/haer.66.3.n47r06u264944865

Menard-Warwick, J. (2005). Both a fiction and an existential fact: Theorizing identity in second language identity and literacy studies. *Linguistics and Education, 16*, 253-274. doi:10.1016/j.linged.2006

Ministry of Education, Culture, Sports, Science and Technology. (2013). *English education reform plan corresponding to globalization*. Retrieved from http://www.kantei.go.jp/jp/singi/kyouikusaisei/pdf/dai3_en.pdf

Ministry of Education, Culture, Sports, Science and Technology. (2014). *Eigoryoku chosa kekka no gaiyou* [Survey result on English proficiency of high school 3rd grader students]. Retrieved from http://www.mext.go.jp/component/a_menu/education/detail/__icsFiles/afieldfile/2015/07/03/1358071_01.pdf

Morita, N. (2004). Negotiating participation and identity in second language academic communities. *TESOL Quarterly, 38*(4), 573-603. doi:10.2307/3588281

Naruke, M. (2013). *Nihonjin no 9 wari ni Eigo ha Iranai* [90 % of Japanese people do not need English]. Tokyo, Japan: Hagiwara.

Norton, B. (2000). *Identity and language learning: Gender ethnicity and educational change*. Edinburgh, UK: Pearson Education Limited.

Okado, H. (2015). Eigo kakusa gensho wo megutte [Aspects of English divide]. In T. Sugino & T. Hara (Eds.), *Gengo to kakusa* [Language and stratification] (pp. 80-82). Tokyo, Japan: Akashi Shoten.

Otsu, Y. (2005). *Shogakko deno eigo kyouiku ha hitsuyou nai* [English education in elementary school is not necessary]. Tokyo, Japan: Keio University.

Phillipson, R. (1992). *Linguistic imperialism*. Oxford, UK: Oxford University.

Phillipson, R. (2009). English in globalization: A lingua franca or a lingua frankensteinia? *TESOL Quarterly, 43*(2), 335-339. doi:10.1002/j.1545-7249.2009.tb00175.x
Reay, D. (2004). "It's all becoming a habitus": Beyond the habitual use of habitus in educational research. *British Journal of Sociology of Education, 25*(4), 431-444. doi:10.1080/0142569042000236934
Saito, T. (2004). *Kikai fubyodo* [Inequality of Opportunities]. Tokyo, Japan: Bunshun Bunko.
Shin, H. (2014). Social class, habitus, and language learning: The case of Korean early study-abroad students. *Journal of Language, Identity & Education, 13*(2), 99-103. doi:10.1080/15348458.2014.901821
Skutnabb-Kangas, T. (2009). What can TESOL do in order not to participate in crimes against humanity? *TESOL Quarterly, 43*(2), 340-344. doi:10.1002/j.1545-7249.2009.tb00176.x
Terasawa, T. (2015). *"Nihonjin to eigo" no shakaigaku: Naze eigokyouikuron ha gokai darake nanoka* [Sociology of "Japanese people and English": Why are discussions of English education full of misunderstanding?]. Tokyo, Japan: Kenkyusha.
The Prime Minister's Commission on Japan's Goals in the 21st Century. (2000). *The frontier within: Individual empowerment and better governance in the new millennium.* Retrieved from http://www.kantei.go.jp/jp/21century/report/pdfs/01cover.pdf
The Provisional Council of Education Reform. (1986). *The second report on education reform.* Retrieved from http://www.mext.go.jp/b_menu/shingi/chukyo/chukyo3/015/siryo/04070501/009/001.htm
Thompson, J. B. (1991). Editor's introduction. In P. Bourdieu, *Language and symbolic power* (pp. 1-31). Cambridge, MA: Harvard University Press.
Torikai, K. (2010). *Eigo kouyougo ha nani ga mondai ka* [What is the problem about English education?]. Tokyo, Japan: Kadokawa.
Vandrick, S. (2011). Students of the new global elite. *TESOL Quarterly, 45*(1), 160-169. doi:10.5054/tq.2011.244020

CHAPTER 3

IDENTIFYING AND IDENTIFYING WITH:
A Critical Look into Student Interaction with Peace, Activism, Altruism, and Love in a Japanese University Setting

Kirk R. Johnson and Tim M. Murphey

Quoting Mahatma Gandhi to start a chapter such as this could be perceived as somewhat of a cliché, yet the concise statements attributed to him express the desired message so well: "There is no path to peace. Peace is the path." Or slightly paraphrased, "As the means, so the ends" (TEDx Talks, 2017). With this thought in mind, shouldn't it be logical for formal education to explore the paths of peace? Our societies are full of platitudes meant to guide us through life with a sense of happiness: "Follow your heart," "Find your passion," "Practice what you preach," are but a few examples. If we can accept that there is importance in investing and unleashing the potential underlying these statements, then we should be exploring the ways to bring these ideals to fruition. Yet, too often in the field of language acquisition, educators neglect the richness that might be found within the realms of positive peace and critical, shared understandings. What we are seeing in our exploratory action research (Smith, 2015) is that we need to identify crucial areas of concern before we can expect people to identify with them and commit themselves to action. Creating spaces to reflect about core concepts of peace, love, altruism, and activism (which many of our students superbly interconnect) created a foundation of respect and opportunities to allow their agency to be expressed.

Unfortunately, instead of engaging our students to explore their understandings and experiences, we educators too often set up lessons on structures that predominately rely on the "banking" of knowledge and information (Friere, 1970). While we are not arguing against fact-based information exchange, we believe that learning is much more than just a one-way transmission of information and this also applies to language acquisition in general. Learning can be a dialogic avenue for growth for all parties within the classroom. Hooks (2017) notes that people learn more from talking together than from being lectured to (as cited in Bell & Kondabolu, 2017). According to hooks, conversation itself is an essential learning tool. Mitsunaga (TEDTalentSearch, 2012) noted through her research and experiential interactions with students in Korea that better acquisition of knowledge happens in situations that evoke "with learning" versus "at learning." Being lectured "at" is a one directional process, often demotivating and not ideally suited for collaborative learning in a language learning setting. This truism also has applications across fields in the hard sciences as well. Freeman et al. (2014) found in a meta-analysis of 225 studies that reported on examination scores in undergraduate science, technology, engineering, and mathematics (STEM) courses that active learning produced more successful classes, while students in classes with traditional lecturing were 1.5 times more likely to fail than those in classes with active learning.

Crookes (2013) proposes that both humanistic and critical language teaching should not only teach deeper life-enriching concepts but that these should be activated in the real world of students and teachers. Thus, teacher-centered classrooms are generally not conducive for the dynamism of peace education methodologies (McLeod & Reynolds, 2010). It might mean for many instructors a leap of faith, a giving up of the security blanket, or a pedagogic shift. If we are looking to enhance the creative capabilities of our students, then properly implemented, active student-centered learning creates a much more advantageous platform. By exploring their own understandings of critical concepts within peace and love, sharing, and sympathizing, the classroom experience can generate the learning of language needs as well as social growth and comprehension.

Kielburger and Kielburger (2008) have been trying to shift paradigms through decades of activism. Through their work, they have emphasized the concept of eudemonic happiness, which is rooted in the fundamental human needs for meaning, connection, and personal growth. It is precisely these fundamental constructs underpinning eudemonic happiness that we hope to bolster in our instructional spaces. Embracing the underlying premises of peace education and positive psychology, we have set out on a series of experimentations in our second language (L2) classrooms over the last several years. We have found that even at introductory levels, when teaching English to speakers of other languages (TESOL) in Japan, our students have generally risen to the challenge to give their opinions and thoughts, albeit sometimes through drawings when words failed them.

We set out on this quest with a variety of daring ideas and questions and ended up with a variety of answers (some to questions we had not asked). We wanted to know to what extent intermediate level English learners might be put off by abstract concepts that people rarely openly discuss even in their native languages. Would they see these concepts as distinct or overlapping? Would they be embarrassed or afraid to discuss things in English that they may have rarely brought up in their lives using their native language? How might they see the connections between these big ideas? To what extent would they *identify* these concepts as important in their own lives, and to what extent would they *identify with* these concepts as major guiding points in their lives? Is it accurate to say that in order to create structural change, students first have to *identify with* a cause and then realize perhaps their voice might have an impact (agency)?

Why Focus Attention on Peace?

Peace can certainly be a vague and elusive concept, especially if it is not challenged. We struggle at times, trying to succinctly understand and express it. However, the notion that peace is passive or weak is a misnomer, whether that might be the result of lazy thinking, missed opportunities, or calculated misinformation. Too often, the institutions and systems of our societies suppress critical thinking that challenges a status quo built on the pillars of consumerism, personal gain, and artificial divisions of otherness. While it is not within the purview of this chapter to investigate such realities, it is within this chapter that we hope to show the valuable space our class times offer to challenge the complexities of peace.

The teaching of peace requires a curriculum that allows for an open exchange of information and opinions. It flourishes in a setting where critical thinking, questioning, and compassion are encouraged. Peace education (PE) works to understand and transform conflicts without the use of violence, not to avoid them entirely (Wells, 2003). Toh (2007) advances the notion that educating for peace is a call on all sectors of society: from government and business leaders to ordinary citizens of all ages and social standings. He postulates that a holistic approach is needed but that there are many intersecting pathways or tracks that can be traveled to make the journey. Holding this to be accurate, educators have an array of approaches with which to broach the fundamentals of PE. We posit that this holds true across academic disciplines and furthermore that the pedagogical settings within Japanese universities offer appropriate platforms to confront such a necessary undertaking. While we recognize the complexities and difficulties in creating such capacities, it is essential to find such space if we hope to counter the pervasive violence and damage afflicting our modern world.

Identifying and *Identifying With*

Identifying with is at the fundamental level developing the senses of empathy and cohesion. While the distance and intensity of the relationship will vary, *identifying with* is much more intricate than just obtaining knowledge or identifying a thing or concept. Thus, our hope is that students will sense connectivity with issues of importance and at a minimum understand they are not entirely external observers to an issue, nor are they helpless in creating positive change. Our goal with this concept within our class pedagogy is not to create activists on any particular issue. On the contrary, we just want to create learning spaces where students can feel empowered to envision and possibly engage in actions of change. This is a huge distinction as it is an attempt to provide opportunities for agency among our language-learning students.

At some point in this chapter it is essential that we acknowledge that we certainly harbor our biases, hopes, and desires for peaceful change. However, our goal on this educational journey is to make sure that our students understand they have both individual and collective powers to positively or negatively affect the world around them. Trying to counter hegemonic modern societies, which overwhelmingly compartmentalizes individuals and applies social pressures to passively conform them to various status quo hierarchies, is quite challenging (Freire, 2000). So much so that we educators often just give up on providing a learning space that encourages critical thought, agency, and alternative paradigms.

With a focus on human rights education, McLeod and Reynolds (2010) found that students can identify content knowledge, but first such knowledge must be put into language that is accessible to the students. This would seem to be even more relevant while learning in a second language context. Also of significance, they discern that the classroom structure and instruction must emulate the values of human rights. Consequently, invoking or *identifying with* the values of peace involves two dimensions. The first is an immediate creation of space based on more equiw conditions and opportunities and the second is a longer-term development of attitudes, beliefs, and values that form the basis for future learning, actions, and interactions. However, with a focus on creating long-term behavioral transformations, McKenzie-Mohr (2000) found that a gap exists between psychological knowledge that promotes sustainable behavioral changes and those who design environmental programs meant to enact such behavioral changes. It has created a situation where the literature is largely invisible to those who can most benefit from it. Unfortunately, that gap means behavioral changes needed in order to mitigate the effects of climate change and pollution are often not expediting long-term shifts. Extrapolating that to the next level, without pressure from the grassroots level, the colossal economic and political institutions that are the main causes for climate changing pollutions will not change their behaviors. Hence, one objective with our research is to help fill in that gap between theory, knowledge, and pedagogy within critical language studies.

Our activity to have students explicitly work directly with the four terms of peace, activism, altruism, and love (PAAL) was in part an attempt to give students a chance to fill in any gaps of knowledge. To exemplify this we will use a case study from a content-based class with a focus on building a culture of peace. This class was well primed to share and interact with the concepts. In total, we explicitly reflected on PAAL as distinctive terms in three stages over a three-week period. In the first stage, students were allotted approximately 30 minutes to write about two questions: the first asked for a definition of each term and the second a chance to explain how they engage with or see each concept being incorporated in the real world.

The initial student interactions with PAAL were then minimally reorganized by the instructor and reintroduced to the class. In a manner of speaking, we were asking our students to perform a critical discourse analysis on their own output (Johnson, Johnson, & Murphey, 2018). Murphey and Falout (2010) refer to this peer and self-analysis of their own comments given back to them as critical participatory looping (CPL). The usefulness of CPL is multiple. First, it offers students the opportunity to learn what their peers are thinking and to detect commonalities in their ideas in a language range that is familiar to them. This looping of their own ideas back to the group also works as motivation as students can see their own ideas having intrinsic value in the lesson. Furthermore, we believe it also helps students identify with the viewpoints, as these literally are their own viewpoints.

Student Generated or Organized Data
Unfortunately, the first two stages of this project suffered from time design flaws. Many students did not have enough time to fully explore all four terms. Generally, activism and altruism suffered and were not addressed to the same level of thoroughness as peace and love. This also carried over into the second stage when we looped their comments back to them to encourage deeper processing via CPL. In this stage, students collaborated in small groups to deconstruct and organize their writing into general themes within each term. From these groups, a class understanding was then developed through languaging (Swain, 2006) to reveal a meaningful range of understandings. After the whole class negotiation process, it was determined that the understandings of peace taken from student output could be categorized into seven overall themes:

- Contentment in daily life
- A sense of justice or fairness
- Having security or safety

- Having opportunities
- Positive relationships
- Healthy natural environment
- Absences of negatives

Of course, the involvement with the activities and the complexity of expressions varied within the class. *Identifying* or gaining knowledge is already a challenge. *Identifying with* such esoteric and malleable constructs calls for a deeper commitment and thinking and not all students were ready to take those steps. Some of that was due to the range of English capabilities, but the reality that some students did not fully embrace the tasks needs to be conceded. Yet those who did, revealed that their interactions went beyond mere knowledge acquisition to magnify the socio-emotional and cognitive benefits within their groups. Those seven overall themes originated from the students own written output and negotiation. Their subsequent classifications matched up well with other analytical attempts to gather such data on the meanings of peace (Parrish & Oxford, 2013).

Turning briefly to the construct of love, the same process produced similar results. The looping (CPL stage) of student output back to the class resulted in the class construction of six general themes of love. One noteworthy point was a strong presence of negative aspects associated with love: obsession, jealously, and loss. So it seems love comes with some baggage or risk of pain along with the pleasure.

- Romantic
- Loved ones (family, friends, pets)
- Social/Society
- Happiness
- Feeling/emotion (beyond happiness)
- Negative (obsession, jealously, loss)

A further upshot from these cooperative learning sessions was that students recognized the value of their classmates' thoughts on the themes. Research shows that students are particularly motivated by people who share similar identity features as they (Murphey & Arao, 2001). Murphey and Arao refer to these people as near peer role models (NPRM). By looping back our students' own reflections on PAAL, we created a classroom full of interacting NPRMs. Dörnyei and Murphey (2003) demonstrated that this scenario creates a potential venue for strengthened relationships and group dynamics in the classroom. One prominent feature of journaling in the third stage of this activity was how students credited their classmates for providing previously unthought-of interpretations and thus expanding their own understandings. Their comments from the journaling stage reflected a sense of pride that they could create multiple understanding of peace and love and also some amazement at the erudite depth of their NPRMs, and all this working primarily in the target language.

Student Data in an Online Forum
The third stage of this project involved student journaling via an online class forum. A critical analysis of these comments exposed a range of understanding and connectivity to the activities and concepts. The following reflections highlight how students learned from other students in their respective groups. For example, one student commented:

> When I talked about "peace" with my group members, I picked up that "no argument" is the one of "peace" things from the papers. But, a member of my group said she thought "no argument is not peace, it is just quiet world and argument is needed to make more peaceful world." I thought it was right and good idea. I did not have ideas like her, so I agreed her opinion and I could find a new view of "peace."

This clearly reveals a new, deeper understanding of peace, negotiated and formed via horizontal student dialogues. Additionally, the following example on love shows students can embrace the concepts as both enlightening and enthralling to discuss.

> We talked about "love" so deeply it's too long but I was able to listen to the story and their experiences I've never got, so I was surprised. It was great for me to rethink about "love." In addition, in that sheet there are many genre of "love." For example, shape of love, same sex love, jealous and connection to peace. I was surprised by these views because I've never expected. The discussion was interesting.

This last exemplar shows that this student could understand the intersectionality of PAAL through our class activities: "By doing this activity, I realized they all are connected each other. Peace needs love. Altruism needs activism in order to make country peaceful."

Embedding *Identifying With* Through Sharing and Journaling

One aspect of critical pedagogy (CP) and PE that we try to emphasize is the lack of learning boundaries in respect to time and space. By this, we are not simply referring to out of class assignments (i.e., homework), but instead, that learning acquisition should not have a set on-off switch, especially when dealing with fundamental living constructs such as PAAL or trying to get students to *identify with* an issue. So it is not the work we are focused on here, but the process of our students being reflectively engaged.

Through journaling and sharing activities, students can implicitly interact with the concepts of PAAL beyond the class boundaries. One such method is what we have labeled the "take it home" (TiH) sharing and journaling forum and was implemented in Kirk's content-based class focusing on various global issues. The action needed is remarkably simple—find someone and share something you learned in class with that person, then record your reflections of the interaction on the class open forum.

Analysis of the students' journaling shows a number of positive markers. First, through such interactions students become "active" and take on a form of ownership as to what and how to share the information. This moves the students beyond the role of passive receptors of info. Furthermore, it gives students an opportunity to bond with and maybe learn from someone in their life. Beyond this, the open forum allows classmates to notice commonalities and differences in their shared experiences, as well as allowing the instructor a number of beneficial markers to monitor progress, including linguistic output. Inspection of the journaling shows that students primarily shared with siblings and friends, but mothers were also commonly sought out for dialogue.

Below is a representative example of a TiH journal in which the student writes about how she shared acquired information about how diamonds became a major source of funding for a series of internal wars. The report of their interaction also acknowledges the social status given to diamonds in modern Japan along with a rather perceptive comment as to our responsibility as citizens.

> I shared the information on conflict diamonds with my friend. She was surprised that such a serious conflict happened in African countries because of diamonds. I told her that Japan was the second (largest) consuming nation of diamonds in the world, only after the U.S., and lots of women long for beautiful diamonds because it's regarded as a symbol of beauty and love. However most of them didn't realize the background. She was greatly shocked to hear that there are citizens who had (their hands chopped off over those)[1] diamonds. (My friend) said we must be more conscious of such countries' present condition, nothing is more dangerous than ignorance.

As this student's writing should clearly indicate, we *identify* some quite serious realities in our learning. Yet, research on teaching about global issues has shown that studying only the problems can be counterproductive as it can overwhelm those being engaged (Hicks, 2002, as cited in Hicks 2004; Rogers, 1998). This is highly relevant to this class as for each issue we investigate we attempt to link it to our lifestyle choices, usually consumerist ones. Once students recognize that connections exist, we then explore opportunities to "be the change." So while this journaling activity does not necessarily address the problem of being overwhelmed by the immensity of an issue, it does offer the students a chance to share and observe how a person in their local sphere of influence reacts to the issue at hand. In my student's interaction above, her friend offered up the connections between knowledge, power, and making informed decisions. Could we extrapolate that this is building some hope and understanding of a sense of empowerment? Could we say that this is a step towards *identifying with*?

The Japanese educational culture has a long history of "reflections on learning" *(seikatsu dayori)* beginning in elementary schools, which tends to stop in junior or senior high school. Thus, getting students to reflect through what Murphey (1993) has called action logs is quite easy and helpful for their learning and their dialogic interaction with deep ideas. The *action logs* can also act as Kirk's TiH journal. Murphey more recently has given what he calls "everyday homework" for students to write "call reports" (after they call and talk to that day's partner about that day's topics) and "teaching reports" in which they teach others out of class something they have learned in class (Murphey, 2017).

When *Identifying With* Leads to Student Activism Beyond the Classroom
2005-2008 – Taking Action Against Landmine and Cluster Munitions

When students *identify with* an issue, wonderful things can materialize. Kirk's first experience with this as a teacher came about when a class was so moved by the horrible realities of landmines that they surprised him by collecting donations for a Japanese NGO that supported landmine survivors. This move, from just learning about an issue as an abstraction that has no effect in their lives to taking an action by seeking some positive change, came about when a few students decided that "just learning" was not enough. However, noting that simple donations are not usually transformative actions, Kirk took an estimated gamble and signed up for a two-day interactive display to be done at the yearly school festival. Providing this opportunity to create and share allowed students to become agents of action on the humanitarian problems of landmines and cluster munitions and not just mere classroom observers. The core group of volunteers, about eight students, kept the activities of this group going for four years and included such actions as collaborating with NGOs and professional photographers, marching with mine victims/survivors and their allies in public rallies, creating community awareness displays and inviting guest speakers to come and speak at the university.

In 2008, during the height of worldwide efforts to get countries to commit to a new treaty to ban cluster munitions, this group of students organized a spontaneous massive "die-in" at the school festival (see Figure 3.1) with the hopes of sharing knowledge of the issue with the greater school populace and also to join the calls to pressure the Japanese government to quickly sign the treaty. What this shows is that these students *identified with* this issue enough to take up various forms of activism. Activism is, of course, not completely unusual to university students in Japan contrary to stereotypes, but the succession of these actions flourished merely from the focus of our class studies, along with the creation of a little scaffolding and some opportunities, which the students themselves helped construct. From these factors came transformative changes and actions by the students to create a better world. Unfortunately, an infrastructure to maintain sustainability over the attrition rate of student graduation was not established; or simply put, the student volunteers graduated without finding students who wanted to continue the efforts. Additionally, the move from simply identifying to *identifying with* and then having actions outside the classroom take place, probably needs to be organically nurtured and grown by willing students alone, like social movements themselves. There are numerous variables in play, but most certainly some scaffolding and support networks will need to be put in place.

Figure 3.1 Student die-in demonstration in combination
the world effort to ban cluster munitions.

2016 to Present – Developing a Space for Peace

With an explicit and focused desire to understand how students and others interact with the constructs of peace, we opened up the possibilities for additional action by students once again at the school's yearly school festival. As we wrote early about our classes, one strand of this research was to explore how our students interacted with the concepts of PAAL. Hence, we attempted to construct course materials that would allow us to both implicitly and explicitly investigate these terms with our students. However, we were not satisfied with the compartmentalized nature of the classroom so we asked for student help in creating an interactive project to be shared with the university populace and local community at the school festival. Inspired by a community peace project by Parrish and Oxford (2013), we collected the messages of willing participants to build a wall of peace that would serve as a public display of their critical understandings of PAAL.

At the most basic level, these peace wall projects were just opportunities to get people actively engaged and connected to fundamental constructs of a harmonious and peaceful society. A concurrent objective was to provide an occasion for our students to express their notions of *identifying with* these ideals of peace and sharing them with their peers and others. Simply put, we wanted to share our feeling of peace and love locally and ascertain what people in our community were thinking about these ideas. In the first incarnation of *the peace wall* (see Figure 3.2) we asked participants to express their understanding of the terms of PAAL. *One step to peace* was the focal point of the 2017 peace wall project (see Figure 3.3). For this, people expressed what they thought was a necessary step to obtain a sustainable peace in our society, including concepts of positive peace or social equity. The output from these events is being analyzed but for a future paper. Our focus here is with the relationships between peoples and the concepts. The genuine value of the projects can mostly be found within the intragroup and intergroup interactions of our six student volunteers at the first project and the eight the following year. One volunteer student made such a strong connection to this project that she participated in all three peace wall incarnations, twice at the university school festival and once more at a renowned national language conference as well as being an active recruiter of other volunteers (Johnson, Johnson, & Murphey 2018). Her feedback comments about participating in the latest event, we think, clearly express strands of *identifying with* and then taking action: "I took your class last year and I could learn a lot of things I had never thought in my life as problems, or what is peace? I wanted people to think about these themes but in a fun and easy way." Other volunteers also expressed similar ideas of wanting to work together and share the concepts of peace with others in our greater community.

Figure 3.2 The Peace Wall 2016 – Peace, Activism, Altruism and Love.

Figure 3.3 The Peace Wall 2017 – What is your one step to peace?

Conclusion

"As the means, so the ends" was our guiding principle with the activities described in this chapter. *Identifying* a means can often take us to the end and through strange twists of fate leave us *identifying with* our tools. As noted in this chapter, the pathways of peace are multiple and local. The groundwork for much of our research found in this chapter focused on the constructs of peace, activism, altruism and love. Hicks (2004) found that when students study about complex problems, they also need chances to investigate the range of solutions for those issues at hand. To overlook this opportunity might lead one down the path of alienation, despair, and disempowerment. Yet, addressing this appropriately can develop a sense of empowerment and encourage the needed steps to become locally active as global citizens. We do understand that problems found in our world can be overpowering and that is precisely why we need to be empowering our students and communities with hopes and tools that will engage them to be an active part of the solutions. When we implement opportunities for our students to explore fundamental concepts such as PAAL in their learning, we are expanding the possibilities to discover those hopes. Through *identifying* them some of us have begun to *identify with* them as core constructs within our lives. While we currently have no longitudinal data to back up a claim that we have shifted our students to identifying with an interconnected coexistence on our planet, we believe we have sufficiently shown that short-term accomplishments can be *identified*.

References
Bell, W. K., & Kondabolu, H. (2017, September 14). Speaking with bell hooks and talking DACA [Podcast]. Retrieved from https://www.politicallyreactive.com/
Crookes, G. (2013). *Critical ELT in action*. Philadelphia, PA: Routledge.
Dörnyei, Z., & Murphey, T. (2003). *Group dynamics in the language classroom*. Cambridge, UK: Cambridge University Press.
Freeman, S., Eddy, S., McDonough, M., Smith, M., Okoroafor, N., Jordt, H., & Wenderoth, M. (2014). Active learning increases student performance in science, engineering, and mathematics. *PNAS, 111*(23), 8410-8415. Retrieved from http://www.pnas.org/content/111/23/8410.full?sid=0e3bbb72-8c1f-4b8e-a98f-1d752f9d7b58
Freire, P. (2000). *Pedagogy of the oppressed* (30th anniversary edition). New York, NY: Continuum.
Freire, P. (2006). The banking model of education. In E. F. Provenzo (Ed.), *Critical issues in education: an anthology of readings* (pp. 105-117). Thousand Oaks, CA: Sage Publications. (Original work published 1970)
Hicks, D. (2004). Teaching for tomorrow: How can futures studies contribute to peace education? *Journal of Peace Education, 1*(2), 165-178.
Johnson, K., Johnson, T., & Murphey, T. (2018). Becoming actively altruistic for love and peace. *Research Institute of Language Studies and Language Education, 28*, 91-121.
Kielburger, C., & Kielburger, M. (2008). *Me to we: Finding meaning in a material world*. New York, NY: Simon & Schuster.
McLeod, J., & Reynolds, R. (2010). Teaching human rights across the curriculum. *Ethos, 18*(3), 17-21.
McKenzie-Mohr, D. (2000). Promoting sustainable behavior: An introduction to community-based social marketing. *Journal of Social Issues, 56*(3), 543-554.
Murphey, T., & Murakami, K. (2001). Identifying and "identifying with" effective beliefs and behaviors. *NLP World, 8*(3), 41-56.

Murphey, T., & Arao, H. (2001). Reported belief changes through near peer role modeling. *TESL-EJ, 5*(3). Retrieved from http://tesl-ej.org/wordpress/

Murphey, T., & Falout, J. (2010). Critical participatory looping: Dialogic member checking with whole classes. *TESOL Quarterly, 44*(4), 811-821.

Murphey, T. (2013). Adapting ways for meaningful action: ZPDs and ZPAs. In J. Arnold & T. Murphey (Eds.), *Meaningful action: Earl Stevick's influence on language teaching* (pp. 172-189). Cambridge, UK: Cambridge University Press.

Murphey, T. (2017). Asking students to teach: Gardening in the jungle. In T. S. Gregersen & P. D. McIntyre (Eds.), *Innovative practices in language teacher education: Spanning the spectrum from intra- to inter-personal professional development* (pp. 251-268). Cham, Switzerland: Springer.

Parrish, T., & Oxford, R. (2013). The people's peace. In R. Oxford (Ed.) *The language of peace: Communicating to create* (pp. 329-354). Charlotte, NC: Information Age Publishing.

Smith, R. (2015). Exploratory action research as workplan: Why, what and where from? In K. Dikilitas, R. Smith, & W. Trotman (Eds.), *Teacher-researchers in action* (pp. 37-45). Kent, UK: IATEFL.

Swain, M. (2006). Languaging, agency and collaboration in advanced second language proficiency. In H. Byrnes (Ed.) *Advanced language learning: The contribution of Halliday and Vygotsky* (pp. 95-108). London, UK: Continuum.

TEDTalentSearch. (2012, June 25). Kyla Mitsunaga: Why teachers must learn "with" their students [Video file]. Retrieved from https://youtu.be/0y4FKH1cQNM

TEDx Talks. (2017, November 17). David Smith: Talking about peace [Video file]. Retrieved from https://www.youtube.com/watch?v=8M5iXMFzf_o

Toh, S. (2007, July). Pathways to the building of a culture of peace. Paper presented at the Peace Education Workshop in Uganda. Organized by the Ugandan national commission for UNESCO and the Korean National Commission for UNESCO.

Wells, L. (2003). A culture of teaching peace. Proceedings of the UNESCO Conference on Intercultural Education (pp. 1-46). Helsinki, Finland: UNESCO.

Notes

1. Referring to an infamous tactic used by the rebel forces in the country of Sierra Leone

CHAPTER 4

PEACEBUILDING AND SOCIAL JUSTICE IN ENGLISH AS A FOREIGN LANGUAGE:
Classroom Experiences from a Colombian High School

Yecid Ortega

"Nuestro pueblo se llama Mundo, y nuestra raza se llama Humanidad." (Our people are called World and our race is called Humanity.) Juan Manuel Santos, Colombian President (Nobel Prize Ceremony, December 11, 2016)

Introduction and Context

Colombia has experienced more than 50 years of political violence characterized by violent conflict amongst various left-wing organizations, guerillas, paramilitary groups, and organized crime (González González, 2014; Sherman, 2015; Vargas & Caruso, 2014). Teenage students suffer the repercussions of this violent societal conflict—youth experience school violence, social isolation, and sexual harassment on a daily basis (López de Mesa-Melo, Carvajal-Castillo, Soto-Godoy, & Urrea-Roa, 2013; Rodríguez, 2014). A peace agreement was signed in November 2016, giving hope that a peaceful post-war reconciliation/state of affairs would emerge. The Colombian government is working to help its citizens move forward towards reconciliation and national unity and prosperity. Consequently, the implementation of peace and social justice curriculum (as detailed in Bill 1732 - *Cátedra de la Paz* [lectures for peace], 2014a) has been identified as crucial for promoting peace and reconciliation among all Colombians.

Typically, history and social studies classes address conflict and peace in the Colombian classroom (Bickmore, Kaderi, & Guerra-Sua, 2017);

Colombian English teachers have traditionally emphasized how English language competency can be beneficial for students' future professional careers (British Council, 2015); however, they rarely engage in discussions related to social justice issues (such as bullying, racism, classism, and other forms of discrimination) in their classrooms. Furthermore, the English curricular content proposed by the Ministry of Education—*Colombia Bilingüe 2014-2018*—(Ministerio de Educación, 2014b) states that English language teaching should be directed towards preparing students with the professional and academic skills needed to compete in the global market. This curriculum, aimed at positioning Colombia as the economic leader of the Latin American region, contradicts the overarching goals of Bill 1732 to promote peace. Although learning the English language is important to function in an international market, the English as a foreign language (EFL) curriculum largely ignores issues surrounding peace and social justice that Colombian society must address in the post-peace accord era. Critiques have recently emerged about the contradictory policy guiding EFL in education and how English classes have mainly focused on uncritically teaching linguistic content that is often culturally unrelated to the urban and rural contexts where it is taught (Usma, 2015; Usma & Pelaez, 2017); however, more research is needed to explore the possibilities of social justice and peacebuilding curriculum (SJPBC) in EFL classrooms.

I argue that issues of violence and social justice could be addressed in Colombian English classes through the lens of SJPBC, which encourages students to learn about themselves, their communities, and their culture. If education is a "task that demands a critical intellect, an ethnic of justice and compassion and a spiritual recognition of the precious and inviolable nature of human life, as well as the web of being that connects life" (Shapiro, 2010, p. 23). EFL instruction has the potential power to focus not only on constructing grammatically correct sentences, but on building peace and striving for a just society in post-accord Colombia.

This chapter examines how one EFL teacher, her students, and a "critical friend" tried to connect English language teaching to social justice issues. A collaborative action research approach was used to explore how English language instruction can lead to social change using a pedagogy incorporating peacebuilding competencies (see Chaux, Lleras, & Velásquez, 2004; Diazgranados et al., 2014; Silva & Chaux, 2005) to foster peacebuilding citizenship among students. The ultimate goal of the research project was to examine and better understand the process(es) whereby Colombian students are sensitized and conscientized about social justice issues and peace in their English classes as they become advocates for peace. The inquiry for this chapter has two foci: 1) discuss the concepts of peace education and social justice in relation to EFL in Colombia and elsewhere, and 2) to highlight how these concepts could be used as a framework for pedagogies to promote peacebuilding through EFL.

Conceptual Considerations

This section examines the two main conceptual perspectives that underpin the research: 1) social justice, peace, and violence(s); and 2) peacebuilding and social justice education. In my framework, these interconnected concepts support each other and find their convergence in *praxis* (see Figure 4.1). For Freire (1970), praxis refers to actions and reflections directed towards the transformation of social structures that oppress the marginalized. Praxis empowers the oppressed to acquire critical awareness of the social topography of power and to question their marginal position in society. I argue that both social justice and peace approaches to education, particularly in EFL instruction, are powerful means of critically questioning the status quo. These approaches do this by privileging and including students' voices in teaching and learning, and by connecting learning to students' lived experiences and larger problems confronting their community (Macrine, 2009).

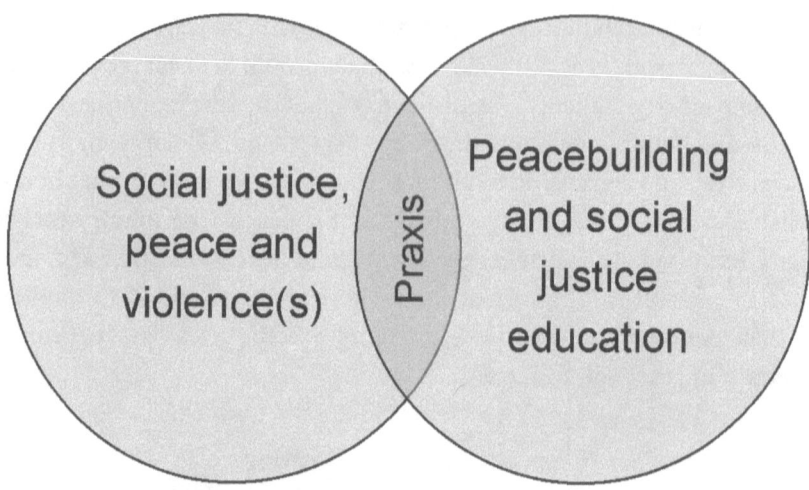

Figure 4.1 A conceptual framework for social justice and peace in language teaching.

Social Justice, Peace and Violence(s)

Social justice is understood in different ways by different people. Some define social justice as a philosophical approach that seeks to treat all people with fairness, respect, dignity, and generosity (Nieto & Bode, 2012). Miller (1999) argues that our understanding of social justice must be practical and *real* rather than abstract and imprecise. Consequently, he conceptualises social justice as the just distribution of benefits and burdens within society. Miller poses questions regarding how ordinary people understand justice and address social justice in their real-life contexts. He proposes three principles for people to use to evaluate the fairness of society: outcomes of distribution according to need; distribution according to "desert" (claiming rewards based on performance); and distribution based on equality. Like Miller, Zajda (2010) also understands justice as a set of principles. Her concept of social justice includes economic, legal, and political dimensions that are guided by a sense of responsibility to work with others. Capeheart and Milovanovic (2007) encourage us to examine the conceptions of dominant and non-dominant justice and how these are applied to people or groups. They explain that social justice is not a narrow system preoccupied with justice for individuals, but a complex and challenging task for humans to change and transform society (Johannessen & Unterreiner, 2008). In short, social justice integrates both fairness and practicality. Although it is based on a philosophy of equality and fairness, social justice is more than an abstract idea—it is manifested and rooted in people's everyday experiences and realities. Social justice includes economic, legal, socio-cultural, and political dimensions that must be addressed at different personal and social levels.

Theorizing around peace—what it is and how it is constructed in our societies—hails from a very different academic tradition than the scholarship surrounding social justice. However, the two concepts have important similarities worth exploring. Peace is often best understood by defining and delineating its opposites: violence and conflict. Galtung (1990) describes three types of violence: 1) *direct violence*—any form of physical or verbal abuse (e.g., killing or torture, rape and sexual assault, and beatings); 2) *cultural violence*—beliefs and attitudes that have been inculcated since childhood and which prevail with us in our daily lives; and 3) *structural violence*—groups, classes, genders, and nationalities that tend to have more access to goods, resources, and opportunities than others. These three forms of violence are interrelated and often manifested in the structural and unequal advantages built into the very social, political, and economic systems that govern societies. Galtung's (1990) conceptualization of peace is linked to the triangle of violence above; notably, he differentiates between "negative peace," which he defines as the absence of direct physical violence, and "positive peace," which he theorizes more broadly as the absence of structural and cultural violence. Therefore, the concepts of positive peace and social justice are quite similar.

Nixon (2011) provides further nuance to the concept of violence by adding a temporal dimension. He argues that many types of violence are "slow" and temporally distant from the causes of this violence; this "slow violence" is largely imperceptible except to the poor and marginalized, who suffer disproportionately from its effects. Although Nixon uses the concept mostly to examine the impact of environmental pollution on the disempowered, "slow violence" is also a useful lens for thinking about how Colombia and other states affected by violent conflict suffer from the effects of hidden, incremental violence.

Valenzuela (2005) states that peace can be manifested in each person, their family, and the sociopolitical and economic community. He believes the individual can create a culture of peace by challenging and dismantling hidden manifestations of structural and cultural violence. Valenzuela guides individuals on how to positively affect the sociopolitical, economic, and religious dimensions of life that foster a culture of peace and eradicate war. Furthermore, UNESCO and United Nations (1997) highlight that a transdisciplinary approach must be pursued in which Valenzuela's principles, school initiatives, and other social ideas can be enacted to foster respect for fundamental rights and freedoms, understanding, tolerance, and solidarity with the marginalized. For nation states that have lived with violent conflict such as Colombia, education has a pivotal role in pursuing a culture of peace and the social transformation our planet needs in times of crisis (Lin & Oxford, 2011). To this, Oxford (2017) presents an array of activities that look at peacebuilding in the English language classroom in Argentina. She asserts that teacher education programs are sites where educators can (and should) learn how to directly and indirectly challenge violence and become agents of change.

Challenging violence can be addressed with social transformation and this one can only be undertaken if structural and cultural forms of violence are made visible (Galtung, 1990). Identifying hidden violence(s) creates space for humans and communities to respond to real-life problems, which Lederach (2006) calls "conflict transformation." This journey recognizes the dialectic nature of relationships. Conflict is socially created by humans; therefore, conflict can also be *transformed* by humans. Consequently, as social beings we do not need to take the world "as is"—we can work to transform it. For Lederach (2006), this transformation must occur at the personal and system levels. At the personal level, conflict transformation is characterised by the pursuit of awareness, growth, and commitment to change. At the system level, conflict transformation includes the elimination of oppression, the sharing of resources, and the promotion of non-violent conflict resolution between disputing groups. Education is seen by many scholars and educational professionals as a means of transforming both interpersonal and societal conflict.

Peace(building) and Social Justice Education

Before I examine how education can work to transform conflict, foster peace, and dismantle problematic social structures, I will briefly outline how schooling can also reinforce and reproduce many different forms of violence and social injustice. First, Bickmore (2017) notes that "...education may legitimize beliefs and narratives of national, ethnic or gender-based chauvinism and social inequity, or normalize (some or all) violence and militarism" (p. 1). Davies (2011) created a useful five-point continuum for conceptualising how education may work to reinforce or mitigate direct and structural violence (which she labels "fragility"; see Figure 4.2). She notes that education can work to actively reinforce violence/fragility or to make inroads towards building peace.

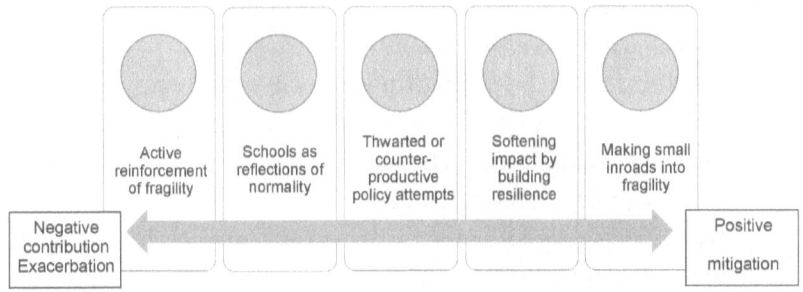

Figure 4.2 The spectrum of impact of education on fragility (adapted from Davies, 2011).

If education is needed to help build a positive, socially just peace, what would this education look like? Mthethwa-Sommers (2014) argues that although schools may serve to perpetuate inequalities and social injustices that exist in society, schools should be also sites for democratic discussions of ideological, cultural, religious, and social diversity issues. To accomplish this goal, theories and practices related to social justice education and peacebuilding can be used to serve the oppressed and transform policies and practices. With this in mind, education becomes a vision of a holistic system in which humans move to a less violent, more cooperative and caring mode of existence and foster a "call to focus on peace in education [that] is necessarily a call to re-envision the very way we educate young people, away from the deadening and confined forms that currently dominate our classrooms" (Shapiro, 2010, p. 8).

The concept of social justice is a useful lens for examining social inequities in schooling; it enables teachers and students to envision teaching and learning for social justice and equity (Johannessen, 2010; Ukpokodu, 2010). I strongly feel that educational concepts of social justice and peace interrogate systems of power and therefore require a critical stance. For example, Giroux (1994) noted how questions of audience, voice, power, and evaluation actively work to construct particular relations between teachers and students, institutions and society, and classrooms and communities. Ukpokodu (2010) highlights that social justice is an action-oriented process that pursues social reconstruction; therefore, a social justice approach to education inherently challenges hegemonic ideologies and tries to confront and dismantle unequal structures in the educational system and society. Mclaren (1988) argues critical education must commit to empower the powerless to transform their conditions which perpetuate injustice and inequity. Critical pedagogy ultimately looks at questioning power relations and the structures that reproduce the injustice, exploitation, and oppression of the status quo while hindering students' liberation (Freire, 1970).

In practice, the social justice approach to education helps create social change by empowering students to become active critical producers of meaning and texts. Teachers can facilitate this in two ways: (1) through understanding the sources of inequalities and privileges in society; and (2) by knowing students' personal histories, learning experiences, and understandings of social justice (Darling-Hammond, 2005; Lee, 2011). Teaching for social justice is based on some important conceptual and pedagogical foundations. Dover (2013), for example, proposes a model that integrates principles of equity and accountability-driven schooling. She argues that education must include critical pedagogy, democratic education, and multicultural education. Kelly (2012) suggests anti-oppressive curricula and pedagogies can make students aware of injustice in schools and motivate them to counter cultural imperialism, marginalization, systemic violence, exploitation, and narratives of powerlessness. Picower (2012) offers six hands-on ways to organize social justice in the curriculum. These look at understanding students' social and linguistic backgrounds and how these backgrounds can be drawn on to help students respect others and take concrete action to create change in their communities. Efforts to integrate social justice into classrooms require a focus on the sociopolitical context of schooling. Teaching for social justice involves more than pedagogical techniques—it must pursue political and ideological goals to affect change. This is especially true in contexts like Colombia emerging from decades of violent conflict.

Education has been identified as a crucial avenue for promoting social cohesion, resolving conflict, and fostering peacebuilding approaches to reduce violence (Bickmore, 2017). Specifically, peace education has emerged "as a field of scholarship and practice that utilizes teaching and learning not only to dismantle all forms of violence but also to create structures that build and sustain a just equitable peace [and] world" (Bajaj & Hantzopoulos, 2016, p. 1). Harris (2009) conceptualizes peace education as the creation of an environment in which students acquire the necessary skills to solve problems caused by violence. He posits that peace education has both long-term and short-term goals. In the short-term, Harris argues that peace education should respond immediately to threatening situations caused by various forms of violence. However, in the long-term he argues that peace education should aim to instill in humans the conditions to transform human values and promote nonviolent action. In the end, educators for peace must teach peace to create peaceful conditions for students to manage conflict and violent situations. Peace education must target both direct and structural violence, very much similar to Lederach's (2006) argument that violence must be transformed at both the personal and systemic levels. Bajaj and Hantzopoulos (2016) argue that in addition to academic research, systemic violence should be named and transformed through curricula, pedagogy, participatory learning, dialogue-based encounters, and teaching multiple perspectives.

Peace education envisions schools as sites that engage in community healing and improvement as a project for human development (Shapiro, 2006). In contexts of violence, Gill and Niens (2014) argue that humanization and critical dialogue are two potential educational strategies for peacebuilding. Bickmore (2005, 2011) defines peacebuilding as a framework which allows for dialogue, problem-solving, and collective decision-making. She asserts that the ability to manage conflict equitably and non-violently is key to citizenship in a socially just democracy. History and social study classes have been identified as key in peacebuilding, peace, and social justice in Colombia (Bickmore et al., 2017); however SJPBC approaches enacted in language classrooms would help ensure that pedagogies and curriculum are culturally responsive, sustaining, and relevant to students' contexts (Billings, 1992; Paris & Alim, 2017).

To conclude this section, I posit that rather than being confined to social studies and history classes, social justice issues should be discussed across the curriculum. Teachers and researchers need to attempt to connect theory and practice towards social change—*praxis*. Chapman and Hobbel (2010) specifically suggest that social justice education should use multiple curricular perspectives to invigorate students to know the world through critical understanding of themselves, the communities in which they live, and the larger society in order to transform the world. Nieto and Bode (2012) propose that social justice should challenge, confront, and disrupt misconceptions and stereotypes that lead to structural inequality and discrimination based on race, social class, gender, and other social and human differences.

The Action Research Project: "Peace in Action"

At first glance, Colombia may appear quite homogenous: Colombia has arguably only one official national language (Spanish), and unlike many Western countries Colombia does not have a recent history of immigration, or the mosaic of foreign languages and cultures that come with it. Nonetheless, Colombia is a heterogenous, multiethnic, and pluricultural country; Spanish and other indigenous languages and cultures live together (Baca, 2006; Fearon, 2003; Ng'weno, 2004). This diversity is evident in the nation's public schools, where indigenous peoples, Afro-Colombians, farmers, and people forcibly displaced by war study side-by-side in both rural and urban areas (OECD, 2013). Although the Colombian government has made significant efforts to promote peace education and citizenship awareness across the curriculum (Ministerio de Educacion, 2014a), these efforts are not necessarily reflected in the EFL curriculum or practices.

Despite the lack of government support for SJPBC in EFL classrooms, some English teachers remain interested in exploring concepts of peace and social justice with their students. One of these teachers, Liliana, is an English teacher at a secondary school in Bogota, where she works with students in grades 9, 10, and 11. Liliana became concerned after she had witnessed bullying and aggressive behaviour from some of her students in her English class. I met her through other professional connections when she began looking for pedagogical solutions to help minimize this aggression. After several meetings exploring and reflecting on the issue, we decided to collaborate in an action research project that Liliana called *Peace in Action*. We used the following question to frame the research and connect theory and practice: What are the students' perceptions about social justice issues in the school/classroom?

School Setting and Participants
The school where the research project was carried out is in Bosa, the 7th locality of the Capital District of the Colombian capital, Bogotá. Bosa is located in the southwestern part of the city and is the 8th largest locality and 9th most populated. Bosa covers the Indigenous territory; the name, Bosa, means "second day of the week," coming from the Chibcha language word "Boza" (School teacher, personal communication, November 16, 2016). This locality has approximately 280 neighborhoods, 63% of which are legally recognized, another 23% are in the process of becoming legally recognized, and the other 14% are unrecognized. Bosa has high rates of internal immigration from other regions of Colombia and most of its inhabitants are of a low socio-economic status (Secretaria Distrital de Planeación, 2009). According to the school's principal, the school educates up to approximately 3,500 students a day in three different shifts in the academic stream; this includes morning and afternoon shifts for secondary students and evening shifts for adult education.

The participants in the study were 42 students of grade 9 aged 14-16 who came from diverse ethnic backgrounds (Afro-Colombians, farmers, and students of indigenous descent). These students received four hours of English per week, and although there are curricular suggested guidelines provided by the government, the teacher and the students collaborated in the creation of their own lessons based on perceived social problems that the school has, such as bullying, school violence, family violence, teenage pregnancy, among others.

Maria participated as a teacher researcher and was key in the data collection process. According to conversations with Maria, she has over 20 years of experience teaching English as a foreign language in public schools and private universities. Her Christian background and her commitment to social justice-oriented pedagogies have influenced her educational philosophy. She respects her students as individuals who deserve a quality education; however, she views the teaching of strong values as important at the development of academic knowledge. During the course of her career, she has become interested in action research initiatives as a way to improve her teaching; this experience was invaluable in the conception and implementation of this *Peace in Action* project.

I have known Maria for four years from different professional networks, and since then we became friends. Maria occasionally came to me for emotional and technical support; emotional support to help deal with difficult moments at school, and technical support regarding EFL pedagogies, resources, and assessment techniques. Over the years we have developed a strong, respectful working relationship that helped me to act as a "critical friend" (Elliot, 1985) throughout the action research project. I acted as a remote facilitator of the research process as well as a professional and academic supporter. Maria's students knew me because she always told them about my helping her with feedback and supporting her ideas for classroom planning.

Methods

This collaborative action research project examined how Maria's high school students learned the necessary social and citizenship competencies needed to discuss conflict as they practiced English. Students were encouraged to talk about peace in the class; they wrote scripts and performed sketches in English to discuss violent events in their school. This research drew on traditions of collaborative action research; more specifically, the research was action oriented and it sought to solve problems at both the institutional (school) and community levels with a practical orientation (Hinchey, 2008).

The research project was carried out during the morning shift 6:45 am to 12:30 pm in the English classroom during the second semester (June to November) of the 2016 academic year. During the research process, Maria took videos and photos of the students' projects as data instruments to reflect on her pedagogy and document the students' outcomes. As a critical friend, I communicated remotely with Maria over the phone and instant messaging programs such as Skype and WhatsApp.

This research project cycle had five different steps (see Figure 4.3); during the data collection Maria and I undertook this cycle five times over the course of 12 classes. The first step of the cycle was the collaborative reflection and planning stage. This step involved planning meetings with Maria to reflect on challenges and opportunities and discuss possibilities for implementing SJPBC activities in her classroom practice. Maria also used this time to complain about the many issues she was experiencing in her class, as well as other school issues and other personal problems. Acting as a critical friend, I gave her advice and emotional support where possible to help her continue her valuable work. In the second step of the cycle, Maria drafted lesson plans with her teaching ideas and shared them with me. We would discuss the plans and modify them until she felt they were ready to be used in class. This led to the third step—implementing the lesson in the classroom. During these classes, Maria would take photos or videos of classroom activities and document students' reactions to our SJPBC activities. To augment these observations, Maria implemented a fourth step in the action research cycle: at the end of class whenever possible Maria would record audio reflections or write reflective notes about what transpired with her students. She would record what worked, what had not, and identify challenges and opportunities to be addressed in future classes whenever possible. In the fifth step of the cycle, Maria would ask students for feedback about the activities in the class. During this stage, the students gave suggestions and comments on how the activities could be modified to engage them more effectively (most of the time students proposed activities related to what they liked to learn or issues they would like to discuss). Finally, Maria would gather students' feedback

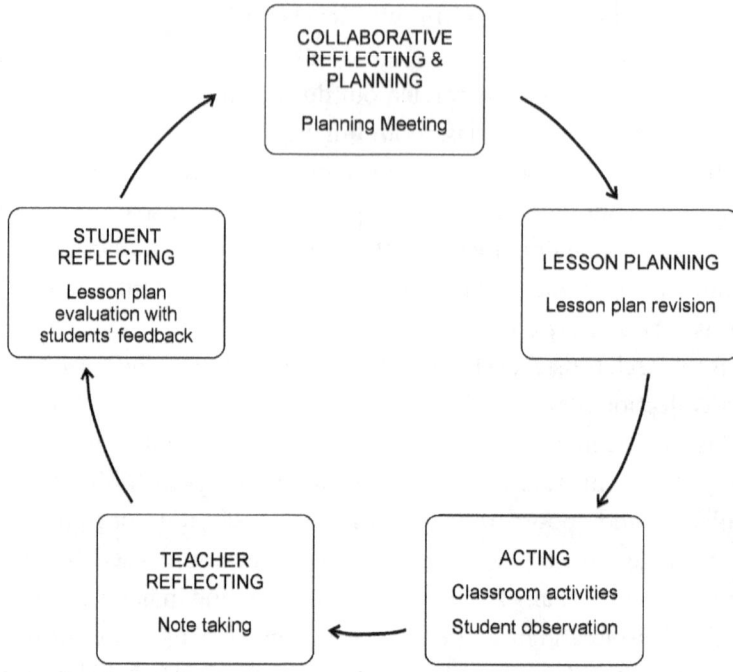

Figure 4.3 Peace in action research cycle.

and suggestions and meet with me and plan more lessons that would reflect what she learned from her classroom experiences.

The iterative action research cycles consisted of an intervention (action plan) in the form of lessons using social justice themes (bullying, classism, racism, and others) that was carried out in Maria's class. The photos, videos, reflections, and meeting and conversation notes were analyzed with Nvivo 11 software using content analysis (Berg, 2009) and a thematic analysis (Ryan & Bernard, 2000). I examined recurring themes to make connections between the research question and Maria's classroom practices.

Implementation and Description

Maria's motivation to integrate SJPBC in her classes stems from the physical, emotional, and verbal violence she increasingly witnessed in her classes and the lives of her students. She noticed that students would physically attack each other for supporting opposing soccer teams or verbally abuse each other in school. She also noticed that students often referred to experiences with domestic violence, street gangs, drug dealing, and financial difficulties at home.

Maria decided to address some of these issues in her English class. Although there are suggested curricular guidelines provided by the government, Maria decided to develop lessons based on the violence, negative conflicts, and social problems she witnessed in the school and her classroom, such as physical violence, bullying, and emotional harassment. In order to address these issues, Maria thought that it was best to start asking her students what the word "peace" means for them. Students wrote some concepts on their notebooks and then shared them with each other. After listening to the students' conceptualizations of peace, Maria felt that these were vague, abstract, and unclear: "(para los estudiantes) la paz es una idea más que una acción en concreto" ([for students] peace is more like an idea rather than a concrete action; August 26, 2016—Maria's audio note).

The students' conceptualizations of peace, although abstract in the beginning of the project, later became a point of entry for other discussions related to the social injustice students and their families lived and experienced. These included family violence, wage inequality, and discrimination based on gender and socioeconomic class. Because the students seemed to understand peace as an abstract ideal rather than a tangible thing or action, Maria encouraged the students to propose concrete activities that could help solve some of the problems mentioned above; she collaborated with her students to create lessons that would take concrete, practical actions for peacebuilding.

One of the first activities students suggested was to create drama-based dialogues in English. Students scripted various sketches based on real-life scenarios of violent or problematic behaviour they had experienced at school. Maria then proof-read and corrected these scripts, and students later performed their sketches for different audiences in the school (see Figure 4.4).

Figure 4.4 Using English to perform sketches about peace.

After several presentations, students revealed that in addition to helping them improve their English skills, participating in the sketches also helped them to be aware of the negative effects of bullying and other forms of aggression. According to Maria's own classroom observations and reflections, this drama-based approach helped students to develop and use skills such as empathy and active listening (Chaux et al., 2008) that empowered them to become advocates for peace and encourage them to learn more English. As she noted, "(este proyecto) fue satisfactorio para mí, porque sentí que en realidad están aprendiendo, están aprendiendo algo más allá de solo lengua" ([This project] was rewarding for me, because I felt that students are really learning something beyond learning just the language; August 26, 2016—Maria's audio note).

Maria realized that for her, the main goal for this action research project was to better understand how her students perceived peace in the school and elsewhere. After several weeks of drama-based and peace-infused activities in the English classroom, Maria's observations suggested that students had become more sensitive and aware of the violent culture that existed in their school. Interviews with students revealed that aggressive practices such as bullying were normalized and had become a part of their everyday lives. Interestingly, bullying was often seen as a sign of friendship and camaraderie rather than a harmful behaviour negatively affecting students' relationships. One student commented, "Teacher, si nosotros buliamos a los otros es porque es nuestro amigo y queremos que mejore, eso es normal" (Teacher, if we bully others is because they are our friends and we want them to improve, that is normal; November 2016, informal interview with students).

Maria's classroom activities were highly successful in that her students were able to communicate ideas challenging violence and encouraging peace with the larger school community. For example, in one activity some students created a picture frame, and walked around the school, taking photos of those who would like to be "in peace." Students would say something like "We are going to take a photo using this frame to those who are in peace." This activity not only helped students practice English outside their classroom, it also created awareness of the issues of bullying and violence and created space for discussions on possible solutions for these negative behaviors.

Peace in Action became an effective initiative for engaging Maria's students in English language learning as they learned the skills to advocate for peace. Several teachers in the school saw the positive results and later worked collaboratively towards a cross-curricular approach that involved most of the teachers in the school. The technology teacher helped the students to make blogs and edit videos to publish on social media and share with the school. Towards the end of the project, the arts and drama teacher worked in collaboration with Maria and other English teachers to use performative approaches to raise community awareness against violence and social injustices.

Analysis of Findings

Peace in Action explored the possibilities for peacebuilding in an EFL classroom. Maria and her students agreed that integrating themes of social justice and peace into English language classes successfully engaged students in learning English and developed skills to discuss problematic situations that happened on a daily basis at school. This project was aligned with two Colombian initiatives to foster peacebuilding and citizenship. First, the lessons demonstrated that a peacebuilding approach to English language instruction can help to operationalize Bill 1732, *Cátedra de la paz* [lectures for peace] (Ministerio de Educacion, 2014a), which has a goal to cultivate a culture of dialogue and peacebuilding among students. Although this action research did not directly or explicitly address social justice or peacebuilding, it fostered a sense of belonging that is a first step towards reducing violence in Colombia and (re)constructing a peaceful society to support democratic participation, respect for diversity, and *convivencia* (i.e., coexistence, or living in harmony; Chaux et al., 2008; Diazgranados et al., 2014; Silva & Chaux, 2005). Second, this project was also aligned with the *Colombian Program of Citizenship Competencies* (Ministerio de Educación Nacional, 2004) because it integrated respect and the promotion of human rights into the English classroom to establish the basic levels of quality education. The project promoted concrete actions that could address real social problems that students and communities face on a daily basis.

Peace in Action encouraged students to promote citizenship and peacebuilding competencies as proposed by Chaux et al. (2008). These can be described as:

- handling anger: the ability to handle emotions without inflicting harm.
- empathy: the ability to feel what others feel.
- distance-taking: the ability to understand others' perspectives.
- creative generation of alternatives: the ability to create alternative solutions to a conflict.
- considering consequences: the ability to understand the consequences of one's actions.
- active listening: the ability to listen actively to others.
- assertiveness: the ability to defend personal rights and others.
- questioning beliefs: the ability to reason and challenge violent and conflictive beliefs.

When Maria's students learned these competencies, they created opportunities for personal and social transformations. These values and competencies can be potentially used by English teachers for both language learning and for transforming behaviours of negative conflict (such as bullying, discrimination, and violence) into positive conflict and dialogue. Additionally, the core values described by Ben-Nun's (2013) "Three Rs" integration model for peace education were also enacted:

(1) **R**espect as a value that means regard for the worth of others with dignity and equality;
(2) **R**ecognition as a process to become aware of the others, understand them and work with them in the process of conflict resolution; and lastly
(3) **R**econciliation as a way to coexist, accept and cooperate with others in search of peace.

Other social competencies described by (Chaux et al., 2008) were promoted such as listening actively to their peers, defending their personal rights and the rights of others, and creating alternative solutions to conflict in their class and school. Furthermore, the research project was anchored in the concept of respect (both self-respect and mutual respect); this encouraged students to engage in meaningful, realistic, and useful pedagogical activities in the EFL class. Students developed their ability to reason and to handle their emotions in a positive, non-violent manner in order to challenge violent and problematic beliefs in the classroom and school. Maria's students learned to respect others regardless of which soccer team they supported. They learned to de-normalize bullying, they created awareness of social injustices in their school and community, and they promoted peace initiatives in the school.

However, despite its accomplishments, *Peace in Action* actually goes against the Ministry of Education's key language policy, *Colombia Bilingüe 2014-2018* (Ministerio de Educación, 2014b), which focuses primarily on developing students' English language skills to increase their economic competitiveness and to position Colombia as the economic leader in Latin America. Maria believes her role as an English teacher is not only to develop English language competencies that will help her students to be economically successful, but also to provide them with the skills to identify challenges and address the inequalities that students and other Colombians face in their daily lives. She asserts that despite the pressure from the government and some parents to focus on economically profitable and marketable English skills, her EFL classes must also ensure that students develop skills to foster and protect their happiness and well-being: "De qué sirve tener estudiantes que sepan inglés si no son felices y no saben resolver problemas cotidianos" (What is the point of having students who know English if they are not happy and are not able to solve daily problems; Communication with the critical friend, November 2016) .

This research project set out to explore students' perceptions of social justice issues in their classroom and school. In the collection and analysis of the action research data two main ideas emerged. First, Maria reconceptualized the curriculum and lesson planning process; she moved from viewing it as a rigid structure imposed on her to viewing lesson planning as a reflective, interactive process co-created with her students based on their comments, feedback, and needs. Data showed that all the activities carried out in the English class were either the product of ongoing discussions with students or the result of discussion and feedback from myself acting as a critical friend. Maria believes that to effectively educate her students, the lesson preparation process and pedagogical decisions should be developed democratically with students and colleagues rather than imposed and developed. Second, students developed something that Maria calls *conciencia social* (social awareness): students became more aware not only of acts of violence in schools (such as bullying and physical aggression), they also became more aware about problems of violence affecting Colombian society more broadly (such as narcotraffickers, guerrillas, and sociopolitical instability). Students shifted from viewing this violence as a "normal" part of their daily lives to understanding that societal violence can (and must be addressed and challenged. In collaboration with Maria and other teachers, students took concrete action to challenge and de-normalize violent behaviors in their classroom, school, and community.

Maria recognized that using a social justice and peace-oriented pedagogy in the classroom is not easy; it requires a lot of work and support. She agrees that this work cannot be isolated; it requires collaboration with students, colleagues, the administration, and "critical friends" to discuss and reflect with. The data strongly suggests that most of Maria's lessons—as well as the learning outcome they produced—would not have been possible if she was working by herself. For example, the support she received from other teachers was key in the accomplishment of some tasks. The arts teacher helped students to develop their acting and performative skills to present the final sketches, while other teachers gave emotional support to Maria when she felt discouraged by many personal challenges.

Maria ultimately described the classroom research experience as extremely rewarding, especially when she saw her students making changes in their lives and helping their peers and family identify and understand social problems. For example, during the students' interview, some students discussed how they talked about issues of family violence with their parents, and other students became friends with some homeless people from their neighborhood and learned about their struggles. Maria concluded that a sense of commitment and collaboration inspired her students to learn English and become social agents of change. In the end, *Peace in Action* was not an individual effort but a collaborative one that advanced peacebuilding in one Colombian English language classroom. For a country entering into a post-conflict era, I believe this is a small but important step.

Discussion and Conclusion

After more than almost half of a century of violent conflict, Colombia is now facing a post-peace accord era. In Colombia, peace, social justice, moral values, and ethical issues have traditionally only been addressed in religion, history, and social studies classes. *Peace in Action* demonstrated that in addition to teaching grammar and punctuation, the English language classroom can become a space to discuss themes of peace and violence that are relevant to students and the communities they live in. This collaborative action research showed that EFL teachers can teach about concepts of peace and violence while simultaneously developing students' vocabulary and linguistic skills. This research can serve as an example of how English classes can encourage and empower teachers and schools to promote peacebuilding skills that students can exercise not only in their English class, but also in their homes and communities.

Peace in Action had a great impact in the school community towards the end that continued to affect change in the year after. Teachers and students worked towards the creation of peace awareness. One example of their work is a collaborative mural (see Figure 4.5) that acts as a daily reminder that all actions must come from a place of love and peace.

Figure 4.5 Collaborative mural to raise awareness for peace.

This collaborative action research may be relevant for emerging social research in two main aspects. First, it breaks new ground in the field of international education by demonstrating how the intersection of social justice and peacebuilding curriculum (SJPBC) and English as a foreign language (EFL) may offer spaces for students to engage in critical peacebuilding through language and literacy instruction. Second, it demonstrates that peacebuilding can be studied across the curriculum, including in subjects like English (i.e., as a second language, foreign language, or teaching English to speakers of other languages—ESL, EFL, TESOL). Furthermore, the ideas described in this chapter may be beneficial for teachers looking for resources to address issues of social justice and peace in their classrooms[1]. EFL students can be encouraged to use language skills to discuss issues that matter to them, their communities, and their families; this may enable them to become advocates for equality, social justice, and peace.

Although peace is commonly defined as the "absence of violence" (Galtung, 1990), Colombia's struggle for reconciliation after of years of violent conflict issues of requires the construction of a positive peace rooted in equality and social justice. This collaborative action research demonstrated that conflict transformation can happen when students are involved in meaningful language practices that promote social competencies which in turn allow students to use respect, resolution, and reconciliation towards actions that embody fairness, respect, dignity, and generosity (Nieto & Bode, 2012). Maria's classroom activities and collaboration with students and encouragement by me as a critical friend suggest that small inroads towards peace can be made when teachers provide spaces for talking about violence and develop competencies on how to build peace and learn the English language skills for communication and challenging social inequality in a country that still struggles with political corruption and a publicly funded healthcare system.

Acknowledgements
I would like to thank Maria (the English teacher), the ethics and drama teacher at the school in Bogotá (Colombia), their students for all their hard work and commitment for social justice and peace and their principal for his ongoing administrative support.

References

Baca, G. (2006). *Nationalism's bloody terrain: Racism, class inequality, and the politics of recognition*. New York, NY: Berghahn Books.

Bajaj, M., & Hantzopoulos, M. (Eds.). (2016). *Peace education: International perspectives*. London, UK: Bloomsbury Academic.

Ben-Nun, M. (2013). The 3Rs of integration: Respect, recognition and reconciliation: Concepts and practices of integrated schools in Israel and Northern Ireland. *Journal of Peace Education, 10*(1), 1–20. https://doi.org/10.1080/17400201.2012.672403

Berg, B. L. (2009). *Qualitative research methods for the social sciences* (7th ed.). Montreal, Quebec: Allyn & Bacon.

Bickmore, K. (2005). Teacher development for conflict participation: Facilitating learning for "difficult citizenship"education. *International Journal of Citizenship and Teacher Education, 1*(2), 2–16. doi:10.1.1.466.8983

Bickmore, K. (2011). Keeping, making, and building peace in school. *Social Education, 75*(1), 40–44. https://www.socialstudies.org/publications/socialeducation/january-february2011/keeping_making_and_building_peace_in_school

Bickmore, K. (2017). Conflict, peace-building, and education: Rethinking pedagogies in divided societies, Latin America, and around the world. In K. Mundy, K. Bickmore, & R. Hayhoe (Eds.), *Comparative and international education: Issues for teachers* (pp. 268-299). New York, NY: Teachers College.

Bickmore, K., Kaderi, A. S., & Guerra-Sua, Á. (2017). Creating capacities for peacebuilding citizenship: History and social studies curricula in Bangladesh, Canada, Colombia, and México. *Journal of Peace Education, 14*(3), 1–28. https://doi.org/10.1080/17400201.2017.1365698

Billings, G. L. (1992). Reading between the lines and beyond the pages: A culturally relevant approach to literacy teaching. *Theory into Practice, 31*(4), 312-320. https://doi.org/10.1080/00405849209543558

British Council. (2015). *English in Colombia: An examination of policy, perceptions and influencing factors*. Retrieved from https://ei.britishcouncil.org/sites/default/files/latin-america-research/English%20in%20Colombia.pdf

Capeheart, L., & Milovanovic, D. (2007). *Social justice: Theories, issues, and movements*. New Brunswick, NJ: Rutgers University Press.

Chapman, T. K., & Hobbel, N. (2010). *Social justice pedagogy across the curriculum: The practice of freedom*. New York, NY: Routledge.

Chaux, E., Bustamante, A., Castellanos, M., Jiménez, M., Nieto, A. M., Rodríguez, G. I., ... Velásquez. (2008). Aulas en paz [Classrooms in Peace]: Teaching strategies. *Interamerican Journal of Education for Democracy, 1*(2), 167. Retreived from: https://scholarworks.iu.edu/journals/index.php/ried/article/download/117/197/0

Chaux, E., Lleras, J., & Velásquez, A. M. (Eds.). (2004). *Competencias ciudadanas: De los estándares al aula, una propuesta de integración a las áreas académicas* (1st ed.)[Citizenship competences: From classroom standards to the integration of academic content]. Bogotá, Colombia: Ministerio de Educación Nacional: CESO: Ediciones Uniandes.

Darling-Hammond, L. (2005). Educating the new educator: Teacher education and the future of democracy. *The New Educator, 1*(1), 1–18. https://doi.org/10.1080/15476880490441379

Davies, L. (2011). Can education interrupt fragility? Toward the resilient citizen and the adaptable state. In K. Mundy & S. Dryden-Peterson (Eds.), *Educating children in conflict zones: Research, policy, and practice for systemic change - a tribute to Jackie Kirk* (pp. 33-48). New York, NY: Teachers College Press.

Diazgranados, S., Noonan, J., Brion-Meisels, S., Saldarriaga, L., Daza, B. C., Chávez, M., & Antonellis, I. (2014). Transformative peace education with teachers: Lessons from juegos de paz in rural Colombia. *Journal of Peace Education, 11*(2), 150–161. doi:10.1080/17400201.2014.898627

Dover, A. G. (2013). Teaching for social justice: From conceptual frameworks to classroom practices. *Multicultural Perspectives, 15*(1), 3–11. https://doi.org/10.1080/15210960.2013.754285

Elliot, J. (1985). Facilitating educational action-research: Some dilemmas. In R. G. Burgess (Ed.), *Field methods in the study of education* (pp. 235-262). London, UK: Falmer Press.

Fearon, J. D. (2003). Ethnic and cultural diversity by country. *Journal of Economic Growth, 8*(2), 195–222. https://doi.org/10.1023/A:1024419522867

Freire, P. (1970). *Pedagogy of the oppressed.* New York, NY: Seabury Press.

Galtung, J. (1990). Cultural violence. *Journal of Peace Research, 27*(3), 291–305. doi:10.1177/0022343390027003005

Gill, S., & Niens, U. (2014). Education as humanisation: a theoretical review on the role of dialogic pedagogy in peacebuilding education. *Compare: A Journal of Comparative and International Education, 44*(1), 10–31. https://doi.org/10.1080/03057925.2013.859879

Giroux, H. A. (1994). *Disturbing pleasures: Learning popular culture.* New York, NY: Routledge.

González González, F. E. (2014). *Poder y violencia en Colombia* [Power and violence in Colombia]. Bogotá, Colombia: ODECOFI-CINEP. Retrieved from http://biblioteca.cinep.org.co:10080/cgi-bin/koha/opac-detail.pl?biblionumber=35803&shelfbrowse_itemnumber=39706#shelfbrowser

Harris, I. (2009). Peace education: Definition, approaches, and future directions. In A. Aharoni (Ed.), *Peace, literature, and art* (Volume 1, pp. 282-301). Oxford, UK: EOLSS Publications.

Hinchey, P. H. (2008). *Action research primer*. New York, NY: Peter Lang.
Johannessen, B. G. G. (2010). Pedagogical ethics for teaching social justice in teacher education. In J. Zajda (Ed.), *Globalization, education and social justice* (pp. 3-13). Dordrecht, Netherlands: Springer.
Johannessen, B. G. G., & Unterreiner, A. (2008). Pedagogical ethics for teaching social justice in teacher education. *Educational Practice and Theory, 30*(1), 27–39. https://doi.org/10.7459/ept/30.1.03
Kelly, D. (2012). Teaching for social justice. *Our Schools/Our Selves, 21*(2), 135–154. Retrieved from: https://www.policyalternatives.ca/sites/default/files/uploads/publications/National%20Office/2012/02/osos106_Teaching_Social_Justice.pdf
Lederach, J. P. (2006). Defining conflict transformation. *Peacework, 33*(368), 26–27. Retrieved from: http://scholar.google.com/scholar_lookup?hl=en&publication_year=2006&pages=26-27&issue=368&author=J.+P.+Lederach&title=Definin g+conflict+transformation&
Lee, Y. A. (2011). What does teaching for social justice mean to teacher candidates? *Professional Educator, 35*(2). Retrieved from https://eric.ed.gov/?id=EJ988204
Lin, J., & Oxford, R. L. (2011). *Transformative ecoeducation for human and planetary survival*. Charlotte, NC: Information Age Publishing.
López de Mesa-Melo, C., Carvajal-Castillo, C. A., Soto-Godoy, M. F., & Urrea-Roa, P. N. (2013). Factores asociados a la convivencia escolar en adolescentes [Factors associated with peaceful coexistence among teenagers]. *Educación y Educadores* [Education and educators], *16*(3), 383–410. doi:10.5294/edu.2013.16.3.1
Macrine, S. L. (2009). *Critical pedagogy in uncertain times: Hope and possibilities*. New York, NY: Palgrave Macmillan.
Mclaren, P. L. (1988). On ideology and education: Critical pedagogy and the politics of empowerment. *Social Text, 19/20*, 153–185. doi:10.2307/466183
Miller, D. (1999). *Principles of social justice*. Cambridge, MA: Harvard University Press.
Ministerio de Educacion. (2014a). *Bill 1732 - Cátedra de la paz* [Peace lectures]. Bogotá, Colombia: Republica de Colombia. Retrieved from http://wsp.presidencia.gov.co/Normativa/Leyes/Documents/LEY%201732%20DEL%20 01%20DE%20SEPTIEMBRE%20DE%202014.pdf
Ministerio de Educación. (2014b). *Colombia bilingüe [Bilingual Colombia]*. Bogotá, Colombia: Republica de Colombia. Retrieved from http://aprende.colombiaaprende.edu.co/es/colombiabilingue/86689
Mthethwa-Sommers, S. (2014). *Narratives of social justice educators: Standing firm*. Cham, Switzerland: Springer. Retrieved from http://link.springer.com/openurl?genre=book&isbn=978-3-319-08430-5

Ng'weno, B. (2004). *Autonomy, self-governance and the status of Afro-Colombian collective territories*. Retrieved from http://oraloteca.unimagdalena.edu.co/wp-content/uploads/2013/01/Autonomy-Self-governance-and-the-Status-of-Afro-Colombian.pdf

Nieto, S., & Bode, P. (2012). *Affirming diversity: The sociopolitical context of multicultural education*. Boston, MA: Pearson.

Nixon, R. (2011, June 26). Slow violence. *The Chronicle of Higher Education*. Retrieved from http://www.chronicle.com/article/Slow-Violence/127968

OECD. (2013). *Colombia: Implementing good governance*. Retrieved from http://dx.doi.org/10.1787/9789264202177-en

Oxford, R. (2017). Peace through understanding: Peace activities as innovations in language teacher education. In G. Tammy & M. Peter (Eds). *Innovative practices in language teacher education* (pp. 125-163). New York, NY: Springer. Retrieved from https://link-springer-com.myaccess.library.utoronto.ca/chapter/10.1007/978-3-319-51789-6_7

Paris, D., & Alim, H. S. (Eds.). (2017). *Culturally sustaining pedagogies: Teaching and learning for justice in a changing world*. New York, NY: Teachers College Press.

Picower, B. (2012). Using their words: Six elements of social justice curriculum design for the elementary classroom. *International Journal of Multicultural Education, 14*(1). https://doi.org/10.18251/ijme.v14i1.484

Rodríguez, E. C. (2014). Hipótesis sobre el matoneo escolar o bullying: A propósito del caso colombiano [Hypothesis about bullying: A Colombian case]. *Intersticios. Revista Sociológica de Pensamiento Crítico, 8*(1). Retrieved from http://www.intersticios.es/article/view/12137

Ryan, G. W., & Bernard, H. R. (2000). Data management and analysis methods. In N. Denzin & Y. Lincoln (Eds.), *Handbook of qualitative research* (2nd ed., pp. 769-801). Thousand Oaks, CA: Sage Publications.

Secretaria Distrital de Planeación. (2009). *Conociendo la localidad de Bosa* [Getting to know the area of Bosa]. Retrieved from http://www.sdp.gov.co/portal/page/portal/PortalSDP/InformacionEnLinea/InformacionDescargableUPZs/Localidad%207%20Bosa/Monografia/07%20Localidad%20de%20Bosa.pdf

Shapiro, H. S. (2006). *Losing heart: The moral and spiritual miseducation of America's children*. Mahwah, NJ: Lawrence Erlbaum Associates.

Shapiro, H. S. (2010). *Educating youth for a world beyond violence: A pedagogy for peace* (1st ed.). New York, NY: Palgrave Macmillan.

Sherman, J. W. (2015). Political violence in Colombia: Dirty wars since 1977. *History Compass, 13*(9), 454–465. https://doi.org/10.1111/hic3.12258

Silva, A. R., & Chaux, E. (2005). *La formación de competencias ciudadanas [The creation of citizenship competences]*. Asociación Colombiana de Facultades de Educación, ASCOFADE. Retrieved from http://www.academia.edu/download/31807215/La_formacion_de_competencias_ciudadanas.pdf

Ukpokodu, O. N. (2010). Engagement and social justice and institutional change: Promises and paradoxes. *The International Journal of Critical Pedagogy, 3*(2), 93. Retrieved from: http://libjournal.uncg.edu/ijcp/article/view/132

Unesco, & United Nations (Eds.). (1997). *Unesco and a culture of peace: promoting a global movement* (2d ed). Paris, France: UNESCO Publishing.

Usma, J. (2015). *From transnational language policy transfer to local appropriation: The case of the national bilingual program in Medellin, Colombia.* Madison, WI: Deep University Press.

Usma, J., & Pelaez, O. (2017). Teacher autonomy: From the conventional promotion of independent learning to the critical appropriation of language policies. In C. Nicolaides & W. Magno (Eds.), *Innovations and challenges in applied linguistics and learner autonomy* (pp. 43-62). Campinas, Spain: Pontes Editores.

Valenzuela, E. (2005). *Cultura de la paz* [Peace culture]. Asunción, Paraguay: Universidad Católica Nuestra Señora de la Asunción.

Vargas, J. F., & Caruso, R. (2014). Conflict, crime, and violence in Colombia. *Peace Economics, Peace Science and Public Policy, 20*(1), 1–4. https://doi.org/10.1515/peps-2013-0062

Zajda, J. (Ed.). (2010). *Globalization, education and social justice.* Dordrecht, Netherlands: Springer. Retrieved from http://link.springer.com/10.1007/978-90-481-3221-8

Notes

1. Some of the ongoing work on social justice for the teaching of languages can be found at: http://www.andjustice4all.ca/

CHAPTER 5

INCORPORATING PEACE EDUCATION INTO EFL

Maki Taniguchi

Introduction

The purpose of this chapter is to explore effective approaches toward incorporating peace education into university English as a Foreign Language (EFL) education in Japan. This chapter is grounded on the assessment of the author's own educational practices in the six compulsory English courses for the first- and second-year students at the University of Shiga Prefecture, Japan. It focuses on the students during the 2015-2016 academic year, whose majors included Engineering, Architecture, Design, Biology, Regional Studies, and Ecology, but not English.

Peacebuilding education can be effectively integrated into English education, because the goal of the two needs to be the same: to cultivate students' compassion and develop their relationships with others. The liberal arts courses analyzed in this chapter were designed to enhance the students' knowledge, skills, and mindsets for English communication as well as for conflict transformation and peacebuilding. Conflict transformation is different from conflict resolution; while the latter refers to resolving a problem, the former refers to transforming a problem into an opportunity to build a sounder society. On the grounds that conflict transformation is inseparable from peacebuilding, the courses focused on developing knowledge about global issues, interpersonal communication skills, and social involvement. The courses paid more attention to social and psychological peacebuilding than political or economic.

Conflict transformation across cultures has never been so urgent as it is today, when the gap between globalism and regionalism is dividing people. War and violence are deriving from people's unmet needs to be respected, included, and humanized. The Preamble of the Constitution of UNESCO (United Nations Educational, Scientific, and Cultural Organization) claims, "since wars begin in the minds of men, it is in the minds of men that the defenses of peace must be constructed." Japan ratified this charter in 1948 after it was defeated in the Second World War. At this point in time, it can be said that Japanese people have the general feeling that they live in a peaceful country. However, peace does not necessarily mean absence of war. It cannot be peace in the truest sense unless hatred, discrimination, and humiliation are dealt with all over the world.

Japan has not experienced any war situations since it committed atrocities and then experienced devastation during the period between the Manchurian Incident in 1931 and the atomic bombs in 1945. It was international intervention that pushed Japan to abandon its militarism. This historical consequence has made many people regard peace not as something they have to build on their own but as conditions or states free from war. Generally, people in Japan maintain passive attitudes toward peace, which is often described as being peace-addicted or indifferent to peace-related issues. However, peace is a holistic process of eliminating root causes of conflict, and peacebuilding depends on not only politicians' or diplomats' efforts but also each individual's.

Under these circumstances in Japan, it is incumbent upon educators to nurture students' knowledge, skills, and sense of responsibility necessary for domestic and international peacebuilding. One avenue for this is to incorporate peacebuilding education into English education, since it is conducive to changing the way students think, listen, and act in situations involving global communication. Peace cannot be achieved by merely wishing and praying. It needs to be strategically planned in the education of language, communication, and culture to promote people's mutual understanding.

Background of the Study

Literature Review

While teaching social justice in the English classroom has been eagerly explored by researchers such as Boyd (2017), there are only a limited number of studies that address the integration of peacebuilding into EFL teaching. The latter includes research by Jakar and Milofsky (2016) and Medley (2016) who see TESOL (Teaching English to Speakers of Other Languages) as the spine, to which peace education can play a supportive role.

Though these studies drawn from educational practices outside of Japan are useful resources for teaching peacebuilding in EFL, it also should be contingent on the Japanese cultural and historical context. As far as the author knows, only three studies are noteworthy in this regard. Two of these, Amanuma (1993) and Shimizu (1996), were completed in the previous century. They went no further than underlining the general importance of educational integration. The third study—Cates (2016)—is the only one which examined practical implications of English pen-pal programs between Japanese and Korean university students.

Regardless of context, international or domestic, and regardless of focus, general or specific, these preceding studies missed one important factor: the incorporation of theory on conflict transformation and peacebuilding into the practice of English teaching. Discussions on the outcomes of integrating peace education into EFL should emphasize theoretical frameworks of conflict transformation and peacebuilding in addition to those of EFL or TESOL. This is the first substantial study that accomplishes both theory and practice of Peace Studies and EFL within a Japanese higher educational setting.

Research Question and Methodology

To elucidate how teaching peace in EFL is possible within higher education in Japan and how that is relevant to other countries, the author employs action research; that is to say, the researcher is not insulated from but rather embedded in applied settings. The role of the author is not differentiated from the role of the practitioner exploring peace education within EFL teaching. This action research is comprised of three case studies on the author's educational practices around three established peacebuilding concepts:

positive peace, building peace as a process, and grassroots initiatives. The assessment and evaluation methods involve preliminary analysis of participant observation and secondary analysis of student interviews, their evaluation reports and writing.

The English Courses
This chapter is predicated on the educational practices of the six compulsory courses of English for the first and second year students at the University of Shiga Prefecture during the 2015-2016 academic year. Each course was two semesters long and comprised 15 classes per semester and 30 classes during the year. From the first-year students, approximately thirty were Engineering majors and thirty were Architecture majors. Among the second-year students, there were thirty each from Design, Biology, Regional Studies, and Ecology. The total number of the students was around 180 in that year.

The goal, contents, and methodologies of these courses were exactly the same. In addition to discussing global issues, it was integral for the courses to cultivate skills, such as critical thinking, relationship building, and taking initiatives. Therefore, the two main goals were (1) increasing the students' English communication skills (writing, speaking, listening, and reading) as tools for creating respectful relationships with others and (2) developing their worldviews as a basis for taking actions to build a trustful society. The contents were selected from an EFL textbook, *Global Issues Towards Peace*, published in Japan in 2014. The methodologies were premised on participatory and experiential styles to involve the students in close work with their peers. Overall, through the content and teaching methods, the students showed remarkable achievements in worldviews, active listening, and social involvement.

Case 1: The Discussion on World Issues
Theoretical Framework: Positive Peace
Absence of war does not necessarily guarantee conditions of peace. Peacebuilding is a continuous process of transforming conflict into cooperation, trust, and harmony among people. In the words of Johan Galtung, who is one of the founders of the field of conflict studies,

peacebuilding is realizing positive peace in contrast with negative peace. The remedies for the former are curative and those for the latter are preventive (Galtung, 1996, p. 2). Whereas negative peace only denotes the state free from war, positive peace refers to the integration of human well-being.

In line with these concepts, the materials of the courses dealt with global issues toward positive peace to provide the students with opportunities to discuss not only how to stop existing conflict but also how to build fair and sustainable communities.

Approach: Strategic Questioning

In Japan, many English teachers give importance to translation exercises to increase students' reading comprehension. Translation helps to understand the content, but it does not always take them much further than gaining information. It helps them construct their knowledge, but it does not necessarily enable them to deconstruct and reconstruct it. Oftentimes it might make students focus on problems rather than solutions when they are exposed to the content of global issues. In fact, acquiring knowledge through reading is not enough to develop their capacity to examine and discuss solutions to world issues. They need practical applications of that knowledge to tangibly understand how to cope with issues.

To that end, the English courses employed some techniques of strategic questioning to stimulate the students' thinking and discussion. The effectiveness of strategic questioning was advocated by Peavey (1994), who defined strategic questioning as a tool which changes both the questioner and the person being questioned (p. 92). Peavey added, "Asking questions and listening for the strategies and ideas embedded in people's own answers can be the greatest service a social change worker can give to a particular issue" (p. 92). The most significant and productive feature of strategic questioning is that it is open-ended, which forces people to go beyond simple yes or no responses. Compared to conventional questioning, strategic questioning is more likely to expand people's critical or creative thinking, and enhance the quality of discussions. This thought-provoking questioning is useful not only for providing chances for better communication in English but also for creating a vision of positive peace.

Exploring Peace through Strategic Questioning
To employ strategic questioning for its intended effect, the students were encouraged to discuss a global issue in each class. The topics the courses covered were selected from the EFL textbook mentioned previously. They consisted of a variety of issues, such as genocide, terrorism, refugees, conflict over water, the dangers of landmines, and nuclear weapons in different parts of the world, including non-English speaking countries. The textbook was well-organized and helped students effectively use the English language to expand their knowledge about world affairs and think how to tackle global problems.

Among these topics, many students seemed to be highly interested in the issue of landmines. One class dealt with landmines particularly in Afghanistan and Cambodia. The students gained a better understanding of landmine clearance in Afghanistan and Cambodia by oral reading and paraphrasing of some parts of the given text. Then they were asked a strategic open-ended question: "How can you use your knowledge and skill to help people affected by landmines?" The students were asked to write down their own answers before a group discussion. One student in the Biology class wrote, "I can bury a lot of seeds of flowers or vegetables instead of landmines,"—an answer that reminded many to keep sowing seeds of peacebuilding throughout their education and career. After writing their answers, they were divided into groups of four, and each one gave their group members a mini-speech based on their writing. Each member had an assigned role, such as facilitator, timekeeper, recorder, and presenter to make the group discussion more active and engaging. For instance, with the help of facilitators, the students conducted their group discussion only in English; the timekeepers managed the presenter's time effectively. After their group discussion, the instructor opened a plenary session in English and asked some presenters to share what had been discussed. The presenters introduced the contents of their discussion by consulting minutes summarized by the recorders. To give an example, in the plenary session of the Biology class, a student presented an idea of one of his group members who was planning to become an agricultural policy maker. He could raise awareness of landmine issues as an agricultural specialist by showing that mine fields prevented people from plowing fields and growing vegetables. The plenary session allowed the students to realize how they could link their various fields of expertise to solving a common issue.

Data and Analysis of the Effects of the Discussions on Global Issues

To assess the effects of the discussions on global issues using strategic questioning, students' testimonials were collected through interviews conducted from April to May 2017. Six students who took one of the author's courses during the 2015-2016 academic year were interviewed. This time lag of one year after the completion of their course was set on purpose. Rather than short term effectiveness immediately after the end of the course, it was important to measure mid-term and long lasting effects. The six interviewees were randomly selected from each of the classes. The interview questions contained (1) what the interviewee acquired throughout the course, (2) what university English courses should focus on in general, and (3) what kind of impact the course had on the interviewee's own major field of study.

Among the threefold findings, the first significant result was a strengthened link between the global issues discussed and the students' own major. One student whose major was Regional Studies stated that she learned how to discuss global issues in English and she was inspired by the author's questions on how she could make use of her major to solve those issues. She emphasized that she had never thought about her major from that angle, and it was always challenging for her to connect her specialized field of Philology with issues including gender, refugees, and genocide. Moreover, she described her realization that her study directly or indirectly pertained to any world issue, which made her resolve to do her share to solve them.

The second finding is related to cultivating the students' points of view. Another student, studying Design as her major, explained that she had become confident about her convictions and her worldviews. The discussions had allowed her to gain knowledge of international situations as well as develop focused and wide perspectives. She realized that it was a great learning experience for her career as a designer, because looking at the world with an informed and nuanced view was the starting point, no matter what product she would design.

The third finding concerns the students' retention of knowledge. An Architecture student recognized that knowledge about global issues continued to engage his thinking even after his completion of the course one year ago. By his own account, what he learned in English, rather than in Japanese, remained fresh in his mind. He affirmed that he became more interested in world problems, especially in environmental issues.

These interviews revealed that the courses encouraged some students to explore international affairs and to establish meaningful relationships between their major and world issues. The strategic questioning developed their critical thinking. In content-based EFL instruction, it is more effective to directly link the content to students' majors so that they can increase their English ability in their specialized field. However, this does not necessarily help them solve interdisciplinary problems using their English competence. Interdisciplinary fields such as conflict transformation and peacebuilding require more versatile knowledge and skills. The reverse is also true. This versatile understanding and competence to tackle a wide range of issues eventually contributes to extending the knowledge and skills required in students' own majors. The students' discussions, strategic questioning, and daily feedback exhibited unexpected results: the discussions motivated the students to keep learning English as well as their own major; along with their knowledge and critical thinking of global issues, their self-confidence also increased.

Moreover, the students could raise their awareness to the point that they could think about their own life in Japan. They learned about sufferings and tragedies in the world; however, they were not overwhelmed and did not despair. They were motivated to find strategic solutions to world problems. Strategic questioning promoted their constructive and creative thinking. It must also be noted that responding to strategic questions in English allowed them to think more attentively than in their native language. As a result, they became conscious of whether their way of living would fuel any problems and do harm to people in other parts of the world. The students recognized their responsibility to figure out the root causes of the struggles and to translate them into fairer, more sustainable, and sounder opportunities.

This entire process of integrating English education with peacebuilding is not about teaching something but about facilitating the students' own learning from various perspectives. By sharing ideas with others, they took a journey of self-discovery of their own interests, beliefs, and values as well as those of others. This provided them with moments to realize that their solution to a problem was inseparable from their classmates', and ultimately, from people in other parts of the world. That is to say, it made them acknowledge that they needed to cooperate with one another and co-create solutions to achieve positive peace. Positive peace in one region or country cannot be achieved without resolving suffering in another corner of the world. In that regard, even the discussions in a small classroom in Japan were already an essential part of global peacebuilding.

Case 2: The Workshop of Active Listening
Theoretical Framework: Peacebuilding as a Process
Peacebuilding is not a static but a dynamic and ever-changing process. In their study in 2001, a peacebuilding non-profit organization, Responding to Conflict, stressed that peacebuilding is not only about producing "peace-enhancing outcomes" but also about "the process" itself (p. 14). It is a whole process of transforming discriminative and unfair treatments into compassionate and inclusive ones. To that end, the author's courses attached great importance to "how" to learn together, as opposed to "what" to learn, in order that the students could be involved in an ongoing process of creating mutual understanding and cooperation.

Approach: Experiential Learning
The acquisition of effective interpersonal skills is an integral part of conflict transformation and peacebuilding. Above all, listening to people's needs and grievances is particularly essential for resolving conflict. Active listening develops students' listening comprehension, and at the same time, helps them cultivate empathetic and trustful relationships with others. However, many Japanese university students care neither about their listening skills in English nor in Japanese; even while under governmental educational guidelines they emphasize self-expression in these languages throughout junior high school and high school. The Japanese ministry of education has been promoting self-expression to counter people's tendency toward shyness, but that leads to less

emphasis on listening to others. Recognizing this conundrum, the author's courses particularly strove to increase their active listening skills along with self-expression. The students were required to non-judgmentally listen to their classmates in the pair or group work that they were assigned.

The educational method of experiential learning is particularly useful for developing students' interpersonal skills, because it helps them co-create learning processes. Kolb (1984) first introduced the cycle of experiential learning. He stated that learning is *"the process whereby knowledge is created through the transformation of experience* [emphasis in the original]" (p. 38). Experiential learning through participating in activities promotes the integration of one's existing knowledge into new knowledge. The cycle of experimental learning consists of experience, its abstraction, and experimentation; when one can produce a reflective observation after a concrete experience, it helps to form an abstract concept. Then, with some active experimentation of the concept it can be confirmed, and thus another leaning cycle begins from there. This experiential learning method prevented unilateral lecturing for more than ten minutes in class. The key part of the students' experiential learning cycles was processing, where they listened to their classmates' ideas and comments and synthesized their own learning. Since this kind of processing requires a high level of cognitive capacity, experiential learning was effective specifically for adult learners like university students.

Experiential Learning of Active Listening
A workshop of active listening was conducted at an early stage of the courses so that the students could practice what they learned and engage in classroom activities with that skill throughout the year. In the workshop, students were paired up and each student in a pair intentionally listened to their partner's talk in English without making eye-contact, giving any feedback, nor showing any interest. Then, they tried to listen to the same talk again which their partner already gave once, but this time with making eye contact, giving some feedback, and showing interest. These pair activities were followed by a processing session where they reflected on the difference between the two listening experiences. Figure 5.1 shows the questions asked of them in the process. The students were not given any lecture on

what active listening was, but they experienced the definition of active listening themselves as they answered the given questions. In all six courses, the students defined active listening as effective listening skills to better understand others and to build better relationships with them by listening non-judgmentally and compassionately. As one can see, those definitions were derived from their own experiences of active listening. The workshop also considered how to apply active listening in their daily life such as on campus, in social situations, and with family.

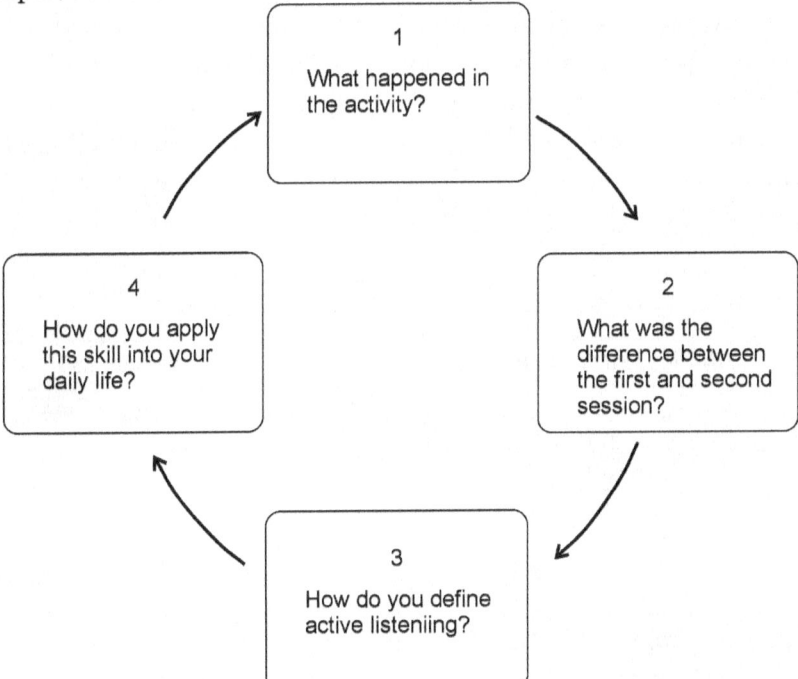

Figure 5.1 Questions for reflection in the workshop of active listening.

Data and Analysis of the Effects of the Active Listening Workshop

The evaluation organization of the University of Shiga Prefecture conducted an official survey of students in all six courses in spring 2015. Its multiple-choice evaluation was composed of 19 questions regarding the effectiveness of their instructor's capacity to manage the courses. Among them, one substantial question revealed how the students applied their interpersonal communication skills in their classroom. The question asked "how the instructor communicated with the students." Why is this question relevant to their communication skills? It is relevant, because every act of communication is mutual, like a reflection in a mirror. The students' evaluation of the author's communication indicated that they had reflected upon the aspects of good and bad communication skills, including their own.

As Table 5.1 demonstrates, almost all students were comfortable with the author's way of communicating with them. This is worthy of attention, because this fact illustrates that they enjoyed communicating with the author, otherwise, they could not have positively evaluated it. More fundamentally, if they had not known what is necessary and useful for interpersonal communication, they could not have enjoyed it and judged the effectiveness of communication itself in the first place. They learned the integral component of communication through their experiences in the classroom.

Table 5.1
The Result of the Course Survey in Spring 2015

Question: How did the instructor communicate with students?						
Course	Answer: Very actively	Answer: Almost always	Answer: Rarely	Answer: Never	Invalid Responses	Valid Responses
1	66.7%	33.5%	0%	0%	0	15
2	81.3%	18.8%	0%	0%	0	16
3	88.9%	11.1%	0%	0%	0	9
4	100%	0%	0%	0%	0	13
5	75.0%	25.0%	0%	0%	0	12
6	88.9%	11.1%	0%	0%	0	18

Note: Not all students responded, because the survey was conducted arbitrarily.

Therefore, the author's well-regarded communication skills were attributed not only to her ability but also to the students' ability. As a matter of course, she tried to lead by example and to cultivate their active listening skills, but at the same time, the students themselves put in tremendous efforts to improve their active listening. Indeed, they actively participated in paired or group discussions and valued their classmates' remarks and opinions. Often it is very crucial for students to achieve high scores in tests such as Test of English for International Communication (TOEIC) or Test of English as a Foreign Language (TOEFL), which they need for higher education abroad. For these tests the training of listening comprehension takes priority over active listening workshops. However, active listening is the foundation of any listening comprehension and communicative activity. In fact, the training of active listening in English is also helpful for listening comprehension for these tests, because active listening requires students to pay more attention to the speaker's perspectives and feelings, which facilitates a much deeper understanding. Active listening is a more comprehensive skill that not only encompasses the limited notion of "listening comprehension" but opens it up to more meaningful and respectful interpersonal relationships.

Cultivating active listening skills is necessary to nurture students' interpersonal relationship building, because it concurrently stimulates understanding about themselves and others. Actively listening to a speaker's experiences and ideas promotes the listener's sympathy and empathy and also develops their self-consciousness and sense of values. It enables the speaker to feel that the speaker's voice is heard and acknowledged, which leads to self-acceptance and self-esteem. Indeed, the students' realization that their ideas were heard did build trustful relationships within the classroom. In this environment, they were more willing to listen to each other, thus creating a virtuous cycle of more active listening. In this way, active listening had mutually reinforcing effects: it helped the students positively engage in communication and mutual understanding. This process of creating respectful relationships would be the basis of any process of peacebuilding.

Case 3: Interacting with a Terrorist's Son
Theoretical Framework: Grassroots Peacebuilding
Building positive peace is a process of people's multi-faceted cooperation. Each individual has a distinct responsibility to take an initiative in the process. Lederach (1997) categorized three "tracks" of the various actors and

their roles in this process: Track I constitutes top leadership, Track II is of middle-range leadership, and Track III encompasses grassroots leadership (p. 39). The top leadership consists of key international political and military leaders who deal with high-level negotiations. The middle-range leadership includes unofficial organizational and academic leaders, such as international NGO workers who help in education and training. The grassroots leadership is composed of local leaders such as social workers who work for local or intercommunal building.

Bearing in mind the categories of actors in peacebuilding, the primary aim of the author's courses was to prepare the students for taking leadership at the Track III grassroots level, by engaging them in an activity beyond their campus and creating a tangible network of peacebuilding. This basic training at the grassroots level is essential for them to become Track II and Track I middle or top range leaders.

Approach: Taking Ownership of Actions

As part of overall educational objectives, students should be trained to give back to society what they learn in their classrooms. They must serve the local and global community by utilizing their knowledge and skills. Nevertheless, not many Japanese university students (nor adults) actively engage in social work. The passive and sometimes apathetic attitude toward social action might stem from the traditional Japanese educational setting, in which students are trained to quietly sit and diligently listen to what teachers instill. This way of learning should not be completely dismissed; however, it is likely to lead to producing passive learners and then passive citizens, not to mention passive teachers or lecturers. In many cases, it causes students to be indifferent toward social, economic, and political issues in their local setting as well in their "glocal" perspective.

With respect to people's responsibility for their social actions, Sharp (2002) reiterated the importance of citizens' initiatives for peace and freedom. He stated that even liberation from dictatorships rested on people's capacity to liberate themselves (p. 13). It is critical to scrutinize the profound meaning of this statement, which requires a significant change in mindset about conflict transformation and peacebuilding. Conflict is not intrinsic in society. Resolution of conflict is not given and it should be achieved through people's interactions with one another. Many people consider a top-down approach; they state that the top leaders, including those in the United Nations or national governments, should devise strategies and implement policies for conflict resolution. However, they must cultivate the mindset not to wait for someone's help to change their social systems or power dynamics. As Sharp claimed, it is the ownership of each individual that can break the cycle of violence and minimize structural violence. People have to liberate themselves from their passivity and act for themselves. University courses must build a bridge between campus and society by providing students with local or global connections to stimulate their initiatives for social change and peacebuilding. They need to find a place outside of their campus where they can apply what they learn in the classroom.

Taking Initiatives for Grassroots Peacebuilding
Toward this goal of social application of education, of initiative and responsibility, the students were provided with chances to share ideas and feelings with a peace activist based in the United States. In 2016, they met with Zak Ebrahim, who confessed that he was a "terrorist's son" and is pursuing his path as an advocate of nonviolence. Here is how the project took place: the students completed a reading comprehension about 9/11 terrorism and counter terrorism measures. This was part of their oral reading and paraphrasing activity of a text given in their textbook. Along with it they watched a TED speech by Ebrahim (2014) in class. (TED stands for Technology, Entertainment, and Design, and it is a nonprofit organization for providing short online talks for free). Then, they were encouraged to send him a message in English, and they eagerly did so. A compilation of some 180 messages were sent to Ebrahim via email. Ebrahim sent back the following message with a note to the students, which they received with great excitement. Ebrahim wrote, "Wow! These were absolutely beautiful and wonderful to read. Thank you so much for these incredible responses and please send my thank you to your students. This is why I do the work that I do!"

This small exchange led to a big encounter. The students' messages brought Ebrahim to the University in January 2016. He gave a talk, and the students asked him many questions ranging from personal experience to global initiatives. They asked him, for example, "Do you still love your father?" or "What can we do to stop terrorism?" Figure 5.2 depicts how they were enthusiastically engaged in this session. They empathically listened to Ebrahim and talked to him, respecting his circumstances and convictions. After the session, one student, whose major was Regional Studies, was still in high spirits and told the author that it was her first real-life encounter with an international figure, and it made her feel she could do something to make the world better.

Figure 5.2 Zak Ebrahim and the students.
Copyright 2016 by the University of Shiga Prefecture. Used with Permission.

Data and Analysis of the Effects of Interacting with Ebrahim

The students' messages to Ebrahim showed that they started taking initiative for social change and peacebuilding in their own way. Among these 180 sincere messages to him, the following three messages particularly described how the students changed their way of thinking and felt inspired to take action as a result of their communication with him.

First, one student described his self-transformation to Ebrahim: "Actually, I have very strong prejudices in my deep heart for long years. But, in these days, I think that is bad and I must abandon the prejudice. Because I heard your speech, my question is transformed into confidence. So I very thank you [sic]." For most students, it was their very first time to listen to a story from someone who had so closely experienced extremism in his own family. It made a deep impression on their minds. Some of these students were bullied as kids, while others had experienced being a minority, such as a Korean Japanese living in Japan. These students could especially relate to Ebrahim's story with their own personal experiences, even though their situations could not be compared with his. Finding common ground to relate to someone even in extremely different life situations allowed them to reaffirm their commitment to transforming inner conflict as well as social conflict.

Second, another student wrote to Ebrahim, after having deeply engaged with worldwide issues and perspectives on terrorism: "I heard your message on TED and I feel that I want to see the realization of world's peace. I think the real peace is not to beat all terrorists but to improve environment around all terrorists. The United States of America must be the leader to realize the real peace [sic]." Other students arrived at similar, deeper insights regarding the causes of terrorism. They expressed that counterattacks on terrorists did not solve the problem; rather it fueled more hatred, hostility, and violence. After learning about Ebrahim's efforts and interacting with him, they could examine terrorism from a different point of view.

Third, another student realized constructive possibilities of translating conflicts into peace and tried to share the awareness with Ebrahim: "I'm a Japanese university student. Hearing your speech, I know that negative feelings and bad experiences aren't necessarily violences and terrorisms, but the power of accepting persons. I hope we change bad things into good things [sic]." This was an empathic message to Ebrahim, because the subject "we" in the last sentence clearly indicated that the student was not simply the audience of Ebrahim's TED talk any more, but took the first step, along with other students, to taking collective responsibility and becoming an agent of social change.

Sending a message to Ebrahim was not merely part of the writing exercises in the course. In addition to reading, speaking, listening, and writing skills, they need one more skill: integrating. In the first place, it was intended to create a connection with Ebrahim across the Pacific Ocean. It is often very difficult with the tight frame of course schedules to devote time to activities outside the classroom. There is no question that managing academic course schedules to set aside time for non-academic activities is a challenge. However, the integration of academics and activism is essential even with limited time. The author often used flip teaching through online lectures, which gave students new material to study at home. This helped in using class time effectively for interactive activities based on what they had learned. Once the students actually shook hands with Ebrahim and gave an embodied expression to their intellectual quests, they could become a collaborator with him to build peace together. In this situation of global interaction between Ebrahim and the students, learning English as a foreign language played a significant role. In fact, learning a foreign language had made the students humble, because the processes of studying it had sometimes put them in an uncomfortable, uncertain, and uneasy place. That enhanced their development of flexibility, patience, and empathy which helped their understanding of Ebrahim as a person.

This entire project showed further that local or global connections increase students' motivation to learn English. They also feel encouraged to engage in social action by utilizing their knowledge about world issues and interpersonal communication tools. Social connections with people in the field help students take initiatives for social change. In the same manner, their initiatives also help their counterparts strengthen the pursuit of their own work. Creating a local or global network brings about such a mutually enhancing action, and develops support, cooperation, and collaboration in society. Taking ownership of world issues from within one's local context constructs their joint future. This is an effective approach toward bottom-up, grassroots leadership for peacebuilding. Social involvements during school days can be an asset to students' own career paths whatever field they pursue and a significant first step of grassroots peacebuilding.

Conclusion

These courses, projects, and cases reveal that peacebuilding through English education is possible and beneficial at the university level in Japan and can be implemented in classrooms in other parts of the world as well. First, peace education can be successfully incorporated into EFL especially when it is packaged as a liberal arts course, because promoting the culture and the language of peace can be connected to every field of study. Moreover, it prepares students to venture outside of the classroom and out into the world. Peacebuilding and English education can pursue a coherent goal: to nurture students' compassion and empathy. Finally, participatory and experiential learning in the integrated Peace and English curriculum encourages students to take leadership of social change.

Integration of peace education into English is not simply about the "how" of incorporation, but about the "why." Why is incorporating peacebuilding into EFL crucial? It is because peacebuilding is indivisible from building human relationships. Building peace is not only building political or economic infrastructures in conflict-torn areas but also building people's social communication and interaction in their immediate surroundings. Peacebuilding is a future-oriented process of changing a troubled relationship into a respectful and trustful one through communication. Cultivating knowledge, skills, and initiatives for better communication in the classroom is already an integral part of peacebuilding.

References

Amanuma, E. (1993). Peace education in the English classroom. *Bulletin of Nippon Veterinary and Animal Science University, 42*, 41-49.

Boyd, S. A. (2017). *Social justice literacies in the English classroom: Teaching practice in action.* New York, NY: Teachers College Press.

Cates, A. K. (2016). Healing colonial pain: English as a bridge between Korea and Japan. In C. Hastings & L. Jacob, *Social justice in English language teaching* (pp. 67-79). Alexandria, VA: TESOL International Association.

Ebrahim, Z. (2014). I am the son of a terrorist: Here's how I chose peace. Retrieved from https://www.ted.com/talks/zak_ebrahim_i_am_the_son_of_a_terrorist_here_s_how_i_chose_peace?language=en

Fisher, S., Abdi, I. D., Ludin, J., Smith, R., Williams, S., & Williams, S. (2000). *Working with conflict: Skills and strategies for action.* London, UK: Zen Books.

Galtung, J. (1996). *Peace by peaceful means: Peace and conflict, development and civilization.* London, UK: Sage Publications.

Jakar, S. V., & Milofsky, A. (2016). Bringing peacebuilding into the English language classroom. In C. Hastings & L. Jacob (Eds.), *Social justice in English language teaching* (pp. 41-48). Alexandria, VA: TESOL International Association.

Kolb, D. (1984). *Experiential learning: Experience as the source of learning and development.* Englewood Cliffs, NJ: Prentice-Hall, Inc.

Lederach, P. J. (1997). *Building peace: Sustainable reconciliation in divided societies.* Washington, D.C.: United States Institute of Peace.

Medley, R. M. (2016). Tension and harmony: Language teaching as a peacebuilding endeavor. In C. Hastings & L. Jacob (Eds.), *Social justice in English language teaching* (pp. 49-66). Alexandria, VA: TESOL International Association.

Peavey, F. (1994). Strategic questioning. In T. Green, P. Woodrow, & F. Peavey (Eds.), *Insight and action: How to discover and support a life of integrity and commitment to change* (pp. 89-116). Philadelphia, PA: New Society Publishers.

Sharp, G. (2002). *From dictatorship to democracy: A conceptual framework for liberation.* London, UK: Serpent's Tail.

Shimizu, S. (1996). The roles of English education in peace education and global education. *Kanagawa University Studies in Language, 18*, 97-110.

Tatsukawa, K., Davies, W., Tagashira, K., Yamamoto, G., & Takita, F. (2014). *Global issues towards peace.* Tokyo, Japan: Nan'un-do.

UNESCO (1945). Constitution. Retrieved from http://portal.unesco.org/en/ev.php-URL_ID=15244&URL_DO=DO_TOPIC&URL_SECTION=201.html

CHAPTER 6

CRITICAL FOREIGN LANGUAGE PEDAGOGY:
*Peace Education and Confronting
and Negotiating Aggressive Situations*

Gerrard Mugford

Introduction

English-language teacher training in Mexico is more often than not considered to be an objective, apolitical, and value-free process where the aim is to help aspiring teachers identify and respond to pre-identified language needs, build up a structural and functional pedagogic knowledge of the target language, develop appropriate teaching methodologies and techniques, and implement testing and evaluation procedures. However, I argue that such teacher training schemes largely fail to respond to the Mexican students' real-life language needs and communicative challenges as they enter the target-language environment and where they may encounter difficult and hostile situations.

In this chapter, I contend that teacher trainees of English as a Foreign Language (EFL) need to be prepared to help learners not only actively participate in pleasant, agreeable, and routine target-language encounters but also to equip them to negotiate a darker side of foreign language interaction—that of difficult, aggressive, and conflictual situations. To pursue this line of argument, I adopt an emic approach which examines real-life antagonistic situations that Mexican EFL users have actually faced. Focusing on EFL peace education—the promotion of cross-cultural harmonious relationships, attitudes, and values—and English language teaching (ELT), I collected data from Mexican EFL users regarding conflict that they had experienced, especially in terms of xenophobia and aggression. Using EFL users' data, I developed a critical pedagogical framework for helping students negotiate and overcome such adverse situations by working with 32 students pursuing a bachelor's degree in Teaching English as Foreign Language (TEFL). The trainee teachers examined how they can help their language learners to negotiate antagonistic and hostile transactional and interpersonal situations, specifically those that involve rejection, racial insults, linguistic discrimination, and intimidation. Whilst it may be impossible to predict the communicative difficulties that their students might face in the target-language context, foreign language teachers can provide learners with a range of pragmatic and discursive resources and choices that allow them to actively choose a communicative stance and select an appropriate response as opposed to purely reacting, often passively, to circumstances.

Review of Literature
Teacher Training
Often reflecting a "banking approach" (Freire, 1993) to foreign language teacher education, ELT training programmes in Mexico place heavy emphasis on methodology, especially by encouraging teachers to faithfully adhere to the communicative approach (for a description see, for instance, Larsen-Freeman, 1986). Importance is also given to the ability to present grammar structures, promote the four skills (reading, writing, speaking, and listening), introduce new vocabulary, model correct pronunciation, and practise communicative functions. Teacher trainees are tested and assessed on their ability to give model classes where timing, efficiency of language presentation, and tangible and measurable results are key evaluation criteria. Teacher training programmes aim to produce professionals who, with their pre-established prescriptive knowledge and bank of teaching techniques, pedagogical formulas, and classroom activities, can hopefully develop successful and proficient foreign language users.

Ignored in this drive for efficient and effective teaching are the learners themselves since the focus is on developing a declarative knowledge of language for its own sake and not on what language users might want to do with language, especially in terms of procedural knowledge. Giroux (1997) described this decontextualisation as follows:

> Classroom knowledge is often treated as an external body of information, the production of which appears to be independent of human beings. From this perspective, objective knowledge is viewed as independent of time and place; it becomes universalized, ahistorical knowledge. Moreover, it is expressed in a language that is basically technical and value free. (p. 21)

Therefore, the target language can be seen as a monolithic stationary linguistic mass which learners have to record, memorise, and repeat (Freire, 1993, p. 52). Successful teaching and learning in Mexico is often framed in terms of the attributes of the "good" or effective language teacher (Johnson, 2004) and the characteristics of the "good" language learner. In this pedagogical environment, Apple (1986) remarks that "[g]ood learning is only the accumulation of atomistic skills and facts and answering the question in standardized achievement tests for students" (p. 147). Following Apple's line of argument, the atomisation of language into structures, functions, and skills may actually undermine learners' communicative abilities since they may be able to express linguistic declarative knowledge but are unable to develop their procedural knowledge (Johnson, 1996).

This stance is often at odds with what language learners actually want to do with the newly-acquired language as argued by Crookes (2013):

> Many students of a second language around the world are taking courses that focus on the structures of language. But many of those who study a second language want to communicate, that is, do things with words (cf. Austin, 1962). The idea, clearly, is that words are for active purposes: we humans use them to perform particular functions (rather than consider the structures on which those functions are hung); among other things we use them to act on the world (and act with each other). In this functional conception of language, language connects with social structures and patterns of interaction to get things done. (p. 87)

Language learners are not normally interested in practising language for its own sake. They are not usually concerned with understanding the intricacies of grammar structures or in differentiating between minimal pairs in pronunciation. However, an objective focus on language usage, rather than on its use, helps to promote a hidden agenda: teachers do not have to focus on the privileged discourses of certain interactants and can quietly ignore how others are silenced. Focusing on the decontextualised discourse in education, Giroux (1997) argues:

> Defined primarily in technical terms (mastery) or in terms of its communicative value in developing dialogue and transmitting information, language is abstracted from its political and ideological usage. For instance, language is privileged as a medium for exchanging and presenting knowledge, and, as such, is abstracted form its constitutive role in the struggle of various groups over different meanings, practices and readings of the world. Within dominant educational theory there is no sense of how language practices can be used to actively silence some students or of how favoring particular forms of discourse can work to disconfirm the traditions, practices, and values of subordinate language groups. (p. 131)

Consequently, foreign language teachers in Mexico are shielded from having to deal with the darker side of foreign language use where Mexican English-language users may face discrimination, verbal abuse or racial, ethnic, or linguistic rejection. In the next section, I argue that difficult and hostile situations are an all too common feature of foreign language interaction for the Mexican EFL users.

Peace Studies
Real-life foreign language use reflects the rough and tumble of everyday interaction as participants engage in both pleasant and antagonistic experiences. In a recent study of Mexican language users' experiences, Mugford (2017) found that in 108 responses from 305 questionnaires, EFL users said that they had faced rudeness and impoliteness when interacting in English in either target-language communities or in Mexico. In a follow-up study 76 out of 197 participants said that they had suffered hostility and

aggression. The results indicate that Mexican EFL users need to be made aware of (and perhaps face up to) antagonistic and belligerent situations. Just as importantly, they need to be given the communicative resources with which to react. This means that Mexican EFL teachers have a vital role to play in raising learner awareness about key issues concerning peace and violence. Peace education cannot be treated as yet another item in a textbook check list on a long litany of world problems to be discussed in the isolated comfort of the EFL classroom. A lack of peace, coupled with violence, is very much local real-world concern for many foreign language users.

To prepare learners for how to deal with violence and aggression in the target language context, concepts of positive and negative peace (Galtung & Fischer, 2013) can help promote meaningful peace education. Negative peace, such as an absence of violence or lack of exploitation, reflects avoidance of conflict but does not necessarily lead to the construction of harmonious and congenial relationships. In contrast, positive peace actively attempts to repair relationships and promote understanding and consideration.

The concepts of positive and negative peace provide a useful framework for foreign language teachers in trying to help their students negotiate aggressive and difficult situations. Negative peace reflects acceptance and tolerance when confronted with conflicting attitudes, actions, and beliefs. This may support the stance of the submissive and compliant foreign language users who put up with discrimination, and aggression. In contrast, positive peace is a proactive attempt to understand and negotiate aggression, overcome racism and other forms of discrimination, and find ways to promote more meaningful and harmonious relationships. However peace education needs to go further and promote the development of a pedagogical framework for confronting aggression and conflict. Such a framework involves foreign language users identifying underlying hostile intent, developing evaluative routines to weigh up their communicative response options, and, finally, acquiring defensive strategies to combat aggression.

Language that signals hostile intent can be identified through conflictual speech acts, aggressive communicative styles, and aggravating strategies. The use of certain speech acts may alert foreign language users to potential hostile interaction. Context plays an important role in determining conflictual intention. For instance, in service encounters, target-language users may falsely claim not to understand the foreign language user or ask them to unnecessarily repeat information. The omission of social "speech acts" such as greetings and farewells may be suggestive as target-language speakers fail to adhere to politeness norms and display a lack of civility. Additionally, impoliteness may be detected through the deliberate flouting of normative discoursal practices such as not interrupting other interlocutors or respecting turn taking patterns.

Whilst the identification and categorisation of aggression and conflict may ultimately be subjective, language learners can be helped at the basic and intermediate levels to recognize interactional styles which are friendly/unfriendly, supportive/non-supportive, rude/impolite, among others. At more advanced levels, learners should be able to identify mocking, ironic, sarcastic, and jocular language use. Within a given interaction, early recognition of interlocutor style can give a preliminary indication regarding how the ensuing interaction may proceed.

Besides identifying potentially threatening speech acts and aggressive styles, language learners can be made aware of aggressive strategies as outlined by Lachenicht (1980):

1. Off Record: ambiguous insults, insinuations, hints, and irony. This strategy is ... designed to enable the insulter to meet an aggrieved challenge from the injured person with an assertion of innocence.
2. Bald on Record: directly produced FTAs and impositions ('Shut the door', 'Do your work', 'Don't talk', etc.)
3. Positive aggravation: an aggravation strategy that is designed to show the addressee that he is not approved of, is not esteemed, does not belong, and will not receive cooperation.
4. Negative aggravation: An aggravation strategy that is designed to impose on the addressee, to interfere with his freedom of action, and to attack his social position and the basis of his social action. (p. 619)

Off-record aggression may be especially challenging for the foreign language user who may not be aware of the indirect use of language. Consequently, the identification of irony, sarcasm, and the jocular use of language should be an important component of any language course as they are characteristic of everyday conversation. Bald-record strategies are easier to recognise since they are blatant face attacks. They are categorised by such obstructionist tactics as deliberating seeking disagreement and ridiculing interactants (see Bousfield, 2008; Culpeper, 1996). Positive aggravation is manifested when it is made clear to the foreign language user that he/she is not "one of us" and, furthermore, is not seen as a legitimate target language user. Negative aggravation surfaces when the foreign language user is not allowed to participate in a given interaction and is not granted the normal sociality rights in terms of equity (i.e., personal consideration) and association rights (i.e., involvement with others; Spencer-Oatey, 2008).

Peace studies needs, therefore, to identify the tools with which to confront aggression and conflict and this leads to the teacher's role in developing a pedagogy that allows foreign language users to react to violence and aggravation.

Pedagogy

Peace education needs to be related not only to the learners' perceived future needs but also, just as importantly, to their current realities, concerns, and worries. All too often, real-world issues are presented in pre-packaged, decontextualised, and abstract terms such as "world peace" and "universal understanding." Conflict, war, and lack of peace is frequently approached in the conventional EFL classroom in terms of the transmission and assimilation of knowledge. For instance, in the ESL textbook *NorthStar* (Robinson Fellag, 2006), learners study different perceptions of war and the work of peace organisations in the unit titled "Perspectives on War." Learners are asked to consider any possible legitimacy and necessity for war. However, there is little discussion of the root causes behind war (e.g., seizure of power, quest for domination, perceived and real threats to security, dwindling economic resources, etc.). Giroux (1983) summarises this approach as follows:

> A pedagogical model built on the transmission of a given body of information, values, and beliefs does not ask whether these are warranted, it asks under what conditions they can be maintained. Teachers and students within this context are expected to be either passive consumers or transmitters of knowledge, rather than negotiators of the world in which they work and act. (p. 179)

As Giroux (1983) argues, no real attempt is made to understand "the relationships among issues such as ideology, knowledge and power" (p. 73). So whilst key manifestations of violence may be identified (such as discrimination, hostility, and aggression), the possible implications, consequences, and conceivable solutions are not examined in any depth. Such a synthetic treatment of peace may be a far cry from the lack of peace in family homes and violence on city streets that may be experienced by the foreign language students themselves. Rather than constructing their own knowledge by interrelating experience and theory, students are acted upon:

> By emphasizing the transmission of information, the pedagogy used in this approach represents a top-to-bottom model that removes the student from any active participation in either the construction of knowledge or the sharing of power. (Giroux, 1983, p. 214)

Teachers need to critically relate the topic to the learners' own experiences, histories, and attitudes and, just as importantly, offer a plan of action so that learners are in a position to act upon their world.

A liberal approach to peace education examines the underlying reasons behind conflict, hostility, and violence and grapples with its various manifestations which may range from racial discrimination and attacks on minorities to ethnic cleansing and genocide. Such an approach can be seen in *English Vocabulary in Use Advanced* (McCarthy & O'Dell, 2013) which, in the unit on "War and Peace," gives students an extensive range of vocabulary (e.g., *child poverty, brutal suppression,* and *massacres*) so that they can reflect on the causes of aggression and hostility. This approach provides students with the necessary language to talk about different causes and manifestations of violence. Whilst McCarthy and O'Dell are justifiably focused on developing learners' vocabulary, the radical teacher can use such vocabulary to help students understand and reflect on violence, hostility, and lack of peace.

A critical approach goes further than merely transmitting knowledge and facts or analysing the causes behind confrontation and conflict. It calls for action. After condemning the banking approach which reflects conventional and liberal approaches, Freire (1993) called for a problem-posing pedagogy which relates to the learners and their immediate context:

> In problem-posing education, people develop their power to perceive critically *the way they exist* in the world *with which* and *in which* they find themselves; they come to see the world not as a static reality, but as a reality in process, in transformation' (p. 64, emphasis in original)

A critical approach therefore goes beyond recording instances of violence and understanding their nature. There is a need for an active response as described by Crookes (2013):

> Critical pedagogy is teaching for social justice, in ways that support the development of active, engaged citizens who will, as circumstances permit, critically inquire into why the lives of so many human beings, perhaps including their own, are materially, psychologically, socially, and spiritually inadequate—citizens who will be prepared to seek out solutions to the problems they define and encounter, and take action accordingly. (p. 8)

In practical terms critical pedagogy can be seen in the work of Auerbach and Wallerstein (2004) who go beyond empowering second-language users to negotiate difficult situations and attempt to help them contest and resist target-language discriminatory and violent practices. Whilst not specifically dealing with peace and war, Auerbach and Wallerstein (2004) examine aggression in the workplace and especially key issues such as harassment, racial discrimination, and employer abuse of power. Besides identifying, describing, and analysing negative incidents, they outline plans to take action so that ESL users can weigh up and consider their options. Mirroring Freire's problem-posing approach, Auerbach and Wallerstein (2004) state that:

> The problem-posing cycle starts with participants' experiences, draws out themes or problems for deeper exploration through dialogue, digs deeper at their root causes, introduce new information and skills, explores strategies for action, moves toward action, and invites reflection on the whole cycle in order to move toward a new cycle. (p. 315)

Therefore, peace education goes beyond the descriptive and analytical stages and involves concrete action that provides language users with a range of resources with which to respond and act. This approach is summarised by Crookes (2013) who outlines the underlying teaching objective behind a critical approach:

> ... critical pedagogy is teaching for social justice, in ways that support the development of active, engaged citizens who will, as circumstances permit, critically inquire into why the lives of so many human beings, including their own, are so materially (and spiritually) inadequate, be prepared to seek out solutions to the problems they define and encounter, and take action accordingly. And then, within that whole area of education, as second language teachers we focus on language and culture, which to a larger extent make us who we are. (p. 77)

Research Objectives
This study aimed to ascertain whether student teachers can be prepared to help their students cope with conflictual and aggressive situations. Student teachers were asked to examine data from real-life incidents which foreign language users felt to be hostile and aggressive. In this research, I endeavoured to expand student teachers' pedagogic resources when trying to develop their learners' responses as opposed to providing student teachers with the "correct" reaction to any given situation. Since all language users are different, they will want to respond in their own way. Whatever their decision, foreign language users should at least have the necessary resources to react in the way that they want to.

Methodology
The research was carried out in three stages. The first stage aimed to raise student-teacher awareness of their own histories, attitudes, and experiences regarding peace and hostility. During a second stage, student teachers reflected on and analysed four hostile situations and considered the response options that their students could adopt in order to react to a face attack (Brown & Levinson, 1987). In a third stage, the teachers were

introduced to possible stances and response options that their learners could adopt.

In the first stage, when examining the concepts of peace and hostility, the student teachers were encouraged to develop their own voice by reflecting in writing about their concerns and worries. The session gave them an opportunity to identify and build up their own language of peace so that as teachers they had the necessary linguistic resources with which to discuss the issues.

During the second stage, the student teachers examined ways of identifying hostility and aggression in four situations and reflected in writing on ways learners could react by taking into consideration contextual and interpersonal factors. The four situations that had actually been experienced by foreign language users are as follows:

- **Walking on the streets: verbal abuse**
  I was walking with some friends and classmates (talking about school and everything else) and all of the sudden a lady started to scream to us in a very aggressive and racist way. She said bad words and looked at us extremely angry. (HS7)

- **Going to the store: linguistic aggression**
  I was living in GDL at the time and I went grocery shopping with my roommate. We went to the Mercado and we were waiting at the vegetable stand for someone to help us. We were having a conversation while we waited to be helped and it was in English. We had been waiting for about 5 minutes then one of the attendants looked at us and was finishing another customer's order and turned to his co-worker and began to say, "Ahi mira, otra gringa piojosa, a ver que quiere" [Oh look, yet another lousy gringa, let's see what see wants] (RD69A)

- **In the family: social rejection**
  I was living in Sacramento, California. My family and I would live with one of my aunts. My aunt's children were around my age but some were older. When I was alone with my cousins, I would get called nasty names. I did not know the meaning of these words; so, they would find it amusing. Because I could not respond back to these intimidations, I was told that I should learn English if I was to live here. (H59)

- **Public transport: racial rejection**
  Yes. I remember I was in the bus one day in my hometown with a friend from Nigeria. Her Spanish was not really good, so we were speaking English. Suddenly, the man sitting in front of us –who was American– turned around and said: "The two of you should feel embarrassed to be contaminating my language." Black people and Mexicanos (mah-hee-cah-nus) should not be allowed to speak or study English. (H44)

The four situations reflected verbal abuse, linguistic aggression, social rejection, and racial rejection. These are problems that Mexican English-language users have faced in the target-language community on a somewhat regular basis.

During the third stage, also in writing, respondents were asked to consider ways in which their learners could be helped to respond to the conflictive situations. First of all, the student teachers examined Lachenicht's (1980) categorisation of aggravation strategies (off record, bald on record, positive aggravation, and negative aggravation) which offer one way with which to identify aggression and hostility. After being able to identify aggravation strategies, student teachers evaluated different ways of responding to aggression and conflict as categorised by Bousfield (2008) which can be divided into: accept the face attack or counter the face attack (which may be offensive and defensive; p. 193). In the context of foreign language interaction, offensive strategies include arguing back and attacking the face of the aggressor. Defensive strategies may involve explaining one's position/behaviour or by appealing to a third party for assistance. Bousfield's strategies offer choices. Interactants may just accept the face attack and not offer any response. Whilst this represents an easy option, the implication is that the foreign language user is compliant and submissive. If the interactant decides to counter the face attack, he/she may retaliate assertively or subversively. Assertive action may involve a counter face attack whilst subversive action is characterised by indirect response. It is important that teachers offer language users a range of options that allow them to choose how to come across when faced with aggression and hostility.

Participants
The 33 participants in the investigation were in their first year of their bachelor's program in Teaching English as a Foreign Language. They were studying at a Mexican public university and their language English-level was between B1 and B2 on the European Common Framework since this was the entry level of English required for the B.A. There were 20 women and 13 men and their ages ranged from 18 to 25. They were all middle-class and Mexican.

Data Collection and Data Analysis
Research was carried out over a four-week period. In the first session, participants were asked to reflect on and write down their histories, attitudes, and experiences regarding peace and hostility in their own environments. They were free to write about any aspect and were under no time limit. Answers were analysed in terms of whether students' were able to articulate their perceptions, concerns, and worries rather than the actual topics discussed.

In the second stage, the four hostile situations were shown through a PowerPoint presentation and classroom discussion examined the characteristics of each situation so that the student teachers could focus on the response options that their students' could adopt. Again, the participants answered in writing and there was no time limit.

In the third stage, after looking at ways to deal with aggressive and hostile situations (see above, Methodology), participants examined, and reflected on, their previous written answers and determined whether they were satisfied with their answers as to whether they provided their learners with communicative resources with which to respond to hostile and aggressive acts.

Results

The First Stage
To understand peace and violence issues faced by Mexican EFL learners, I asked student teachers to reflect on how important peace is in their own world. The results offer a sociocultural context with which to focus on their personal concerns and fears. Issues that emerged included insecurity on the streets, discrimination, and fear for their family. A key concern was personal safety when going to university and going out at night: "I feel insecure in my way to school or in my way home because of all the insecurity of the streets" (Michelle) and "We don't feel safe going out any more. We always have to be aware of what's happening around because if you probably get stolen" (Marisol). Respondents were particularly concerned about their immediate family and domestic tranquillity: "I have son and I worry about the world he is going to grow in" (Norma) and "It is really important for me,

because if I don't have peace in my house, I couldn't do my daily tasks and I'd be irritated, and the same with my school" (Jaime). An underlying fear of discrimination was expressed by gay members of the class: "Well before I came out to my family, I was living in fear thinking a lot about what people said and thought but now that I'm out I feel comfortable and I do care about other opinion" (Diego) and "Being gay I would get some offensive comments in the past. I still do but since I came out of the closet, it has been easier to handle them …." (Burke). It seems that student teachers now feel more at ease in managing intolerance from others.

The results indicated that peace and violence were not distant and isolated concepts on the other side of the world but very much part of their everyday concerns and fears. Since these were real-world issues, it was easier to encourage student teachers to think about the challenges that their own students might have to face in the future.

The Second Stage
During the second stage, the student teachers were presented with the situations (see above) which closely matched the concerns that they had expressed in the first stage.

In the first situation (Walking on the streets: verbal abuse), silence was seen as the safe option for 24 respondents when giving advice to the students. For example, Perla noted "I would tell them to keep calm, and don't say anything, sometimes silence is the best weapon." Another suggestion was, "Keep walking, ignore them, know that you are better than that" (Norma). However, nine respondents felt that they wanted to give their students options, such as, "I would help my students giving them security in their new language" (Paola). Marisol added, "As a teacher, I would prepare my students with some intelligent ways on responding to things like that." However, answers suggested that these student teachers did not have the linguistic or pragmatic resources with which to prepare their students to confront this situation.

In the second situation (Going to the store: linguistic aggression), the number of respondents who advised to do nothing was reduced to eight. The most common answer, from 15 participants, was to make a comment in Spanish so that the shop assistants knew that this English-speaking client knew Spanish. For instance:

> So what people should do is speak in the language in which they got insulted and tell them "Tambien hablo español y no deberias insultar a alguien por hablar otra idioma" [I also speak Spanish and you should not insult someone for speaking another language] or something like that. (Ricardo)

Mariana added, "As a customer, in this case, you have the right to say something back, perhaps clarifying you speak Spanish and you understand." Meanwhile ten respondents adopted more defensive strategies and advised their students to be much more assertive. For example, Alondra said, "I'd tell my students to say something in Spanish making clear that they are going somewhere else where they treat them right." Susana admitted, "I would [in a] polite way [say] that I will take my 'pijoso' [lousy] money and do business somewhere else."

In the third situation (In the family: social rejection), 17 respondents said that they would do nothing, whilst another 11 said that they would talk to a third party (e.g., a close relative) as seen in the following examples. Adith suggested, "She could probably talk to her/his parents about the situation so her cousins can be punished," while Mariana recommended that "in this case you should have told someone in charge, like your parents, to take care of the situation since learning English takes time and they should have been supportive."

Another five respondents were more assertive in their reactions with advice. Perla stated "not respond at all, just smile. If you don't know English very well. If you know English try to say something like 'Yeah, I'll keep it in mind' to let them know you don't care what they said." Norma, on the other hand, advised to "give them the same treatment, you know other words that they don't understand, and they won't know if you are insulting them or not."

In the fourth situation (Public transport: racial rejection), 17 respondents said that they would do nothing. This strategy may be more antagonistic as the aggressive passenger may feel that he is being ignored. Another two said that they would just laugh at him. The remaining 14 said that they would confront the aggressive bus passenger with comments such as, "I would respond in not a rude way to ask for respect but never go further" (Joseph) or "It's none of your business so I'm not listening to you anymore" (Ricardo).

In conclusion, doing nothing seemed to be the student teachers' overall advice to language learners. Whilst it may be appropriate in certain contexts, foreign language users themselves may feel that they want to have more communicative options and at least be able to face up to aggression and hostility to some degree.

The Third Stage
For the third stage, the student teachers examined the different strategies with which to deal with aggression and conflict (i.e., Lachenicht's [1980] categorisation of aggravation strategies and Bousfield's [2008] offensive and defensive strategies). Subsequently they were given the opportunity to review their previous responses to the four situations. Rather than rewriting their answers, respondents reflected on which aspects they would try to reinforce (e.g., linguistically, pragmatically, or communicatively.) Of the 33 respondents, 21 modified their answers whilst 11 left the answers the way they were. It should be stressed that they were not obliged to make any changes.

In the first situation (Walking on the streets: verbal abuse), respondents said that they would work on building up their students' vocabulary range and develop their ability to reply with stock phrases such as "deal with it." Respondents often adopted a metapragmatic approach and said that they would discuss Bousfield's (2008) offensive and defensive strategies directly with their students. For instance, Itzel argued, "I would also give them the weapons to use sarcasm, irony, and the most-important: self-confidence, so they can adapt to any situation." This approach sees language learners as capable of making their own decisions rather than having to following pre-packaged language formulae. Furthermore, student teachers felt that building up their learners' self-confidence was an important dimension to helping foreign language users react in the way that they wanted to.

In the second situation (Going to the store: linguistic aggression), respondents felt that action was called for rather than acquiescence. This often involved speaking in Spanish and leaving the store without making a purchase. Marisol admitted, "I would tell them to leave the store and say 'Hablo español' [I speak Spanish] and then something between polite and aggressive." Susana said, "I have the right to take my money elsewhere." Given the customer service context, respondents argued that the foreign language user could show a certain level of antagonism by making comments in Spanish to the shop assistants such as "Are you gonna to serve me or not?" (Omar Paredes). Recognising their own limited knowledge, student teachers were also interested in developing their own teaching skills. Dhamar, for example, revealed, "I am not good at using sarcasm or irony but I am willing to, so as to help my students to defend themselves in safe contexts." Such comments also reflected a more metapragmatic approach to dealing with conflictive situations by the student teachers (e.g., by presenting Bousfield's [2008] offensive and defensive strategies.)

In the third situation (In the family: social rejection), student teachers emphasised the need to build up the language users' confidence when expressing themselves in English and, at the same time, develop their understanding of contextual considerations, especially the limits and options available when it comes to dealing with family relationships. This included not taking things too seriously and accepting some of the rough and tumble that goes with family life.

In the fourth situation (Public transport: racial rejection) respondents felt they had to provide their learners with communicative options and explored different strategies. For instance, the use of silence was seen as one way to unnerve the aggressive passenger. Other respondents, like Marisol, said that they would dismiss the aggression with the use of phrases such as "I'll keep it in mind" whilst actually working on their language. Other respondents discussed the parameters and options available when faced with confrontation in a public setting.

Analysis

Analysis indicates that student teachers can relate to difficult and aggressive circumstances through their own personal histories and experiences. However, when asked to respond and to react to actual situations in English, they feel that they do not have the necessary linguistic and pragmatic knowledge. On the other hand, they do appear to have the necessary resources in Spanish to deal with hostile situations.

Results from the first stage indicate that violence, discrimination and fear are real-life issues for the student teachers and therefore they are in a strong position to highlight these concerns to their own students as opposed to merely presenting textbook topics on remote and far-removed topics such as conflict, war and lack of peace. An ability to identify with problems does not mean that the pedagogical resources to deal with them are available. Student teachers who approach foreign language teaching through Freire's (1993) banking approach or Apple's (1986) atomisation of language are not going to be in the best position to teach the target language for active and critical purposes (Crookes, 2013).

Findings in the second stage appear to confirm the student teachers' lack of necessary resources to deal with hostility and aggression. Inaction and silence characterised the student teachers' responses. These stances seem to confirm Giroux's (1997) concern regarding "how language practices can be used to actively silence some students" (p. 131). Peace studies must promote courses of action as articulated by Galtung and Fischer (2013) through the concept of positive peace which dynamically tries to remedy social relationships and foster tolerance and thoughtfulness.

Meanwhile, in the third stage, student teachers seem to be well aware of their need to be able to develop the learners' linguistic, cultural and communicative resources. In the first situation (Walking on the streets: verbal abuse), student teachers showed their willingness to discuss communicative options and choices on equal terms with their own students (e.g., the use of use sarcasm and irony). However, it is important to note that reactions and responses involve consequences. Foreign language learners need to understand the risks and outcomes when following a given course of action. At the same time, this approach reflects a much more equitable teacher-student relationship in the classroom as opposed to teachers having to know all the answers when reacting in a given situation. In the second situation (Going to the store: linguistic aggression), student teachers examined ways of acting rather than just talking (or not talking). Importantly, they examined the options available to the customers who were criticised for using English. This included the judicious use of code switching between English and Spanish, the assertion of customer rights (e.g., equity and association rights; Spencer-Oatey, 2008), and the ability to take one's custom elsewhere. Again, student teachers said that they would openly discuss with their students possible strategies for reacting and responding to insults. In the third situation (In the family: social rejection), student teachers looked beyond language and felt that their learners needed help to develop their self-confidence both when speaking in English and reacting to difficult situations (e.g., being criticised by relatives). Building up self-confidence is often ignored in foreign language teaching where the emphasis is on accuracy and fluency rather than on learners establishing a sense of security and a positive self-image. In the fourth situation (Public transport: racial rejection), student teachers explored the use of silence and pre-established routines (e.g., stock phrases) as ways to have a quick response to denigrating remarks. However, student teachers were aware that there are limits to what one can do in a given situation.

The third stage underscores the need for Freire's problem-posing pedagogy as foreign language users examine possible options and resources and supports Crookes (2013) call for a critical pedagogy that "is teaching for social justice, in ways that support the development of active, engaged citizens…" (p. 8). This analysis indicates that teaching training needs to go well beyond knowing how to present and practise language structures in the target language and evaluate learners' language performance. Student teachers need to be able to relate to their students' communicative realities and provide the necessary pragmatic resources so that those students' can interact, respond, and react in hostile and uncomfortable environments. Student teachers therefore need to critically engage with students in order to provide learners with communicative choices regarding how they want to participate in the target-language environment.

Conclusion

Research indicates that student teachers can be encouraged to examine possible pragmatic resources for dealing with difficult and hostile situations and, at the same time, reflect on the resources that they may need. Rather than adopting pre-established methodological approaches, student teachers were able to bring their own perspectives (e.g., the need to build up self-confidence when interacting in the target language or the strategic use of silence). This teaching approach tried to cater to learners' needs rather than filling them with methodologies, structures, and didactic material. The focus is on how student teachers can become effective teachers who respond to their students' needs.

Furthermore, the student teachers used their experiences to reflect on the level of response that could be exerted in the different contexts. For instance, being verbally abused on the street may call for no response whilst foreign language users can be much more assertive as customers in a shop. At the same time, student teachers strongly identified with the feelings of their students when faced with conflict and aggression. Feeling confident as a foreign language user is fundamental so that one can reply in the way that one wants to and this may be far more important than having an accurate and fluent command of language where one cannot express what one truly feels.

References

Apple, M. (1986). *Teachers and texts: A political economy of class & gender relations in education*. New York, NY: Routledge.

Auerbach, E., & Wallerstein, N. (2004). *Problem-posing at work: English for action*. Edmonton, Alberta: Grassroots Press.

Bousfield, D. (2008). *Impoliteness in interaction*. Amsterdam, The Netherlands: John Benjamins.

Brown, P., & Levinson, S. (1987). *Politeness: Some universals in language usage*. Cambridge, UK: Cambridge University Press.

Crookes, G. V. (2013). *Critical ELT in action: Foundations, promises, praxis*. New York, NY: Routledge.

Culpeper, J. (1996). Towards an anatomy of impoliteness. *Journal of Pragmatics, 25*, 349-367. https://doi.org/10.1016/0378-2166(95)00014-3

Freire, P. (1993). *Pedagogy of the oppressed*. New York, NY: Continuum.

Giroux, H. A. (1983). *Theory & resistance in education: A pedagogy for the opposition*. New York, NY: Bergin & Garvey.

Giroux, H. A. (1997). *Pedagogy and the politics of hope: Theory, culture and schooling: A critical reader*. Boulder, CO: Westview.

Galtung, J., & Fischer, D. (2013). Positive and negative peace. In J. Galtung (Ed.), *Johan Gultung: Pioneer of peace research* (pp. 173-178). Berlin, Germany: Springer.

Johnson, C. (2004). Characteristics of effective EFL teachers in Mexico as perceived by students and teachers. *Mextesol Journal, 28*(1), 9-21.

Johnson, K. (1996). *Language teaching and skill learning.* Oxford, UK: Blackwell.

Lachenicht, L. G. (1980). Aggravating language: A study of abusive and insulting language. *International Journal of Human Communication, 13*(4), 607-687. https://doi.org/10.1080/08351818009370513

Larsen-Freeman, D. (1986). *Techniques and principles in language teaching.* Oxford, UK: Oxford University Press.

McCarthy, M., & O'Dell, F. (2013). *English vocabulary is use advanced: Vocabulary reference and practice.* Cambridge, UK: Cambridge University Press.

Mugford, G. (2017, July). *Politeness, choice and interpersonal stance in a foreign language: Routines and conformity vs. individual polite understandings?* Paper presented at the 15th International Pragmatics Conference, Belfast, Northern Ireland.

Robinson Fellag, L. (2006). *NorthStar: Building skills for the TOEFL iBT advanced.* White Plains, NY: Pearson Longman.

Spencer-Oatey, H. (2008). Face, (im)politeness and rapport. In H. Spencer-Oatey (Ed.), *Culturally speaking: managing rapport through talk across cultures* (2nd ed., pp. 12-47). London, UK: Continuum.

CHAPTER 7

SOCIAL DISPOSITIONS AGAINST WOMEN IN BANGLADESH:
Using Critical Media Literacy to Promote Social Justice

Sabiha Sultana and K. C. Nat Turner

Literacies are skills used to infer meanings from texts that differ across cultures (Mahiri, 2004). Literacies in today's world go beyond the traditional idea of only reading and writing skills, since graphs, diagrams, images, symbols, artifacts, sounds, and many other modes work as mediums of communication as well. Multimodal texts, or texts that integrate language and audio-visuals have a broader impact than what only one mode of communication can accomplish (Gee, 2003). Traditional idea of literacy thus expands into media literacy. Critical media literacy further refers to the learners' ability to read and produce multimodal texts that address social justice issues (Turner, 2005). To cultivate multimodality and critical media literacy Multimodal Media Production (MMP) proves to be a very effective tool. MMP involves understanding and portraying people's lives using documentaries, digital stories, music, digital video poetry, multi-user virtual environments (MUVEs), public service announcements, youth radio, websites, blogs, wikis, and other mediums (Gubrium & Turner, 2010, p. 469).

As co-authors of this paper, we bring you a compelling case study of MMP. It focuses on my, Sabiha Sultana's, critical media literacy as it unfolds through a self-critical examination of gender issues in Bangladesh. I completed my Master of Education (M.Ed.) in Bilingual/Multicultural English as a Second Language (ESL) studies at a large public university in the Northeastern United States. During my studies, one of my courses titled "Researching New Literacies: Multimodal Media Production and Social Justice" required me to showcase my multiliteracies by creating an MMP on a social justice issue related to my life in Bangladesh. I had to give a presentation of the MMP to the College of Education for scholarly feedback as well as upload it on YouTube for public consumption. The MMP can be accessed at https://www.youtube.com/watch?v=_Dh466e3Mps (Sultana, 2016).

I chose to portray my life in the MMP project by using multiple modes: Google images to display abstract ideas, screen shots of newspapers and educational data from the Internet, background music from Google, my own voice, and of course, English subtitles. I used the MMP project as a research method to analyze social dispositions toward Bangladeshi women and the resulting effects on their creativity. Making the MMP helped me read my world critically and understand my socially constructed identity as a woman in Bangladesh. In this chapter, I will describe, section by section, how this process unfolded. During the project, I not only became increasingly self-aware and socially conscious, but also gained confidence that neglected social issues can actually be productively addressed and even solved using multiple modes of communication. The philosophical foundation that worked as a basis for this research was *advocacy/participatory knowledge claims*, which considers an inquiry as a political agenda to raise awareness, to change the lives of the participants, and improve their circumstances (Creswell, 2003, p. 9). As a Bangladeshi woman, creating my MMP and cultivating my critical media literacies was an enormous learning experience. It helped me critically self-analyze the way Bangladeshi women are viewed from an ethnic and gender perspective.

Literature Review
Critical Literacy for Social Justice
Giroux (1987) states, "literacy is fundamental to aggressively constructing one's voice as part of a wider project of possibility and empowerment" (p. 7). This literacy-powered "project of possibility" which Giroux articulates has the ability to disrupt hegemonic and manipulative uses of language. Literacy

in this sense has less to do with simply reading and writing than challenging oppressive and unequal social relations. Literacy, and hence education overall, should be geared toward social equality and justice (C. Craig Jr., personal communication, September 15, 2016), and toward raising voices of the oppressed (E. Bonilla-Silva, personal communication, November 17, 2016). The Freirean emancipatory model interprets literacy as a self-critical reading of the world we live in, to empower the oppressed to become active agents of social transformation (Freire & Macedo, 1987). According to Goodman (2003), critical literacy is:

> the ability to analyze, evaluate, and produce print, aural, and visual forms of communication. A critical literacy empowers low-income, urban teenagers to understand how media is made to convey particular messages and how they can use electronic and print technologies themselves to document and publicly voice their ideas and concerns regarding the most important issues in their lives. (p. 3)

A Freirean emancipatory model and the concept of critical literacy were the basis of my MMP project that helped me critically read the world I lived in, portray the oppression of women in Bangladesh, and raise my voice for social equality and justice.

Critical Media Literacy
Kress (2003) argues, "language alone cannot give us access to the meaning of the multimodally constituted message" (p. 35). Since multimodal communication includes not only written texts, but also music, images, films, speech, etc., critical literacy has to expand its scope to critical *media* literacy. Gee (2003) views critical media literacy as enabling people to recognize and produce meaning in a *semiotic domain* (pp. 18-19). It is the skill to identify, analyze, and produce multimodal texts aimed at addressing social inequality. The MMP project, as this chapter will show, gave me an opportunity to build my critical media literacy. That is to say, it enabled me to look beyond language and to understand the complex collage of multimodal communication; it trained me critically to parse this collage in a way that revealed power and patriarchal structures responsible for women's

oppression. Once I was able to do that, I could raise my critical voice and position myself as an active agent of social transformation.

Technology, Media, and a Pedagogy of Multiliteracies
As the role of literacy has shifted from consuming information to actually producing it (Beers, 2007) and as the idea of multiliteracies has flourished (New London Group, 1996), the pedagogical role of technology has also changed. Apart from becoming a ubiquitous part of our lives, media and technology are important for being "the major contemporary means of cultural expression and communication" (Buckingham, 2003, p. 5). Even though social networking or video games might not seem like educational tools, such activities have been shown to involve constructive and critical thinking; they also go a long way in addressing learners' identity conflicts (Gee, 2003; Ito et al., 2008; Morrell & Duncan-Andrade, 2005; Squire, 2006). "The Multiliteracies approach suggests a pedagogy for active citizenship, centered on learners as agents in their own knowledge processes, capable of contributing their own as well as negotiating the differences between one community and the next" (Cope & Kalantzis, 2009, p. 72). As we all become increasingly technologically savvy and multimodal in our daily communication, it is imperative that our pedagogy also integrates effective use of technology, media production, and multiliteracy to ensure learners' active participation in their own learning. Along with becoming efficient high-tech multi-taskers, this active agency can help learners become critical thinkers engaged in issues of social justice.

Multimodal Media Production (MMP)
Gubrium and Turner (2010) argue, "increasingly, the public is using MMP to publicly document, comment upon, and create their own meaning of events around them" (p. 469). But MMP takes us into another dimension, from single-authorship to a kind of collective intelligence (Levy, 1998) that works as an effective tool to produce emancipatory projects. Collective intelligence refers to a situation when multiple authors with diverse intelligences analyze and resolve issues from different perspectives. Hypertext is an example of such a collective intelligence. Similar to multiple authorship in hypertexts,

MMPs can thrive on collective or collaborative intelligence at every stage, from perceiving social issues, writing personal stories, to devising various aspects of media production. MMP is also a form of social research with a digital story-telling approach; even though the participants may not be experts in the field as such, they produce their own life stories, which have a claim to truth and honesty. There are examples of how such collective/collaborative intelligence and genuine grassroots initiatives have yielded favorable results for social justice. Turner (2007), in his MMP named "Part 1 of 2: The Lower Ninth: Ground Zero for Reparations and Education," shows how communities in New Orleans could claim reparations against injustice.

Clearly, this was a motivating project for my own story telling. Through my MMP, I could recall how my freedom was denied to me in my childhood in Bangladesh and how I challenged patriarchy to be where I am today. My MMP project gave me an opportunity to analyze how multimodal texts that portray women negatively still exist and circulate, but how I can truly become an agent of social change, gender equality, and offer encouragement to others in my situation by voicing my story.

Intertextuality

Largely, intertextuality refers to referencing outside texts within a given text. For example, within one secondary text (i.e., literary, semiotic, or social discourses) there can be many references to a broad range of primary texts. We comprehend intertextuality based on our previous experiences of understanding texts. Hence, intertextuality as a meaning making process can vary from a text maker's perception to a text reader's perception. Intertextuality can also be implicit or explicit. Since language is a social element (Labov, 1972), intertextuality is defined as a social construction by Bloome and Egan-Robertson (1993) as well. They also argue that one significant feature of intertextuality is that it is not an art of writers alone; it depends on the meaning making process and expertise of the readers, too. Intertextuality is controlled by and understood within the discourse of which it is a part. Words, signs, images, and the like are used to textualize people's experiences of the world they live in. In my MMP I use intertextuality, implicitly and explicitly in many ways; for example, I use existing images, which may not by themselves refer to gender violence or social justice, but juxtaposed with other images and inserted within my discourse and narrative, they carry that context. The viewers of my MMP may interpret the meaning of those images differently and from diverse perspectives.

Methodology

I began my inquiry into social justice and gender issues including those of "empowerment, inequality, oppression, domination, suppression, and alienation" from a feminist perspective (Creswell, 2003, p. 10). Throughout the course and the MMP project I was in consultation with the second author of this chapter, K. C. Nat Turner, who also served as the course instructor in the fall semester of 2016. As mentioned earlier, *advocacy/participatory knowledge claims*, to which feminist perspectives are integral, served as the central framework of this research.

I strung together many components: free still gif images from two sources, Google and Access to Information Program at the Prime Minister's Office, Dhaka; screen shots from *The Daily Star*, *The Financial Express*, *Dhaka Tribune*, *The Daily New Nation*, and *Harvard Business Review*; data from *Bangladesh Bureau of Educational Information and Statistics*; free background music from Google; my own written text as subtitles; and my own video and voice. I adopted a qualitative approach where these multimodal texts were collected, created, and analyzed using thematic analysis and synthesis. Stringing these items together into my coherent digital story and statement was an exercise in critical media literacy.

My co-author and instructor, Prof. Turner, explained theories and research on multimodality and semiotics throughout the semester. This included secondary literature, pictures, videos, and existing MMPs. Additionally, hands-on technology was showcased to develop our technical skills. Afterwards, Prof. Turner provided guidelines for selecting topics from our life, work, and specific experiences. Prof. Turner asked us to choose a research topic by brainstorming issues of social justice that would have a long-term effect on society. We students chose our topics drawing upon our own lives, selecting issues we found important in our context, drafting how they could be represented through an MMP effectively to raise awareness.

I chose my topic—gender issues in Bangladeshi society. I wrote a think piece describing the rationale and methods of producing my MMP to address the issue. This had to be followed by a chronological story board to maintain the sequence of the MMP. I had to reflect on a number of issues. I had to carefully choose the type of pictures I could use, decide where they would stem from (Google, magazines, or personally captured), whether they would be moving or still images, etc. I had to enhance the images with background music, comment on the images with my own voice over and narration, and think of other ways to make the MMP fluid and effective.

Finally, I made an MMP using diverse software: Microsoft PowerPoint for screen recording, Paint for image editing, Free Audio Cutter for cutting voice and background music, Atube Catcher for audio/video editing and converting, Easy Video Maker, Windows Movie Maker, Camtesia, Debut Video Capture Software, Videopad Video Editor, digital cameras, and cell phones. At every step, Professor Turner and my peers provided feedback as I presented my MMP to the classroom. The professor held individual consultation meetings with the students to know the progress of MMPs and gave constructive feedback.

In the process of creating the MMP I faced some challenges. First, as metaphors I had to use some images that were borrowed from different contexts, because appropriate and authentic pictures from Bangladesh were unavailable. Second, some instances of women's oppression were too abstract to portray using semiotics. Third, my location was limited to the northeast of the United States. Hence, it was not possible to bring a live vibe using interviews from the Bangladeshi girls who actually suffer gender violence in Bangladesh.

Research Questions and Researcher's Positionality

When I wrote the think piece for my MMP I only thought about portraying a social issue in Bangladesh. Once the MMP was completed, I conducted qualitative research to analyze it as a multimodal text. I focused on two research questions:

1. How do social dispositions toward women in Bangladesh affect their creativity?
2. How does that MMP demonstrate the researcher's critical media literacies?

In consultation with Prof. Turner, who has been an advocate for women's rights and human rights for over two decades, I looked back on my own life and experience in the Bangladeshi society. I compared and contrasted my childhood lifestyle with a boy's upbringing. I looked closely at how my own childhood development affected my opportunities later in life for higher education and employment. I found that my childhood was not as free as that of a boy, which had long-term effects on my creativity. For example, back then I was not supposed to go anywhere alone, talk to strangers, have conversations with people, all of which boys were allowed to do. These practices impeded my communication skills. Since I did not learn the norms of conversation with unknown people as a child, I continued to feel afraid, even later in life, to talk with people at my workplace. I did not acquire the skills of resolving issues with people through conversation. I realized that mine was not an isolated case; I represented how most girls in Bangladesh society are treated. Needless to say, my position and firsthand experience was tightly knotted in the research process.

Findings
Social Dispositions that Affect Female Learners' Creativity

The research questions and qualitative approach yielded further guiding concerns:

1. What is the significance of talking about creativity?
2. How do the people of Bangladeshi society perceive women?
3. What are the consequences of these perceptions?
4. What common solutions have been identified to address the consequences?
5. What measures should be taken to resolve the issue?
6. What are the long-term effects of these solutions?

Learners' creativity as a controversial issue in Bangladesh. To illustrate this issue within 12-30 seconds of my MMP, I used screen shots of public exam results in Bangladesh published on the National Education Database, supported by news debates. To enhance the data, I used background music, my own voice narration, and good images depicting imprisoned minds. There are an increasing number of students every year who get an A+ on their tests; however, there is also a growing debate on whether these public tests ensure students' creative development. Maasranga Television broadcast a piece nationwide, in which it was shown that secondary school students who earned an A+ on their public exams performed very poorly in general knowledge (Rony, 2016). This was a very controversial documentary. The grading system for secondary and higher secondary examination was introduced in 2001 in Bangladesh. Since then, the number of highest grade acquirers (Grade A+) has been increasing dramatically each year. However, these students do not do well on university admission tests, in the job market, in the work place, or in other practical situations. The general public and educators have begun to criticize the quality of education and the validity of standardized exams seeing the discrepancies between students' test results and their real-life performances (Choudhury, 2014; Hossain, 2016; Jahangir, 2016; Molla, 2016). The World Bank Enterprise Skills Survey (2012) reveals that graduates who completed higher education and other training programs were deemed inadequately skilled for today's and tomorrow's labor market. Public education is unable to nurture Bangladeshi learners' creativity and critical thinking. World Bank stated in 2016 that the overall quality of Bangladesh's human capital needed improvement.

According to Franken (1993), "creativity is defined as the tendency to generate or recognize ideas, alternatives, or possibilities that may be useful in solving problems, communicating with others, and entertaining ourselves and others" (p. 396). The education system in Bangladesh does not provide enough opportunities for learners to think critically, challenge others' ideas in student-centered classrooms, solve problems using hands-on activities, or communicate with others in pair and group work. Ensuring the quality of education is critical (Richards et al., 2008), however, lack of creative thinking cannot only be ascribed to poor education system in Bangladesh. It is a consequence of long standing social norms.

There are a number of factors, some specifically affecting girls/women, others affecting both boys and girls, men and women alike, that are to blame for hindering learners' creativity and critical thinking. For example, children do not have enough freedom to make their own decisions in their household or classroom situations. They do not feel they can shape their personal lives or their education in a manner of their choice. Children are taught that asking questions is rude behavior. Children follow teachers' instructions in the teacher-directed classrooms without any analytical discussion. The classes are not student-centered and the overall pedagogy does not encourage communication, arguments, challenges, or debates.

As this was my first-hand experience, it was very important for me to actually appear in front of the camera in my MMP and voice my concerns (40 seconds to 1 minute 25 seconds in the MMP). I reflected on my own childhood, when my family would decide where I could go and whom I could speak with. This familial and social structure had deep rooted patriarchal fears: our society was considered "unsafe" for girls. I was also not supposed to critique my family members' decisions or behavior. Consequently, in school, I was not really equipped to ask questions, let alone challenge or critique my teachers' statements. There was no context or activity in school, in which we could develop our communication abilities, discussion and debate skills. These structures and pedagogy imprisoned my mental faculties. Now that I am a teacher, I am seriously plagued by this. I want to develop my own students' creative energies, but wonder how far I am capable of doing that given the fact that I was never trained to go beyond predefined boxes.

People's perceptions about women in Bangladesh and its consequences. The second part of the MMP (1 minute 37 seconds to 3 minutes 40 seconds) shows how society perceives women in Bangladesh, what the consequences of this perception are, and most importantly, how it hinders their creative development. This part of the MMP includes still images from Google, along with background music and written text. This section reveals the diverse roles of women in an oppressively patriarchal society. The focus is their bodies, which are set on par with other products to be sold for profit, in magazines and shopping malls. They are products to be exported from underdeveloped countries. Their primary role is to entertain men using their beauty.

The consequence, of course, is sexual harassment. Girls are harassed on the streets and in the work place. There is domestic and other violence against women. The rate of publically or legally reporting sexual abuse is low and child rape instances are growing (Khan, 2015).

With increasing use of technology in Bangladesh, the image of women created in the media is abundantly accessible to the children. Their perceptions of women are based and built on such images. Both national and international media present women as subordinate to men or as possessions of men. Children primarily see women playing the same roles, doing only household work or using their beauty to make men happy—both of which demonstrate women's inferiority to men in Bangladeshi society. In national and international news, they also get to see human trafficking, Bangladeshi women being sold in foreign countries, or women refugees being abused. It reinforces their perception that women are vulnerable around the globe. This, in turn, reinforces patriarchal structures, a sense of superiority and dominance for men, which perpetuates the cycles of harassment, abuse, violence, and rape that have been present in Bangladeshi society for centuries.

Common solutions and its long-term effects. In the third part of the MMP (3 minutes 37 seconds to 5 minutes 37 seconds) MMP slides show how Bangladeshi society uses common solutions to protect girls from harassment and violence and what the effects of these typical solutions are. Protecting girls from harassment actually results into more oppressive patriarchal solutions: forced early marriages, confining girls at home with dolls, indoor toys, and games. These so called protective measures limit their creative and critical thinking. They do not develop the skills to communicate, to understand an issue with diverse perspectives, or to solve problems collaboratively.

These girls, when they grow up to become mothers and teachers, they reinforce the same roles and restrictions. Their own mental imprisonment prevents them to cultivating their children's creativity. They perpetuate the same patriarchal rules and structures that they internalize early on in their lives.

Measures to ensure a gender sensitive environment. The fourth part of the MMP (5 minutes 35 seconds to 6 minutes 6 seconds), suggests ways in which this vicious cycle of gender violence could be challenged and broken. We all need to play our part in breaking stereotypes and creating gender sensitive environments. For this, it is indispensable and imperative to teach everyone to analyze media depiction of women. From casual to serious sexism is taken for granted in Bangladeshi society, and hence it must be an educational goal to discern it and question it. Blind belief in anything the media has to offer needs to be replaced by critical media literacy. A nationwide mass movement is needed to address every aspect of gender inequality. I must mention here that at this juncture in my MMP, after seeing images of gender violence, it was important to show a positive, empowered image that would establish hope for achieving the goal of gender equality. I chose to show a picture of the Bangladeshi women's cricket team. These strong and self-assured sportswomen indicated we are indeed active agents of social transformation, that we are working toward our goal in the present moment, and a democratic equal future for all can be achieved.

Measures for nurturing learner's creativity. The last part of the MMP (6 minutes 8 seconds to 6 minutes 26 seconds) is dedicated to the measures that should be taken in society to nurture learners' creativity and critical thinking. It should start at home in family environment. Beginning with small creative tasks, parents should let children make their own decisions. They should help them analyze pros and cons of every choice. Classrooms should be student-centered. Teachers should train the students to look at a problem through different perspectives; they should encourage discussions and debates. From family to school, such measures taken at an early age will build critical thinkers and creative problem solvers of the future. They will create an equitable and respectful society.

New Literacy Practices Involved in this Research
To tell a digital story in the MMP manner I had to acquire new literacy skills. Apart from learning how to use new software (i.e., movie maker, or easy video maker) in making a video, I had to think critically in every essential stage of my production about what Lambert called the seven elements of digital story telling: point of view, dramatic question, emotional content, voice, soundtrack/music, economy, and pacing (as cited in Gubrium & Turner, 2010, p. 472). I started by orientating my interest by reading literature on the topic and watching MMPs about other issues of social justice. These practices initiated critical literacy because the brain was "being challenged at every turn by new forms of media and technology that cultivate sophisticated problem-solving skills" (Johnson, 2005, p. 145). All of the ICT literacies I acquired prior to taking the MMP course were used in this research to raise my voice critically analyzing

existing media and producing a counterhegemonic media product (Sholle & Denski, 1993).

The multimodal pedagogy in the "Researching new literacies: Multimodal media production and social justice" course empowered me to analyze the media and to produce the MMP raising my own voice as a representative of oppressed Bangladeshi women. I viewed this process as my critical literacy. In producing the MMP, I had to observe my own lived experiences (Freire & Macedo, 1987) with a critical distance. With reading my own world, I had to "investigate, solve problems, understand ideologies, understand texts" (Luke, 2015) as well. With critical analysis, I had to redesign existing multimodal texts (Cope & Kalantzis, 2009) using intertextuality. My MMP actually helped me align my life with my formal education, connect my childhood in a developing country to my adulthood in the US, my real experiences with acquired educational skills. It was a multifaceted unfolding of my multi-literacies.

My MMP assisted me in expressing my opinions in a nuanced, critical, yet personally grounded way. Morrell calls this *cultivating voice* (Morrell, 2014). Throughout the process of MMP I learned how to raise my voice for social justice. Apart from the content of my MMP, I had to think about the audience for whom I made the MMP. This sense of audience made me think about the language and visuals for the MMP as well. Hence, the process of MMP built my sense of creating a product for intended viewership, their dispositions and expectations, and the role the MMP would play in helping them rethink the issue at hand. Furthermore, the feedback from Prof. Turner and my peers worked as a source of collective intelligence throughout the process of the production. To sum up, the process of MMP reflected my emotional, academic, oral, media, cultural, technological, visual, musical, informational, critical, and creative skills.

Discussion

To address an issue of social justice using an MMP has two-fold implications. To begin with, those creating the MMP have to introspectively and with civic consciousness, discover important social issues that need to be addressed and solved. On the other hand, for making an effective MMP with successful semiotic presentations, they need to acquire critical media literacies. An MMP in this regard, is an effective research method as well as a hands-on pedagogy. In fact, it could be tailored for Information and Communication Technology (ICT) curriculum in Bangladesh. In Bangladesh, I had some experience in making video tutorials for online courses which were only made for academic purposes. The target group was only limited to the academic contexts. However, my MMP research made me realize how those limited skills and audience could be expanded to a much broader context and to important social justice issues. I see great benefits of MMPs as a pedagogical tool especially for those learners who live in rural areas in Bangladesh. Practicing MMP as a pedagogy, rural learners can be made conscious about the digital divide and unequal access to educational resources. They can realize the extent to which they are deprived of good facilities and opportunities; they can reflect on their oppression and demand what they deserve. In addition, it would help to make the learners active agents of social transformation, for decentralization of development in Bangladesh.

Telling the stories of social dispositions against women in Bangladesh using the MMP, expanded my vision of women's freedom. I realized the complexity of barriers in developing women's creativity. The process and outcome of creating the MMP helped me recount my own stories and experiences and come to terms with their emotional impact. Granted that my focus was Bangladesh, but I realized in the process that my findings were equally applicable to other communities around the world. Hence, my multimodal MMP could engage audiences beyond borders. Making it publically available online also made it more accessible to those women across the world who could identify with my experiences and join me in our collective struggle and pursuit for a better world.

Conclusion

Given the number of incidents involving abuse and harassment every year, Bangladeshi society can be said to be rather unsafe for women. Parents are often concerned about their daughters' safety. The impulse to protect their daughters, however, results in limiting their freedom. This limitation ranges from not being able to go outside alone to not being able to take advantage of higher education opportunities around the world. This tremendously impedes women's creativity and critical thinking. Even though, girls are being educated in the society, their mind remains unnurtured.

Describing these social dispositions against women in Bangladesh, my MMP examined ways in which gender inequality could be addressed. Multimodal portrayal of women's oppression also helped the audience understand the intensity of the issue. The actual and intended audience of my MMP was teachers, students, educators, social activists, and policy makers from Bangladeshi ministries. I hope that I have played a small part in motivating them to take measures to transform Bangladeshi society for the better. My MMP, as an easily accessible YouTube product open for global viewers, can potentially provide a critical perspective to international organizations that work to eradicate gender violence.

My MMP has been well received by the audiences. They see it as a significant tool to raise awareness of pressing social issues. When I presented the MMP in an international conference in June 2017, a teacher from Pakistan showed her interest in showing my MMP in her country. She could relate her own experiences with mine and stated that women's issues in her country are similar to what Bangladeshi women face. When I presented my MMP at my own university, as the course required, other doctoral students found my digital story telling as a great example that truly reflected my critical media literacies. A teacher from Western Massachusetts appreciated my MMP making and asked me whether I was interested in making MMP commercially with a media company. Almost all viewers confirmed with me that creating MMPs is a great tool to critically reflect on social issues and take productive action.

The circumstances that hindered my freedom in childhood changed over time. Now education in Bangladesh is becoming more student-centered where the students can ask questions, discuss with the teachers and peers, and critically work through various perspectives. However, women still face physical and mental abuse, gender inequality, and violence. I hope to have done a very small part in addressing these issues that are both very personal to me and yet experienced in many cultures and societies across the world. Much needs to be done to achieve true equality and empowerment. Yet, we ourselves are the agents of our own transformation.

References

Beers, K. (2007). The measure of our success. In K. Beers, R. E. Probst, & L. Rief (Eds.), *Adolescent literacy: Turning promise into practice* (pp. 1-13). Portsmouth, NH: Heinemann.

Bloome, D., & Egan-Robertson, A. (1993). The social construction of intertextuality in classroom reading and writing lessons. *Reading Research Quarterly, 28*(4), 305-333. http://dx.doi.org/10.2307/747928

Buckingham, D. (2003). *Media education: Literacy, learning and contemporary culture*. Cambridge, UK: Polity Press.

Choudhury, Z. (2014, September 30). Politics of education: Debate over student exams. *The Daily Star*. Retrieved from http://www.thedailystar.net/politics-of-education-debate-over-student-exams-43902

Cope, B., & Kalantzis, M. (2009). "Multiliteracies": New literacies, new learning. *Pedagogies: An International Journal, 4*(3), 164–195. http://dx.doi.org/10.1080/15544800903076044

Creswell, J. W. (2003). *Research design: Qualitative, quantitative, and mixed method approaches* (3rd ed.). Thousand Oaks, CA: Sage Publications.

Franken, R. E. (1993). *Human motivation* (3rd ed). Belmont, CA: Wadsworth Publishing.

Freire, P., & Macedo, D. (1987). *Literacy: Reading the word and the world*. Westport, CT: Bergin and Garvey.

Gee, J. P. (2003). *What video games have to teach us about learning and literacy*. New York, NY: Palgrave Macmillan.

Giroux, H. A. (1987). Introduction: Literacy and the pedagogy of political empowerment. In P. Freire & D. Macedo (Eds.), *Literacy: Reading the word and the world* (pp. 1-28). Westport, CT: Bergin and Garvey.

Goodman, S. (2003). *Teaching youth media: A critical guide to literacy, video production, and social change*. New York, NY: Teachers College Press.

Gubrium, A., & Turner, K. C. N. (2010). Digital storytelling as an emergent method for social research and practices. In S. N. Hess-Biber (Ed.), *Handbook of emergent technologies in social research* (pp. 469-491). New York, NY: Oxford University Press.

Hossain, S. (2016, November 22). Education suitable for 21st century. *The Financial Express*. Retrieved from http://www.thefinancialexpress-bd.com/2016/11/22/53939/Education-suitable-for-21st-century

Ito, M., Horst, H., Bittanti, M., Boyd, d., Herr-Stephenson, B., Lange, P. G., . . . Tripp, L. (2008). *Living and learning with new media: Summary of findings from the digital youth project*. Retrieved from http://digitalyouth.ischool.berkeley.edu/files/report/digitalyouth-WhitePape.pdf

Jahangir, R. (2016, November 11). Teaching students to seek quality knowledge. *The Financial Express*. Retrieved from http://www.thefinancialexpressbd.com/2016/11/11/52772/Teaching-students-to-seek-quality-knowledge

Johnson, S. (2005). *Everything bad is good for you: How today's popular culture is actually making us smarter*. New York, NY: Riverhead.

Khan, M. J. (2015, August 5). 280 children raped in the first six months of 2015. *Dhaka Tribune*. Retrieved from https://www.dhakatribune.com/uncategorized/2015/08/05/280-children-raped-in-the-first-six-months-of-2015

Kress, G. (2003). *Literacy in the new media age*. New York, NY: Routledge.

Labov, W. (1972). *Language in the inner city: Studies in the Black English vernacular*. Philadelphia, PA: University of Pennsylvania Press.

Levy, P. (1998). *Becoming virtual: Reality in the digital age* (R. Bononno, Trans.). New York, NY: Plenum Press.

Luke, A. [jonathanrajalingam]. (2015, March 31). Allen Luke - Critical literacy [Video file]. Retrieved from https://www.youtube.com/watch?v=UnWdARykdcw

Mahiri, J. (2004). New literacies in a new century. In J. Mahiri (Ed.), *What they don't learn in school: Literacy in the lives of urban youth* (pp. 1-18). New York, NY: Peter Lang Publishing.

Molla, M. A. (2016, August 19). The GPA 5 rat race. *Dhaka Tribune*. Retrieved from http://www.dhakatribune.com/bangladesh/2016/08/19/gpa-5-rat-race/

Morrell, E., & Duncan-Andrade, J. (2005). Popular culture and critical media pedagogy in secondary literacy classrooms. *The International Journal of Learning, 12*, 1–12. https://doi.org/10.18848/1447-9494/CGP/v12i09/48068

Morrell, E. [grpsmychoice]. (2014, October 2). *Literacy summit 2014: Ernest Morrell* [Video file]. Retrieved from https://www.youtube.com/watch?v=dWKabHtlvS8

New London Group. (1996). A pedagogy of multiliteracies: Designing social futures. *Harvard Educational Review, 66*(1), 60-92. https://doi.org/10.17763/haer.66.1.17370n67v22j160u

Richards, J., Austin, S., Harford, W., Hayes-Birchler, A., Javaherian, S., Omoluabi, O., & Tokushige, Y. (2008). *Improving the quality of education in Bangladesh*. Madison, WI: La Follette School of Public Affairs, University of Wisconsin–Madison.

Rony, R. [redwanrony]. (2016, May 29). I am GPA 5, I got GPA 5 [Video file]. Retrieved from https://www.youtube.com/watch?v=rkwiEWm43X8

Sholle, D., & Denski, S. (1993). Reading and writing the media: Critical media literacy and postmodernism. In C. Lankshear & P. McLaren (Eds.), *Critical literacy: Politics, praxis, and the postmodern* (pp. 297-321). New York, NY: State University of New York Press.

Squire, K. (2006). From content to context: Videogames as designed experience. *Educational Researcher, 35*(8), 19-29. https://doi.org/10.3102/0013189X035008019

Sultana, S. [sabihasultana]. (2016, December 5). Social dispositions against women: Using critical media literacy to promote social justice [Video file]. Retrieved from https://www.youtube.com/watch?v=_Dh466e3Mps

Turner, K. C. N. (2005). *Critical media literacy: A tool for transforming inequalities in society*. Unpublished manuscript, University of California, Berkeley, CA.

Turner, N. [natturner]. (2007, January 30). Part 1 of 2: The lower ninth: Ground zero for reparations and education [Video file]. Retrieved from https://www.youtube.com/watch?v=xliPhDei0d0&feature=plcp&context=C33180b7UDOEgsToPDskJPKfk6exhWHPo9pfEvnKVm

CHAPTER 8

BILINGUAL TEACHER CANDIDATES SPEAK OF PEACE, LANGUAGE AND IDENTITY:
Reflecting on Era of Restrictive Language Policies in CA

Ana M. Hernández

Introduction

The passing of Proposition 227 (1998), the anti-bilingual education law instituted for 18 years by 61% of California voters, sealed the fate for English Learners (ELs) to receive instruction "overwhelmingly in English" through Structured English Immersion (SEI) programs lasting no longer than one year and then transferring to mainstream English-language classrooms. The term *English Learner* (EL) is used by public schools, authors, and researchers when referring to students who speak a primary language other than English (Abedi, Hofstetter, & Lord, 2004). The term is still used throughout public schools in State and US Departments of Education. However, there is a concerted movement to eradicate this term by experts in the field and replace it with *emergent bilingual or dual language learners* to recognize the students' linguistic assets.

SEI is defined as a methodology in which ELs learn English through structured and sequential lessons. Lessons designed for ELs are based on the mainstream curricula (Haver, 2002), differing from other alternative instructional programs where the primary language is taught and maintained, such as dual language immersion or bilingual maintenance programs. The law prompted restrictive language policies in schools, and teachers were forced to shift instructional practices with lack of clarity and guidance (Gandara & Hopkins, 2010; McField, 2014). Bilingual classrooms were immediately dismantled and books written in other languages (e.g., Spanish) were removed from classrooms and libraries, some even destroyed and trashed by school leaders. Parents and teachers were notified by schools and districts of immediate programmatic changes for ELs. Parents of ELs were required to sign waivers to permit their children to attend dual language schools, if offered by the district. Bilingual instructional programs were removed by many districts and bilingual teachers were reassigned to English-only/SEI classrooms. In addition, Proposition 227 permitted lawsuits from parents/guardians against teachers:

> Any school board member or other elected official or public school teacher or administrator who willfully and repeatedly refuses to implement the terms of this statute by providing such an English language educational option at an available public school to a California school child may be held personally liable for fees and actual damages by the child's parents or legal guardian. (Article 5 - Legal Standing and Parental Enforcement, section)

Few districts with high numbers of English Learners and successful bilingual or dual language programs at the time enacted the waiver process within the written law to permit parents of ELs to opt out of English-Only/SEI instruction if the school/district offered an alternative program (e.g., bilingual/dual language education option) under the provisions of Proposition 227. Although the law stipulated the right of parents to choose their child's educational program, the law also emphasized teacher and principal input into the waiver decision and approval (Parrish et al., 2006). This pinned parental rights against educator judgment, ambiguity in communication, inconsistencies in the processes, and uncertainty of access to waivers across the state. Even after signing the waiver for an alternative program at the school, Proposition 227 stipulated a mandatory 30-calendar day SEI enrollment for students of parents selecting an alternative instructional program. Teachers noted there was no educational reason to have students enrolled in an SEI program to be removed 30 days later, and argued that students lost one month of grade-level instruction at the onset of school (Parrish et al., 2006). Parents expressed frustration about placing children in a program they had not selected as an option, where little or no comprehension occurred in the 30 day waiting period, and then removing students from a classroom where relationships were already established between peers and teacher (Parrish et al., 2006).

Evidently, 18 years later, voters in California overwhelmingly passed Proposition 58 (2016) as California Senate Bill 1174, *California Education for a Global Economy*, which revoked some of the provisions of SEI outlined in Proposition 227, effective July 2017. However, there is still a need for highly proficient bilingual teacher candidates to deliver content instruction in alternative programs for ELs (Ramos, Harris, & Sandoval-Gonzalez, 2017). This constitutes a critical issue for recruitment and preparedness of candidates for bilingual teacher preparation programs in higher education (Alfaro & Hernández, 2016). This is not only to assure candidates have high levels of bilingualism, but candidates may feel reluctant to apply for such programs believing they lack adequate linguistic skills to become future bilingual teachers (Hernández, 2017).

New pedagogies and exams aligned to California's Basic Educational Skills Test (CBEST), such as the California Subject Examination for Teachers (CSET), Teacher Performance Expectations (TPEs), Teacher Performance Assessments (TPAs), and Reading Instruction Competence Assessment (RICA) are already challenging assessments in teacher credentialing programs, not to mention that bilingual teacher candidates must also pass a proficiency exam to teach in a language other than English, the California Subject Examination for Teachers of Languages Other Than English (CSET-LOTE). The issue facing most institutions of higher education is the critical differences in the bilingual/biliteracy skills (i.e., speaking, listening, reading, writing) of the candidates, due to limited or no access to bilingual instruction in prior K-12 public school years—diminishing the natural linguistic resources of heritage language teacher candidates affected by nearly two decades of Proposition 227 (Hernández, 2017; Hernández & Alfaro, forthcoming).

The range of linguistic skills across bilingual teacher candidates in languages other than English is vast and varied, in addition to a wide diversity of English proficiency skills, as English could also represent their second or third language. The linguistic typologies of bilingual teacher candidates are unique, because each candidate has a distinct K-12 grade schooling experience, language background, and personal investment in the development of their languages (Hernández & Alfaro, forthcoming). This diversity in language identification and proficiency is not generally addressed in teacher preparation programs. It is important for bilingual teacher preparation programs to consider the teacher candidates' linguistic background when recruiting and admitting candidates, since differentiation of instruction will be needed to meet or augment the candidates' language development (Hernández, 2017).

Proposition 227 was one of the topics in a course that I taught titled "Methodology and Cultural Contexts in Bilingual Education" for teacher candidates seeking a Bilingual Authorization in Spanish. We began by examining the 1998 California's voters' guide for Proposition 227, which dramatically affected the education of the bilingual teacher candidates at the time. These teacher candidates, who were wrongly denied the opportunity to receive bilingual instruction as they were growing up, were examining the law for the very first time. Some members of the class had heard about the politics surrounding Proposition 227, but the majority had not made the connections to their own subtractive experiences in school.

This chapter will explore bilingual teacher candidates' narratives on how they maintained, learned, and revitalized their native language, Spanish, in times of restrictive policies and discrimination in public schools under the jurisdiction of Proposition 227. The narratives explain the political contexts and instructional ramifications of their schooling experiences and, at times, feelings of linguistic peace at home. Candidates faced racial and cultural oppression and reflect on ways they or their families interrupted the suppression. By exploring patterns of injustice, the chapter analyzes teacher candidates' liberation and empowerment in the preservation of their language and identity despite the tumultuous times of language loss and schooling in the era of Proposition 227. The following research questions are addressed: 1) How did bilingual teacher candidates learn, maintain, and/or revitalize their heritage language despite the implementation of Proposition

227 - illegalization of bilingual education in California?, and 2) Why do they want to become bilingual educators?

Conceptual Understanding

The theoretical framework draws from peace education (Page, 2008) as the process of acquiring the *values*, the *knowledge*, and developing the *attitudes*, *skills*, and *behaviors* to live in harmony with oneself, others, and the environment. Recently, there has been a convergence between peace education and human rights education in addressing social justice and equity issues in schools and society. It is suggested by Page (2008) that peace education be thought of as:

> Encouraging a commitment to peace as a settled disposition and enhancing the confidence of the individual as an individual agent of peace; as informing the student on the consequences of war and social injustice; as informing the student on the value of peaceful and just social structures and working to uphold or develop such social structures; as encouraging the student to love the world and to imagine a peaceful future; and as caring for the student and encouraging the student to care for others. (p. 189)

Peace education centers on conflict resolution and training individuals to resolve inter-personal disputes through techniques of negotiation and a vision for possibilities. Approaches of this type train participants in the skills of critical thinking, coalition-building, and promoting the values of freedom of speech, individuality, tolerance of diversity, compromise, and critically conscious people (Brabeck, 2001; Page, 2008).

Hence, a more complex examination of peace is the multifaceted notion of critical peace education (Bajaj 2008, 2015; Bajaj & Hantzopoulos, 2016; Trifonas & Wright, 2013) which links education to the goals of social justice by interrupting inequality through critical pedagogy (Freire, 1970). Therefore, critical peace education values a space of transformative education where teachers can view educational opportunities for students who have been historically disenfranchised by inequitable systems. Teachers can transform students into thinkers for social change and active learners in their communities. Students of impoverished communities, who are linguistically and culturally diverse, need to connect knowledge to power and freedom of oppression in order to achieve social reconstruction (Freire, 1970; Giroux, 1988). Structures that allow subtractive language programs for English learners create a "culture of silence and oppression" for groups of students who are perceived as subordinates in educational stratifications. The chapter examines the teacher candidates' narratives through the lens of critical peace education (Bajaj 2008, 2015; Bajaj & Hantzopoulos, 2016; Trifonas & Wright, 2013).

Context and Methodology

This qualitative study captured teacher candidate narratives about their schooling experiences during the two decades of the bilingual education ban in California (Proposition 227, 1998). The research was designed to focus on how teacher candidates developed their biliterate identity despite their schooling in restrictive language environments. Participants sought a California bilingual teaching credential in Spanish (Bilingual Authorization). The certification allows the holder to provide instruction to English learners through the following options:

- *Instruction for English Language Development* (ELD)—designed specifically for EL students to develop listening, speaking, reading, and writing skills in English
- *Instruction for Primary Language Development*—EL students develop listening, speaking, reading, and writing skills in their primary language
- *Specially Designed Academic Instruction Delivered in English* (SDAIE)—subject area English instruction designed to provide EL students with access to the curriculum
- *Content Instruction Delivered in the Primary Language*—subject area delivered in the students' primary language

Participants

The study recruited 36 bilingual teacher candidates from two credential programs: single subject and multiple subject at a state university in Southern California. Within each program there were native Spanish and English speakers with a mix of Latin@ and White students. However, data analysis discussion for this chapter only reflects nine of the participants (7 NSS & 2 NES), selected across programs.

- Single Subject Program (n=9)
- Multiple Subject Program (n=27)
- Native Spanish Speakers (NSS) (n=17)
- Native English Speakers (NES) (n=10), 3 Latin@, 7 Whites

Methods

Data collection and analysis included narratives from reading reflections and two class assignments—PhotoVoice: My Culture and Identity and History of My Languages from nine of the participants. The assignments were required in two of the courses for the Bilingual Authorization Program: 1) Biliteracy I - Contexts for Learning, and 2) Biliteracy II - Methodology and Context.

Class lessons on the political contexts of Proposition 227 set the background for a series of reading assignments related to language and identity. One of the textbooks, *Words Were All We Had: Becoming Biliterate Against the Odds* (Reyes, 2011) is a collection of autobiographical narratives from a generation of Latina/o students whose early schooling was marked by attempts to stifle their bilingualism. Reyes described how individuals triumphed over school systems that suppressed Spanish. The stories recounted literacy events created at home, at church, or in the community that helped the young Latinas access rich linguistic and cultural resources to succeed in life. After reading the book, teacher candidates submitted the reading reflections, PhotoVoice, and History of My Languages.

Measures

The following measures were collected for the study during fall and spring semesters:

Reading reflections. Personal reflections of the book *Words Were All We Had: Becoming Biliterate Against the Odds* (Reyes, 2011).

History of my languages. Teacher candidates wrote a narrative essay about their language learning, describing the experiences that shaped their language acquisition, including the attitudes and beliefs about their language learning and usage. Candidates reflected on their own specific language learning experiences and circumstances by exploring their linguistic identity as a learner, future teacher, and as a bilingual/bicultural individual.

PhotoVoice: My culture and identity. Through the use of photographs and narration candidates told their personal story through visual imagery as a self-study in understanding their culture. They shared the photovoice narratives with classmates to build community, learn about each others' cultures and families.

Data Analysis
The use of descriptive coding (Saldaña, 2009) allowed me to summarize in short phrases the basic topics found in the segmentation or categorization of the qualitative data. This process provided basic codes for the data that later allowed me to organize a codebook with overarching themes. Using second-cycle coding methods (Saldaña, 2009), I returned to the corpus to reorganize and reanalyze the data, combining or reducing codes into smaller sets of constructs. Through this iterative process of interpretation, I identified major themes that captured the essential notions of the data. Analysis of the reflections and two additional assignments demonstrated triangulation of data across all measures, as well as connections to the theoretical framework.

Results and Discussion

As elementary, middle, and high school students during the era of Proposition 227, many of the bilingual teacher candidates in the study had not had the opportunity to learn content in their primary language, read a textbook in Spanish, or have their identities affirmed in their schools. They were products of *subtractive bilingualism* in schooling, the erosion of the primary language by the dominant tongue (Cummins, 1994, 2000). Only two of the 36 teacher candidates (5%) had attended dual-language programs—because their parents had applied for bilingual education waivers at districts offering alternative programs. The goal of dual language education is to serve ELs who speak a common primary language along with "native speakers of English." Both groups of students attain bilingual and biliteracy skills without the risk of native language loss. Students learn academic content in both languages, as well as cross-cultural awareness. Duration of the bilingual program is five to twelve years for both groups of students (Lindholm-Leary, 2001).

A State of Confusion
After reading the book by Reyes (2011), teacher candidates began to recall the dismantling of bilingual programs in their communities. Some teacher candidates recalled being pulled out of their bilingual programs and assigned to English-only classrooms. They shared emotional accounts of confusion in school and at home with their parents. Some shared stories of falling behind in their English classes, because they could not comprehend their teachers and were unable to ask questions or communicate their ideas in English.

Even though many of the candidates had been denied the benefits of bilingual education, they felt a calling to become the bilingual teachers they never had. I knew the teacher candidates needed to have opportunities to explore and reflect on their own bilingual histories and identities within the political and sociocultural contexts that had shaped them. Through critical peace education (Bajaj, 2008, 2015; Bajaj & Hantzopoulos, 2016; Trifonas & Wright, 2013), candidates began to see the social injustices through a critical pedagogy lens (Freire, 1970). Yolanda (pseudonyms used to protect students' identity) vividly recalled the passing of Proposition 227 during her schooling...

> ...*me pusieron inmediatamente en una clase de inglés. Estaba muy confundida porque tuve que cambiar el idioma de mi educación...estas leyes tenían una agenda xenófoba y discriminatoria. Me pregunto, ¿cómo hubiera sido el desarrollo de mi bilingüismo si esta proposición nunca hubiera tomado efecto en California?* (They immediately put me in an English class. I was very confused; because it changed the language of my education... these laws had a xenophobic and discriminatory agenda. I wonder, how the development of my bilingualism would have progressed, if this proposition had never taken effect in California?)

Yolanda's sentiments not only reflected a state of confusion when she was suddenly placed in English-only instruction soon after the passing of the law during 3rd grade, but she speaks of a prohibited opportunity to fully develop her bilingualism in school due to a xenophobic and discriminatory legislation. She wondered what would have been the level of her bilingualism had the proposition not been instituted in California. She clearly cried against a missed opportunity to use her language assets and schooling under an unjust law for nearly two decades. What if I had participated in a bilingual program? What would my biliteracy skills be like today? Why was I denied the right to learn my language while adding English? After efforts to regain her language at home, today, Yolanda is a Spanish as a second language teacher at a high school in southern California.

As I continued to read the teacher candidate reflections, I encountered Raquel's first experience in 4th grade when she arrived in California. Raquel was excited to begin school in a country full of opportunities, yet she explained how she lost two years of schooling, because she could not understand the teacher nor read books shared in class. She described the confusion and the feeling of being devalued as an individual, "*Recuerdo que en cuarto y quinto año no aprendí nada, porque mi maestra solo hablaba inglés. Recuerdo haberme sentido confundida y que no era apreciada*" (I remember that in fourth and fifth grade I did not learn anything, because my teacher only spoke English. I remember feeling confused and not appreciated.). Raquel's statement represents a vanished hope for a student who clearly needed someone to connect the curriculum through her native language and prevent the loss of critical years in school. Through much hard work at home, Raquel maintained her Spanish skills. Today, her younger siblings clearly benefit from Raquel's bilingualism. She helps them with homework in English and translates complex texts into Spanish. She is teaching her siblings both languages and they eagerly wait for her to come home every day, because they do not want to miss their lessons. This demonstrates an inner peace for Raquel, as she finds joy in sharing her bilingualism with family. She is also empowered by the knowledge of two languages to achieve social reconstruction (Freire, 1970; Giroux, 1988). On a side note, Raquel completed her Master of Arts in Education two years after she finished the Bilingual Authorization Program. She is a dual language middle school teacher at a local district serving ELs.

Parents as Language Teachers

In the History of My Languages assignment, the teacher candidates remembered personal stories of literacy contexts at home, despite being forced to choose English over Spanish at school. Their essays described parents becoming more and more responsible for teaching Spanish reading and writing at home during the era of Proposition 227. Some candidates remembered English-only instruction in school, but also recall being engaged in family literacy events in their primary language. Many of the narratives described their mothers' attempts and persistence in teaching them the Spanish alphabet, combining syllables to create words, and/or learning how to read and write simple sentences in their home language. They began to value spaces of a transforming education at home—of parents as teachers who provided opportunities for the development of their native language, despite the sentiments of being disenfranchised by the inequities of the school system (Freire, 1970). Candidates wrote about their processes for "becoming bilingual and biliterate against the odds" just like the narratives in Reyes's book (2011). In one essay, Carla recalled how her mother taught her how to read and write in Spanish even though her schooling was all in English...

> ...*mi mamá me enseñó a escribir y a leer en español... Me daba libros y me hacía copiar oraciones para practicar mi escritura. Cuando entré a la escuela secundaria, ya podía escribir párrafos en español por los esfuerzos que hizo mi mamá.* (My mom taught me to write and read in Spanish. She gave me books and made me copy sentences to practice my writing. When I entered high school, I could write paragraphs in Spanish due to my mother's efforts.)

Mothers played a significant role of inspiration to the candidates as they were growing up. Josefina shared spending time in the crop fields waiting for her mom to finish work. Her mom picked vegetables at a nearby farm as a migrant worker six days a week. In the meantime, Josefina would read Spanish materials left at the lunch tables by the farm workers. Sometimes the reading materials consisted of local Spanish magazines or newspapers, other times there would be Spanish novelas left on the premises, and there were times when Josefina would find discarded leaflets and junk mail near the lunch tables to keep occupied while mom returned from the fields to take her home. She states, *"Le doy las gracias a mi madre, porque siempre nos hablaba en español, nos llevaba a trabajar con ella al campo. Pasábamos las tardes leyendo revistas que conseguíamos sobre las mesas donde comían los trabajadores"* (I thank my mother, because she always spoke to us in Spanish, she took us to work with her in the fields. We would spend the afternoon reading magazines left on the tables where the workers ate). In her essay, Josefina shared a ballad she wrote to commemorate her mom's struggle to keep the language alive at home. She said the ballad brought her peace and memories of cherished time even through the struggles of poverty, but thankful that her mother always spoke Spanish to them. This is evidence of complex examination of peace that is centered on conflict resolution to resolve inter-personal disputes of poverty and language identity (Brabeck, 2001; Page, 2008).

Over 90% of immigrant youth help their parents navigate the mainstream American culture, a process known as cultural brokering (Lazarevic, 2016). Child culture brokering is connected to child emotional distress and family disagreements (Jones, Trickett, & Birman, 2012). When there is a lower English proficiency, families tend to use their children as brokers more often (Reyes, 2011). On the other hand, for older children, culture brokering allows them to stay connected to their culture of origin by having to speak the language and understanding cultural norms and values. They can also gain a better understanding of the new culture and take pride in the fact that they are teaching language to other family members (Jones, Trickett, & Birman, 2012). As in the case of Micaela, a candidate who shared how she maintained her Spanish by translating/brokering for her mom, who as a seamstress needed to communicate with her clients. As a child, Micaela quickly learned the sewing terms related to making alterations to articles of clothing in both languages, so her mom could communicate with her clients. Micaela learned to read and write messages for her mom and clients. She connected her story to similar ones read in Reyes' (2011) book, where children became brokers of languages barriers for parents and families. Micaela spoke of frustration when she did not know how to accurately translate the concepts to her mom in fear that her mother would misinterpret the clients' wishes and potentially lose her job. At times, Micaela experienced shame for her family, due to poverty, lack of language, and the stress placed upon her as a child.

Later in life, she began to identify more with bilingual students in high school, and as an adult, she became an activist for social justice in protests against Proposition 187 (California's anti-immigration measure) and Proposition 227. Today, Micaela holds a Multiple Subject Credential with a Mild/Moderate and Moderate/Severe Disability Education Specialist, a Bilingual Authorization, and a Master of Arts in Special Education. She is a bilingual special education teacher at a local school district with a dual language program. This way of giving back to her community with her bilingual skills represents the convergence between Peace Education and Human Rights in addressing social justice and equity issues in society (Page, 2008). She stated in her essay:

> Me identificaba más con estudiantes mexicoamericanos, porque hablaban dos idiomas y entendían dos culturas, al igual que yo. Formé parte del Club de la Raza y empecé a ser activista de la justicia social...formé parte de las protestas en contra la Proposición 227. (I identified more with other Mexican American students, because they spoke two languages and understood two cultures, just as I did. I joined the Club de la Raza and I became a social justice activist ... I was part of the protests against Proposition 227.)

A Forbidden Language at School and Home
However, not all the teacher candidates' narratives were of support for their native language at home. Laura for example, tells a very different story. She came to the US at age 14 and was placed in all English instruction where teachers and students did not speak any Spanish. She talks about succeeding in her mainstream English math classes, because she could problem-solve using computational skills, not because she understood the teacher. Laura speaks of alienation and stigmatization at school that caused her to feel shame for her cultural identity and language. She would hear her teachers tell her, "If you keep speaking Spanish, you will never learn English. English only!" Laura explained how at home her parents also forbade her to

speak Spanish and demanded she communicated with her brothers only in English, so she could master the new language quickly and also provide her parents with exposure to learn English at home.

> *Cuando llegamos a los Estados Unidos, mis papás me regañaban cuando usaba el español en casa. Mis papás querían que solo hablara inglés con mis hermanos. Así también mis padres podrían aprender el idioma.* (When we arrived in the United States, my parents scolded me for using Spanish at home. My parents wanted me to only speak English with my brothers. So, my parents could also learn the language.)

As a bilingual teacher candidate, Laura felt she identified with the high school students in her clinical practice site, because they shared parallel experiences; however, she also related to her students the benefits of knowing two languages and invited them to share how they learned their languages. This manifestation of Laura's transformation for Peace Education (Page, 2008) allowed her to acquire the values, the knowledge and develop the attitudes, and behaviors to live in harmony with oneself, others, and the environment. She wrote, *"cada día me siento más orgullosa de mis raíces, de mi cultura y de mi idioma"* (Each day I feel prouder of my roots, of my culture, and of my language).

Proposition 227 instilled uncertainties in parent's beliefs about the language of success and status of prestige in America, which impacted the learning environments at home and preference for the power language despite their cultural heritage. Candidates mentioned in their reflections and essays that several of their Latin@ parents quit speaking Spanish at home to them in order to excel the children's proficiency in English. Some of their parents used older siblings to translate messages into English for younger children in their families; therefore, breaking down their means of communication within their own families. Alex wrote in his narrative how his Mexican father refused to speak Spanish at home and insisted in speaking only English to his family, so his children could become proficient in the language and succeed in school. However, Alex realized he could not communicate with his grandparents, so at age 14 he decided to learn Spanish in high school and continued his studies through college.

Alex stated, *"Empecé a estudiar el español para que pudiera hablar con mi familia en México. Después me di cuenta que podía ser maestro de español"* (I started studying Spanish, so I could talk with my family in Mexico. Then, I realized that I could be a Spanish teacher). Alex and his wife are raising their children in a bilingual household. Alex is a Spanish high school teacher and a cooperating teacher for bilingual teacher candidates.

Equal v. Equity in Dual Language Education

Of the 36 participants in the study (bilingual teacher candidates), two of them were privileged to participate in a dual language program, because of the waiver process. The waiver process was a loophole in the law that allowed bilingual education to still function in California even though it had been deemed illegal in public schools. Districts with strong bilingual education programs—and those where White, middle-class parents advocated for dual language programs—could support parents' rights to request waivers for primary language instruction. Both Kyle, White middle class student, and Omar, immigrant from Guatemala, attended a dual language program and received their core content instruction in both languages through 8th grade. However, their experiences differed greatly even though both Kyle and Omar attended the same bilingual program and schools in their district. Proposition 227 required that Omar's parents attend yearly mandatory district meetings to hear about the regulations and renew the waiver. Yet Kyle's parents did not have to sign yearly waivers to register or continue their child's bilingual education, because Kyle was not an English Learner.

Kyle described his schooling as an additive process—he learned Spanish as a second language while maintaining and developing his first language, English. Although Kyle celebrated his biliteracy, he understood that his enriched experience was unlike that of others who suffered the injustices of Proposition 227. He knew that his future students might see him as privileged and part of the dominant culture. In his writings, he clarified his obligation to raise the prestige of Spanish, as the mother tongue that connects his students to their culture. Kyle explained, *"Los estudiantes pueden verme como parte del 'dominant White culture' y es mi obligación de poner las lenguas al mismo nivel y darle al español más prestigio, porque es la lengua materna que los conecta a su cultura*" (Students can see me as part of the 'dominant White culture' and it is my obligation to level the languages by giving Spanish more prestige, because it is the mother tongue that connects them to their culture).

In contrast, Omar described his experience as a challenging one, since his primary language was Q'anjob'al, a Guatemalan Indigenous language. Even though learning Spanish as a second language and English as a third was challenging, Omar felt he benefited greatly from the bilingual program. However, he experienced marginalization from other students for being a Latino, and discrimination from Latin@ students for being of Indigenous background. He described acts of violence against his family and how he felt the need to fight others or clown around in school to be accepted.

> *Mi familia ha sido víctima de violencia por ser guatemaltecos. Como niño, quería pelearme o hacerme el chistoso para que otros me aceptaran, pero ahora marcho adelante para educar a muchos sobre la presencia indígena en esta sociedad.* (My family has been victimized by violence because we are Guatemalan. As a child, I wanted to fight or be the class clown so others would accept me, but now I walk tall to educate many about the indigenous presence in this society.)

Currently, Omar works with various nonprofit organizations that provide educational supplies to Indigenous schools in rural Guatemala. He also mentors young Guatemalan students in soccer leagues, academic programs, and speaks to them in their Indigenous language. Omar received an award from the county office of education for his community work. Most interestingly, both Kyle and Omar are bilingual teachers in the same middle school/district they attended as young children. Kyle is a bilingual science teacher and Omar is a bilingual language arts and social studies teacher. They both serve the same student population of migrant and immigrant students from Guatemala.

Bilingual Against the Odds
We invited the author of *Word Were all We Had: Becoming Biliterate Against the Odds* (Reyes, 2011) to class in spring. The conversations and interactions

enriched candidates' ideology as critically conscious teachers, as they shared their own stories with Dr. Reyes. In their reflections and assignments, candidates shared their own recollection of "spontaneous biliteracy" (Reyes, 2011) informal occurrences of language learning without formal instruction in Spanish, such as watching telenovelas at home or reading prayer books during mass or catechism. Candidates discussed family trips to México, Guatemala or El Salvador to visit relatives and learn more about their heritage. In all their stories, they spoke of someone who made a difference in their lives, as many narratives mentioned champion teachers who, despite personal liability for disobeying the law, provided linguistic support in their native language.

It is unimaginable that in the state that cradled the 1974 landmark case of Lau v. Nichols, students' rights to access education regardless of their primary language, would permit the passing of Proposition 227 (1998) requiring districts to educate English Learners in English-only instruction. In California, ELs represent nearly one third of the state's public school education, approximately over 1.4 million students (22%) in 2015-2016 school year. In spring 2016, a total of 2,664,291 students spoke a language other than English in their homes. This represents about 43% of California's public school enrollment (2016). Although ELs represent 59 language groups in California, 84.7% speak Spanish. Unfortunately, the majority (59%) of secondary school ELs are considered long-term English learners (LTELs), meaning they have spent more than six years without reaching sufficient English proficiency to be reclassified (Olsen, 2010). English Learners who enroll in kindergarten have a 50% chance of becoming LTELs. Failure to meet the needs of ELs in schools has prompted various initiatives to ensure future success rates in California (Hernández & Alfaro, forthcoming):

- Passing California Proposition 58, *California Education for a Global Economy* (2016)
- California State Department of Education $5 million grants towards addressing the bilingual teacher shortage (2017)
- Pathways to reduce the numbers of LTELs in schools, beginning with preschool education in their primary language
- Recognition of students who have studied/attained proficiency in two or more languages by high school graduation can receive the State's Seal of Biliteracy (Californians Together, 2018)
- Increasing the numbers of dual language programs in the state

I culminated the year by having teacher candidates create their own PhotoVoice projects. Candidates incorporated their narratives with family photographs, music, poems, and videos that explored their identity through their life experiences, including their schooling and becoming bilingual. These projects represented a lifetime of challenges and successes to acquire and maintain their dual identities. We celebrated their accomplishments and resiliency against a powerful political storm of restrictive language policies that swept through their schools and communities. We felt peace in our hearts and I could see the pride in the candidates' faces, as they proudly presented their projects to the class.

Today these candidates represent an era of struggle for social justice and linguistic equity in California. They symbolize the thousands of children denied of the legitimate recognition of their home languages in school. People must recognize the families' persistence and beliefs to value their home language and undermine the years of harm imposed by Proposition 227. These future teachers are the new dawn for revitalizing biliteracy in public education. They know the hardships of linguistic discrimination and family struggle to maintain the vitality of Spanish.

Although many had felt unsure of their language abilities at the beginning of the program, the teacher candidates demonstrated a transformation in self-image and academic progress. Those who had difficulty with Spanish proficiency at the onset of the program practiced Spanish grammar through class essays, rewrote papers, took Spanish classes, or received peer tutoring to advance their proficiency. All 36 candidates completed the program. Many now have careers as bilingual/dual-language educators. Sixteen candidates continued to advance their studies: Four earned their Special Education Advanced Credentials, eight went on to complete a Master of Arts in Education with a concentration in multilingual and multicultural education, two completed a Dual Language Certificate, and two are applying to a doctoral program.

Conclusion

As I read their reflections and assignments, I saw candidates' identities reawakened by their passion to become bilingual educators. They believed in breaking the cycle of prejudice and discrimination by becoming change agents in bilingual programs. Candidates were fueled by their commitment to transform the system that wrongly denied them of their right to learn in their native language. The candidates' voices resonated in affirmation and peace for cultural and linguistic equity.

> No one will ever steal my language or my culture, and I will fight for the future of my children and students. Being bilingual is something I will always maintain. I will do what is possible, so that my students achieve and maintain their bilingualism. (Alex)

References

Abedi, J., Hofstetter, C., & Lord, C. (2004). Assessment accommodations for English language learners: Implications for policy-based empirical research. *Review of Educational Research, 74*(1), 1-28. doi:10.3102/00346543074001001

Alfaro, C., & Hernández, A. M. (2016). Ideology, pedagogy, access and equity (IPAE): A critical examination for dual language educators. *The Multilingual Educator* (CABE 2016 edition), 8–11. Retrieved from http://www.bilingualeducation.org/ME/ME2016.pdf

Bajaj, M. (2008). *Encyclopedia of peace education*. Charlotte, NC: Information Age Publishing.

Bajaj, M. (2015). Pedagogies of resistance and critical peace education praxis. *Journal of Peace Education, 12*(2), 154-166. doi:10.1080/17400201.2014.991914

Bajaj, M., & Hantzopoulos, M. (Eds.). (2016). *Peace education: International perspectives*. New York, NY: Bloomsbury.

Brabeck, K. (2001). Justification for and implementation of peace education. *Peace and Conflict: Journal of Peace Psychology, 7*(1), 85-87. doi:10.1207/S15327949PAC0701_09

California Department of Education. (2016). Bilingual authorization, credential leaflet – CL-628B. *Commission on Teacher Credentialing*. Retrieved from http://www.ctc.ca.gov/help/english-learners/bilingual-auth.html

California Department of Education. (2018). Facts about English learners in California. *CalEdFacts*. Retrieved from http://www.cde.ca.gov/ds/sd/cb/cefelfacts.asp

SB-1174, English language education. Sen. Reg. Sess. 2013-2014. (C.A. 2014). Retrieved from http://leginfo.legislature.ca.gov/faces/billNavClient.xhtml?bill_id=201320140SB1174

California Primary Election Voters Information Guide/Ballot Pamphlet. (1998). English language in public schools initiative statute, proposition 227. Retrieved from http://vigarchive.sos.ca.gov/1998/primary/propositions/227text.htm

Californians Together. (2018). State laws regarding the Seal of Biliteracy. Retrieved from http://sealofbiliteracy.org/index.php

Crawford, J. (1999). *Bilingual education: History, politics, theory and practice.* Los Angeles, CA: Evaluation, Dissemination and Assessment Center, CSULA.

Cummins, J. (2000). *Immersion education for the millennium: What we have learned from 30 years of research on second language immersion.* Toronto, Ontario: Ontario Institute for Studies Education, University of Toronto.

Cummins, J. (1994). Primary language instruction and the education of language minority students. In *Schooling and language minority students: A theoretical framework* (2nd ed., pp. 3-46). Los Angeles, CA: California State University, Los Angeles.

Freire, P. (1970). *Pedagogy of the oppressed.* New York, NY: Continuum.

Gándara, P., & Hopkins, M. (2010). *Forbidden language: English learners and restrictive language policies.* New York, NY: Teachers College Press.

Giroux, H. (1988). *Teachers as intellectuals: Toward a critical pedagogy of learning.* Granby, Massachusetts: Bergin & Garvey.

Haver, J. J. (2002). *Structured English immersion: A step-by-step guide for teachers and administrators.* Thousand Oaks, CA: Corwin Press.

Hernández, A. (2017). Bilingual against the odds: Examining Proposition 227 with bilingual teacher candidates. In E. Barbian, G. Cornell Gonzales, & P. Mejía (Eds.), *Rethinking bilingual education* (pp. 311-320). Milwaukee, WI: Rethinking Schools.

Jones, C., Trickett, E., & Birman, D. (2012). Determinants and consequences of child culture brokering in families from the former Soviet Union. *American Journal of Community Psychology, 50,* 182-196. doi:10.1007/s10464-012-9488-8

Lindholm-Leary, K. J. (2001). *Dual language education.* Clevedon, England: Multilingual Matters.

Lazarevic, V. (2017). Effects of cultural brokering on individual well being and family dynamics among immigrant youth. *Journal of Adolescence, 55,* 77-87. Retrieved from https://doi.org/10.1016/j.adolescence.2016.12.010

McField, G. P. (2014). *The miseducation of English learners: A tale of three states and lessons to be learned.* Charlotte, NC: Information Age.

Olsen, L. (2010). A closer look at English language learners: A focus on new directions. In *The Starlight: Research and Resources for English Learner Achievement,* 7. Retrieved from http://www.laurieolsen.com/uploads/2/5/4/9/25499564/a_closer_look_at__long_term_english_learneres_olsen_color_eng.pdf

Parrish, T. B., Merickel, A., Pérez, M., Linquanti, R., Socias, M., Spain, A., ... & Delancey, D. (2006). *Effects of the implementation of proposition 227 on the education of English learners, K–12: Findings from a five year evaluation.* Sacramento, CA: California Department of Education.

Page, J. S. (2008) *Peace education: Exploring ethical and philosophical foundations.* Charlotte, NC: Information Age Publishing.

Ramos Harris, V., & Sandoval-Gonzalez, A. (2017). *Unveiling California's growing bilingual teacher shortage: Addressing the urgent shortage, and aligning the workforce to advances in pedagogy and practice in bilingual education.* Long Beach, CA: Californians Together. Retrieved from https://www.californianstogether.org/wp-content/uploads/2017/07/June-2017-CalTog-Bilingual-Teacher-Full-Brief-r4-1.pdf

Revilla, A. T., & Asato, J. (2002). The implementation of Proposition 227 in California schools: A critical analysis of the effect on teacher beliefs and classroom practices. *Equity & Excellence in Education, 35*(2),108-118. doi:10.1080/10665680290175130

Reyes, M. L. (2011). *Words were all we had: Becoming biliterate against the odds.* New York, NY: Teachers College Press.

Trifonas, P., & Wright, B. (Eds.) (2013). *Critical peace education: Difficult dialogues.* New York, NY: Springer.

CHAPTER 9

THE TATTOOED BODY SPEAKS PEACE:
Centering the Male Brown Body as Language of Rebellion, Resilience, and Emancipation

Mia Angélica Sosa-Provencio and Tamara Anatska

> Read the lessons of ages writ in parable...upon...flesh...in blood...language of bones, of skin. The body speaks in tongues far more eloquent than mere words...Yes. The body speaks in languages left unread.... (Cantú, 2001, pp. 264-265)

Language in its many forms is endemic to human connection for its multilayered pathways of communication by which we make meaning of ourselves and our lives; for though we ourselves make language, it makes us in turn (Gates, 1987; Gee, 1991; Heath, 1983; hooks, 1994). The boundaries of language are ever shaped and (re)framed by our multilayered sociopolitical contexts (Alim, 2005; Anzaldúa, 1987; Fairclough, 2003; Gee, 2003; Gonzalez, 1999). Chicana and Latina Feminists have pushed these boundaries of language to advance an understanding of the gendered *Brown Body* as living language(s) and speaking subject, a site of reclamation and oppositional consciousness that centers Peoples of Color curricularly and epistemologically (Anzaldúa, 1987; Cruz, 2006; Galindo & González, 1999; Hurtado, 2003; Moraga, 1983, 2011; Sosa-Provencio, 2017; Yarbro-Bejarano, 1998). This ethnographic study seeks to understand and illuminate a language of peace often unread: *one of bones and of skin* (Cantú, 2001) as discourse of the male *Brown Body* spoken through the tattooed bodies and lived realities of four Mexican/

Mexican-American (*Mexicano*[1]), struggling-class male tattoo artists: E, JN, JM, and D[2]. Findings reveal a racialized, embodied, agentive epistemology through the knowledge and wisdom of four Mexicano men, as their tattooed bodies and artistry may offer a corporal text of resistance, resilience, and piercing structural critique toward more hopeful pathways of regeneration. For these men, tattooing is the embodied expression of their agentive capacity to reclaim ownership over their bodies and realities and to shape a world of boundless possibilities more worthy of them and their loved ones where peace, justice, and self-acceptance are sacred and enduring.

Troubling Realities

In the U.S., Brown and Black men and youth are overrepresented in manual labor, occupy the most dangerous and fatal occupations, and are disproportionately undereducated, silenced, and criminalized (Byler, 2013; Noguera, 2003; Oesterreich, Sosa-Provencio, & Anatska, 2017; Rumberger & Rodriguez, 2011; U.S. Department of Labor, 2015; Vera Sanchez & Adams, 2011). The U.S. Department of Education (2014) reports that nationwide, Black and Hispanic/Latino male students in middle and high school are suspended and/or expelled at rates disproportionate to their enrollment; for those at intersections of class, language, and/or (dis)ability, the disproportionality of suspensions and expulsions is further evident (U.S. Department of Education, 2014). Pertaining to gender, suspension and expulsion trends are as follows: out of 51% of male students nationwide, 67% are subjected to in- and out-of-school suspensions and 74% are expelled (U.S. Department of Education, 2014). Though this study was conducted prior to the November 2016 election, findings perhaps bear further weight today in an "America" which endorsed the vile rhetoric of a man who took possession of the highest office in the U.S. in large part by depicting Mexicano males as *illegals*, *rapists*, and *thugs*. As these men (re)write their own bodies and identities at intersections of race, class, and gender, they reveal a *Language of the Male Brown Body* which may challenge the dehumanization targeting Brown and Black men and youth (Gonzalez & Immekus, 2013; Gregory, Skiba, & Noguera, 2010).

Theoretical Foundations

We theoretically ground this ethnography within a Chicana Feminist framework which enables us to more deeply understand the complex innerworkings of race, class, and gender in the navigation of power and oppression in these men's lives, a specificity of difference "necessary to decenter the Eurocentric curriculum" (Elenes, 2003, p. 194) and the White supremacy which forms it. This work is further informed by *endarkened epistemologies* (Delgado Bernal, 1998; Hurtado, 2003) which uncovers the embodied, multimodal, ancestral, and pedagogical language of the Brown Body and its power to defy and rewrite the fixed, subordinated identities ascribed within a racialized, classed society. We seek to reveal a *Language of the Male Brown Body*—one of peace, spoken through the epistemological and pedagogical devices (Cruz, 2006) that are the tattooed bodies, lived realities, and artistry of four Mexican/Mexican-American men. In this way, this study seeks to challenge the dominant discourse of tattooing as semiotic expression and reactionary resistance to oppression (Albin, 2006; Benson, 2000; DeMello, 2000; Fisher, 2002; Jeffreys, 2000).

Through their flesh and artistry, these Mexicano men (re)claim sole-authorship over their lives, bodies, and futures. In doing so, they shape a language which reframes the male and Brown Body as a stronghold of resistance to the mechanisms of oppression. By permanently inscribing their passions, desires, and acts of resistance into their very skin in a manner JM says, "they can never steal from you," their bodies become text they alone author. The following research questions guide this work: 1) What is the knowledge/wisdom language spoken through the tattooed bodies and artistry of four Mexican/Mexican-American (*Mexicano*) male tattoo artists of struggling economic backgrounds who live and work along the U.S/Mexico Border? 2) In what ways do these Mexicano men utilize their tattooed bodies to speak to the dynamics of power and oppression within their surrounding worlds? 3) What are the particular experiences of struggle and resilience at intersections of race, class, and gender informing their language?

Literature Review: Language of Body as Navigation for the Social, Political Matrix

[L]anguage must be used to create identities that can be recognized. (Sumara, 2002, pp. 90-91)

I am my language. Until I can take pride in my language, I cannot take pride in myself. Until I can accept as legitimate...all the other languages I speak, I cannot accept the legitimacy of myself...I will have my voice...I will overcome the tradition of silence. (Anzaldúa, 1987, pp. 39-40)

The relationships between self, each other, our histories, and the natural and symbolic world are dynamic and multifaceted. As such, they require schemas of representation that are equally adept, elastic, and which may help us carry the great weight of human experience (Cantú, 2001; Galindo & Gonzales, 1999; Gee, 1991a, 2003; hooks, 1990; Latina Feminist Group, 2001). The position that language holds within the everyday life of any social group is "interdependent with the habits and values of behaving shared among members of that group" (Heath, 1983, p. 10)—namely, language illuminates the ways in which communities organize their physical space, work, and relationships to each other and themselves. Tattooing has been theorized in academic literature as a discourse which is "simultaneously the exteriorization of the interior [and] simultaneously the interiorization of the exterior" (Schildkrout, 2004, p. 321). According to Albin (2006), tattooing represents "a story being told by a body that does not articulate but still speaks" (p. 34), and which places body at the epicenter of language and human experience.

Tattooing as Expression of Individualized Selves
In the production of individual self-meanings through tattooing, the corporal body becomes a canvas, written and painted upon as a resource for expression (Swindler, 1986). This view of tattooing as an intertextual semiotic form of expression "assumes an interplay of content and not form alone. It is not just that the body has been modified, it is the intersection of the modification itself with the individual's meaning and societal ideals"

(Albin, 2006, p. 25). Approached in this way, the body becomes a system of signs mediating the individual with the surrounding world—it becomes text. Through the act of tattooing, individuals alter their bodies, adding images and symbols for their skin to become the "interface between individual and society" (Schildkrout, 2004, p. 319), a corporal vehicle through which "the self is made explicit" (Giddens, 1991, p. 76). Tattoos are images laden with stories and representations contributing to the presentation of the self (Goffman, 1959). Tattoos, then, assist in designing and performing roles assigned or achieved by the individuals inscribing their bodies. For many, tattoos embody selves and convey the act of becoming the self which one wishes to express or conceal.

Tattooing as Expressions of Power and Ownership
In many societies, tattooing has been the landscape upon which executions of power have been wrought, often configured as an instrument used to imprison, cast away, and to mark individuals "deserving" of deprivation of life and liberty. Tattoos exist within a history of social stigmatization (DeMello, 2000; Fisher, 2002; Olguín, 1997) which characterizes it as "patronized largely by criminals...and other undervalued social types" (Sanders, 1989, p. 92). This oppressive instrumentation of the body is reflected in histories of forceful and conspicuous tattooing of prisoners and slaves for the purpose of indelibly marking their subordinated social status as that of property. According to Gustafson (2000), this practice reaches back into third century BC as Roman slaves were tattooed on the forehead with, "*know thyself,*" or more particularly *know your place, know your status* (p. 24). This history perhaps challenges Benson's (2000) assertion that one's body is perhaps the only thing *which we really own*. Whether or not we truly "own" our own bodies, Benson posits that the body is "the only thing that might defend us against the webs of power that entangle us" (pp. 251-253). The body and its skin indeed offer a landscape upon which political struggles of power and resistance are waged (Foucault, 1979). Fisher (2002) theorizes the tattooed body as a phenomenon of continuous shift, an embodied language which gives form to the act of (re)claiming and (re)appropriating one's *socially diseased* identity from the oppressive powers of the state (p. 103). Understanding

the tattooed body as an embodied language of peace offers a potential for emancipation and reflexivity to assist in the (re)alignments of self-identity and action.

Tattooing in the Forked Tongue of Rebellion and Hope

> [F]or a people who live in a country in which English is the reigning tongue but who are not Anglo…what recourse is left to them but to create their own language which they can connect their identity to, one capable of communicating the realities and values true to themselves…We speak a patois, a forked tongue, a variation of two languages. (Anzaldúa, 1987, pp. 35-36)

In addition to its instrumentality in expression of the self, tattooing has been situated symbolically within sociopolitical struggles to write and (re)negotiate self-identities in connection to the structural realities of oppression (Kirkland, 2009; Olguín, 1997; Wagner, 1986). Tattoos assist in designing individual and collective identities and challenging problematic roles etched onto bodies constructed as the foreign and unwanted *Other* even before tattoos were ever inscribed (Baca, 1990; Fanon, 1963; Senger, Villaruel, & Walker, 2004). In Olguín's (1997) work with Chicano convicts, or *pintos*, tattooing plays a central role in maintaining ownership over one's own body as *pintos* tattoo their own captive flesh in scathing defiance to the State's attempt to own them in body, mind, and spirit for perpetuity. In subversively tattooing themselves and each other, there is heard the yet-unconquered warrior cry of "*Los Chicanos*…[who] know how to survive" (Anzaldúa, 1987, p. 44). According to Olguín (1997), tattooing "the brown, *Tatuaje*-marked text of the Chicano…make manifest their challenge to the underlying subtexts: that is, the peonage and proletarianization of the racially marked Chicano people after 1848" (p. 175). The tattooed skin thus becomes a socially and politically mediated canvas of defiance, "always in a state of becoming" (Olguín, 1997, p. 167) amid structural power (Foucault, 1979). Tattooing is thereby a means of authoring spaces of possibility to regain freedom and (re)claim the right to own the very body one inhabits (Kirkland, 2009).

Methodology

Research Site

We conducted this research in a small, locally-owned tattoo shop called "LB" (pseudonym), which was located in a mid-sized city of nearly 100,000 people lying 60 miles from the U.S./Mexico border. At the time of the study, the city's per capita income was under $24,000 with 19.8% of residents living below poverty (U.S. Census Bureau, 2016). We chose this site because of the city's proximity to the U.S./Mexico border and its large Mexican/Mexican-American population. According to the U.S. Census Bureau (2016) estimates, the city's ethnic breakdown is predominantly Hispanic (48.5%) and White (38.1%). The official public school demographics reported a 75.7% Hispanic enrollment with 10.8% English Language Learners (District Office of Accountability, Assessment & Research, 2017). Over 35% of the residents speak a language other than English at home. We chose this tattoo shop in particular because of its general popularity amongst friends, co-workers and previous students. Likewise, one of our research team was loosely acquainted with one of the tattoo artists, who provided a point of contact.

Participants

Participants originally included five working class male tattoo artists: four Mexican/Mexican-American and one White. This paper focuses on the lived realities and voices of the four Mexican/Mexican-American tattoo artists, E, JN, JM, and D, who range in age from 28 to 37 and grew up along the U.S./Mexico Border where they currently reside. We selected participants by their experience, availability, and willingness to participate. Additionally, JN's wife, MG, volunteered and signed informed consent to interview while accompanying her husband at work.

Data Collection

Throughout this study, researchers spent over twelve hours at the tattoo shop engaged in participant observations and interview. All interviews ranged between impromptu informal conversations and semi-structured interviews which were digitally recorded and transcribed verbatim. We chiefly utilized semi-structured interviews which allowed necessary flexibility and fostered follow-up questions to enrich understanding (Marshall & Rossman, 2011). We also used the artists' portfolios to do free listing to distinguish or sort different types of tattoos and styles and to prompt dialogue.

Data Analysis
We clustered analysis around emerging themes in our conversations, interviews, and probes. Emerging themes were categorized in the crosscutting of all the interviews produced and analyzed around the phenomena discovered in the information emerging from our questions. The salient themes were crystallized across our field research. Our analysis aimed at eliciting situated knowledge to generate description of intentions and actions and elucidating how tattoo artists understand their world. With the understanding that knowledge is embodied and entangled in power relations, we sought to analyze findings through a multilayered, complex interpretation.

Positionality
Throughout this ethnographic study, we continuously problematized our ethnic, gender and class identities as sites of possible biases (Maxwell, 2009) as well as our positionalities as outsiders to the world of tattooing. While it is important to stress that neither of us is ethically or morally opposed to tattoos, for various reasons we have not acquired them. As researchers, we attempted to heed Luttrell's (2009) call to, "open ourselves to the acts of seeing" (p. 476). As such, we attempted to maintain validity by continuously engaging critically with the literature, the data, and with our participants. Sosa-Provencio shares geographic, ethnic, and linguistic ties with participants, although it is her light-skinned Spanish and Irish ancestry which are most visible phenotypically. Also White European in phenotype, Anatska moved to the U.S. from Belarus as an adult. By virtue of our roles in academia and respective upbringings, neither of us share particular class status with our participants. Additionally, it must be noted that we are women, and in this world of tattooing, this was yet another site of the (un)shared identity composing the amalgam of our complex insider/outsider status (Villenas, 2009). As such, it was continuously necessary to "question

our own identities and privileged positions" (Villenas, 2009, p. 346) to stave off easy assumptions that impacted interpretation and data theorizing.

Findings
Asserting Dignity Amid a Marked Status and Invisibility in Schooling

> I am a man of substance, of flesh and bone, fiber and liquids...ache[ing] with the need to convince yourself that you do exist in the real world, that you're a part of all the sound and anguish...I am invisible, understand, simply because people refuse to see me... (Ellison, 1995, pp. 3-4)

In line with literature documenting the educational marginalization of Mexican-American and Latino men, schooling for these four men was an experience of invalidation and invisibility. In one interview, JN, a 37-year-old father, recalls, "I only made it to 9th grade and dropped out...I still dream about school...That's one of my biggest regrets." In JN's description of the education he did not receive is a voice of longing. This structural oppression likewise echoes in E's description of schooling. E layers his experience as the 30-year-old son of a Mexican-born mother with the goodness his tattooed body and artistry have brought him. These enabled him to survive the depression and seclusion in the master's house of dominant schooling (Lorde, 1983). He notes...

> I never did go to school, *period*, and all I can remember...I did is draw... I tried to get back in school, but they didn't let me... When I went through a depression, I stayed in my room and made drawings...I felt good...I think it made me wiser...I know myself better...

While E strives to claim a life of hard work and dignity for himself beyond the limited educational opportunities afforded him, he continues to be degraded by people like his girlfriend's parents. E states, "[my girlfriend] comes from a different lifestyle; she went to school, she has a family...the culture is definitely different. I am Hispanic, she is White, so...I think her parents see me as a bad seed." E reveals a marking of "bad" that operates to separate and stratify him as a function of class, social capital, and race. His girlfriend's "different" lifestyle is composed of access to schooling, a dominant family life structure, and White culture which he can never attain. In speaking the opposition to E's transgression of his *lower place*, connection to a long history of the punitive and visible marking of *bad seeds* and criminals emerges (Gustafson, 2000). JM, a 35-year-old father, explains, "tattoos started in prisons because people would put numbers on them, even on their foreheads...They labeled them...I guess [they] rebelled and started getting more tattoos." In E's and JM's words is the reality that these men are not marked by the way of their tattoos; they were "already painted, tainted, and marked by the color of their skin" (Olguín, 1997, pp. 166-167) long before a tattoo was placed.

Although E recognizes that he is marked as *bad* by people like his girlfriend's parents, body tattooing enables a rearticulation of self beyond circumscribed inferiority, beyond the "mirrors of hard, distorting glass" which surround him (Ellison, 1995, p. 3). E shares that his tattoos help shoulder the weight of this marking and his haunting memories from the past:

> I saw some bad things...I am regretting it to this point; it's burning up inside me, so I figured if I put it on my face, it was kind of a punishment towards myself...I felt personally...if I passed away that God would see it and forgive me...

The highly visible positioning of the words, *Forgive Me*, over E's left eyebrow stands as a permanent admission of transgressions he feels he committed in times past—his continued cleansing of what he has seen. E bears that which *burns inside of him* as a plea of forgiveness marked into his face through these words as well as through a diamond tattooed into the corner of his eye that he states symbolizes his tears. While E's tattoos could perhaps be simplistically understood as his desire to "suffer surely... wash[ing] away half [his] crime" (Dostoyevsky, 1968, p. 499), they in fact subvert Puritanical Christian notions of sin, punishment, atonement, and redemption which are further concretized in dominant discourse (Olguín, 1997). E utilizes his face and his flesh to assert that his judgement and forgiveness lies not in the hands of those who would condemn him but in his hands alone. In his semiotic expression is the hope of someday absolving himself not only in the eyes of his God but in his own eyes as well. In much the same way, Gaspar de Alba (1998) speaks to the resistive and redemptive power of language spoken visually through Chicano resistance art, tattooing for E and for these men becomes a means of agency to reclaim and dispel distortions of themselves.

Speaking Peace Amid Social Violence: Tattooing is What Kept Me
These artists position themselves firmly time and again within the salvation that their work holds in their personal and professional lives—as the *terra firma* that keeps them steady amid surrounding social violence. JN recounts, "I've been a bad drug addict...Tattooing is what saved me [from] the demons." By these words, JN reveals that tattooing has provided him the ability to transcend the wreckage of circumstances that some would say is permanent. For these Mexicano men who were denied formal education and economic opportunity since childhood, offering their children a "steady pathway" (JN) in the world is a daunting and uncertain task. JN, who has visible tattoos on his face and arms, recognizes his marked status in dominant society, "I can be the greatest person in the world,...[but] if I try to get a job at a bank, there's no way in hell they're gonna hire me...with my job it's scary cuz I don't know what's gonna happen...." Amid this recognition that more steady occupational paths are closed to him because of the ways in which he as a Mexicano male of working class background is perceived by the outside world, irrespective of his tattoos (Olguín, 1997), the language of tattooing becomes *what keeps them* through its capacity to bind them to each other and to their families. Permanently marking his body as well as the bodies of others provides JN with a means of seeking peace away from the seeming intractability of being "the addict." JN gives credit to his wife and children, "my family helped me and I did it...looking at my kids...I've fallen off...tattooing is what kept me...I got through it...I can never go back...." For JN, as for his brothers in ink, "*tatuajues* represent a victory—a testament to the survival of the human spirit" (Olguín, 1997, p. 170) providing both solidness and fluidity to reinvent himself and his life.

Even as these men hold their tattooed bodies and artistry up as way to "never go back", they acknowledge they hold this victory tenuously amid the crushing injustices surrounding them. In an interview, E shares the fate of another artist who has succumbed to drugs, "He basically ruined himself...I don't wanna do the same thing...I'm trying to slowly go the other way." While maintaining some connection and brotherhood with those who he deems, "ruined" themselves, he notes that tattoo artistry is something that fortifies him to "go the other way." For these men, language scribed into skin is sacred and sanctifying for its ability to bring clarity and wisdom necessary to claim a space for themselves amid the violence of a stratified world.

Binding Safety Between Loved Ones

The art of tattooing acts in large part to (re)claim ownership over one's one body and one's imagined realities against the backdrop of oppressive societal dynamics that would seek to possess and circumscribe body, mind, and possibility. Tattooing instead binds these men to a world in which people, ideas, and even love are made safe. JM asserts that his fascination with tattooing is in part due to its constancy, "I love the fact that it's so permanent. A life changing experience...to me I'm intrigued and amazed by what you can do with a little bit of ink and a needle." According Burciaga (1993), the term *con safos*—which translates almost literally to "with safety" began to emerge as an insignia of sorts in the 1970's within Chicano/Pachuco culture through its uniquely hybridized language of *Caló* melding English, Spanish, and the Indigenous Mesoamerican language Nahuatl. By signing a piece of art, political literature, or work of graffiti with the words *con safos* (or c/s as it came to be abbreviated), a promise of safety and common respect was mutually shared between the artist and his/her audience.

Tattooing in the world of these four stands as a similarly solid covenant—a promise "they can never steal from you" (JM), one that expresses to their families a safety, connection, and loyalty that the outside world lacks. According to E, couples tattoo each other as a symbolic way to mark each one for the other, to "save themselves" in a way that expresses to the world a promise made by two. While these artists commonly bemoan some young couples marking each other with symbols of affection that often fade long before the tattoo, they maintain respect towards the intention of preserving or honoring another, as in the case of E who tattooed his girlfriend in an articulation of their connection, "she wanted to get something from me, so she got a sleeping owl" (E). For these artists, promises echoing the notion of *con safos* have even greater value when this seal of loyalty is expressed within the eternal bonds of family love.

The unshakeable "true love" spoken in symbols and script between JN and his wife MG, who have been married for almost two decades, transcends what they often witness between couples who mark each other as passing fancy. JN speaks of the tattoos that bind his and his wife's bodies and lives to each other, "we've been here for so long…she is still my love you know, so I'll never wanna cover it up." For JN, tattooing his wife acts as a statement that their "trust and love" is safe in them. He becomes visibly emotional as he speaks of the ring he tattooed on her as an unending gift to their family, "we have our kids…we have something special…I carry [my tattoos] everywhere…Even when I die…it represents me…how I feel… what I care about in life, like my kids, and my wife…I have [it] on my face."

For JN, tattoos are a way to permanently etch into his body what is already indelibly on his spirit. JN uses the language of tattooing to translate his desire that his physical form be a space of shared ownership for his family, an inheritance for his children to…

> have something when I am gone…it's not about me anymore…it's about my kids and their future…if I do pass, my kids can get something…I got a rose with my son's initials…I got my daughter's name and crown on there…It's her tattoo… on my body.

JN's body in this way articulates a promise to his children and wife that, amid the brokenness and fragility of the world, his love and role in their lives is unending.

In JN's words echoes the desire which emerges across these four tattoo artists' words and articulating flesh: *amidst racialized social oppression and financial uncertainty, our bodies are a stronghold of unending honor dedicated to you, our children*, that is, "yours until you go to the grave" (JM). According to D, "art doesn't die either; it lives with us." Through tattooing their bodies in honor of their children, these men transform themselves into an alternative space which offers steadiness. For E, unfaltering loyalty is spoken through a large portrait of his mother on his upper arm, "I care about her a lot especially cuz she was a single mother and trying to raise me. It's kinda rough for a single mother to raise a man…I just have unconditional love for her."

These men likewise utilize their bodies and artistry to communicate unflagging loyalty, respect, and faith in each other. Tattooing alongside and onto each other for nearly a decade, they refer to each other as *brothers* and at times *blood brothers*, summoning the literal biological element pulsing through their work. For JN, his brothers at the tattoo shop are more than colleagues—they protect each other's interests, wellbeing, and "keep each other here." These men share their lives, their families, and their artistry, receiving tattoos from each that express their connection and friendship. By offering their tattooed bodies up to their families and to each other to speak bonds that lie beyond the grasp of spoken words, these Mexicano male tattoo artists together (re)claim their right to continue unencumbered along more hopeful pathways.

Conjuring Alternative Spaces of Possibility
Adding dimension to the notion that tattoos are a fixed marking upon the body, D, the youngest artist at 28, affirms that the value of tattooing for him as for many clients is in a mutability mirroring the changes of body and time which are always in flux. He recounts the resistance he has met from clients while attempting to touch up or fix their old tattoos, "some people like their tattoos because it was done at a certain time or by a certain person…I've tried to, like, fix people's tattoos that look like crap and then they're like, 'no, I *like* it. I don't *want* you to change it'." In a similar manner, D speaks of his own process of accepting and claiming the perfect imperfection of his tattoos, "It might not be perfect…but…it's part of me and I *like* it. It's grown on me…the minute you get it…it becomes you." For D, accepting the tattoos upon his body seems to parallel an acquired acceptance of self against the backdrop of imperfection and change. For these participants and many of their clients, tattooing is the power to (re)claim infinite and alternative possibilities through tattoos which D says, "live…breathe…get

darker and lighter with your body." These men shape their own bodies as living, breathing expressions of identities which resist circumscription by an ability to be at once fixed and mutable.

For E, his tattoos represent not only what has been but what *will be*—they convey a reality to him which he has yet to discover. E relays, "I have this thing for eyes which I still haven't found out why...in time I'll find out" (E). Although perhaps at the present time E does not understand the true significance of his desire to tattoo eyes on his body, he opens his body as a space through which he enables meaning to emerge over time. For E, the body is not simply imprisoned by his conscience and soul (Foucault, 1979)—but an instrument which will in time illuminate pathways toward his own emancipation.

JN likewise speaks of a mysterious and dualistic spirituality playing out on his body, "I kinda got this I guess demonic thing going on....I have a little bit of both God and devil...I had to wash my hands, and I've got back up... God was the one who helped me" (JN). This interwoven sacred and profane nature of tattooing JN conveys is reflected in both the classical and medieval worlds, visible in sanctified Christian images and demonic depictions alike (MacQuarrie, 2000). JN utilizes his painted flesh as a "transgressive vernacular *écriture*" existing in the tension between the demonic and the sacred which "facilitates the constant re-elaboration and transformation of the already marked body of the Chicano" (Olguín, 1997, p. 166). This re-elaboration, transformation, and act of reclaiming the body is again evident throughout JN's discussion of not only marking his body in today's world but of a re-imagined reality space where his body can simultaneously be new and unmarked as well...

> If I could redo everything...I wouldn't probably get any tattoos...[if] I didn't have tattoos....I could change...the way I go about my life...I'd be back to clean...like a baby... they got no sins...pure souls...I wish I could rip this off and do it all over...either way they are in my heart...I mean that's history...cuz I was at different points of my life.

JN expresses his desire to be *clean* and *pure* again, new like a baby, while also revering the experiences and history that brought him to this flesh which manifests things *in his heart* that he would never take back.

Conclusion

> *Los Chicanos*...We know how to survive...We know what it is to live under the hammer blow of the dominant *norte-americano* culture...*Humildes* yet proud, *quietos* yet wild, *nosotros losmexicanos-Chicanos* will walk by the crumbling ashes as we go about our business. Stubborn, persevering, impenetrable as stone, yet possessing a malleability that renders us unbreakable, we, the *mestizas* and *mestizos*, will remain. (Anzaldúa, 1987, pp. 44)

For these four Mexicano men at intersections of race, gender, and class, tattoo artistry and their tattooed bodies become a genesis of language that (re)frames their identities—their ability to navigate a racialized and economically unstable world. They forge ultimate devotion to family and to each other and a future of peace and safety. Through words and iconography inscribed into their physical beings, these men consciously (re)iterate themselves in the form of layered and intersubjective communication (Slattery, 2006) within a society that marks them disposable, deficit, and criminal. These men wield their artistry and their bodies to generate life, to speak a "sense of life in which there is always something left to say, with all the difficulty, risk, and ambiguity that such generativity entails" (Jardine, 1992, as cited in Slattery, 2006, p. 115). The landscape of their skin culminates in a vast array of tools and knowledges which enables an internal/external space of continuous "hybridization, juxtaposition, and integration" (Ybarra-Frausto, 1991, p. 156) that buffers them against the outside world. These men speak and shape a world more peaceful and beautiful, one in which they are, "masters of all the material means which make possible the radical transformation of society" (Fanon, 1963, p. 310).

Their emancipatory corporal language is formed by way of *intraembodiment* and *interembodiment*, wherein "the construction of the body and the production of body knowledge is not created within a single, autonomous subject (body), but rather that body knowledge and bodies are created in the intermingling and encounters between bodies" and within them as well (Springgay & Freedman, 2010, p. 230). These men's bodies and artistry write and rewrite an unending story which defies the circumscription of the world in which they live, work, and love. As these men continue to mark their bodies and the bodies of others, they author a living, breathing peace language—one which grows and regenerates in ways mirroring the body itself. In doing so, they assert their dignity and rightful place in a time and space that is never fixed.

Implications

Findings have implications toward a deeper, more expansive, and embodied understanding of language that has the ability to expose and resist structural oppression by speaking and enacting more hopeful social futures (Anzaldúa, 1987; Cantú, 2001; hooks, 1994; Sosa-Provencio, 2017). The lived realities of these four Mexicano men illuminate that the conquest and colonization of land, bodies, and language and constructions of the *criminality, illegality,* and *foreignness* of especially Mexicana/os is ever-present. Through their tattooed bodies and artistry, these four Mexicano male tattoo artists remind us that, "liberation is always a negotiation between what was, what is and what will be" (Taliaferro-Baszile, 2010, p. 490). These findings likewise have implications for more deeply understanding the oppressive educational and social realities facing especially young Latino and Mexican-American males of struggling economic status as well as the agentive language they shape in order to bring about a more hopeful vision for themselves and their loved ones of *what could be*. Findings likewise have implications for educational researchers and practitioners toward shaping schooling spaces as sites of hope and promise. This work may offer dimension to dominant theoretical framings of language as vehicles of peace, agency, and resistance to historical and ongoing oppression, especially for marginalized populations, including Mexican-Americans, who struggle for economic and educational equity within their own ancestral lands and who simultaneously shape lives of dignity and beauty.

References

Albin, D. D. (2006). Making the body (w)hole: A semiotic exploration of body modifications. *Psychodynamic Practice, 12*(1), 19-35. doi:10.1080/14753630500471960

Alim, H. S. (2005). Critical language awareness in the United States: Revisiting issues and revising pedagogies in a resegregated society. *Educational Researcher, 34*(7), 24-29. doi:10.3102/0013189X034007024

Anzaldúa, G. E. (1987). *Borderlands/La frontera: The new mestiza.* San Francisco, CA: Aunt Lute books.

Baca, J. S. (1990). *Immigrants in our own land.* New York, NY: New Directions.

Benson, S. (2000). Inscriptions of the self: Reflections on tattooing and piercing in contemporary Euro-America. In J. Caplan (Ed.), *Written on the body: The tattoo in European and American history* (pp. 234-254). Princeton, NJ: Princeton University Press.

Burciaga, J. A. (1993). *Drink cultura: Chicanismo.* Santa Barbara, CA: Joshua Odell.

Byler, C. G. (2013). *Hispanic/Latino fatal occupational injury rates.* Washington, DC: U. S. Department of Labor, Bureau of Labor Statistics. Retrieved from http://www.bls.gov/opub/mlr/2013/02/art2full.pdf

Cantú, N. (2001). Reading the body. In Latina Feminist Group (Ed.), *Telling to live: Latina feminist testimonios* (pp. 264-265). Durham, NC: Duke University Press.

Cruz, C. (2006). Toward an epistemology of a brown body. In D. Delgado Bernal, C. A. Elenes, F. E. Godinez, & S. Villenas (Eds.), *Chicana/Latina education in everyday life: Feminista perspectives on pedagogy and epistemology* (pp. 59-75). Albany, NY: State University of New York Press.

Delgado Bernal, D. (1998). Using a Chicana Feminist epistemology in educational research. *Harvard Educational Review, 68*(4), 555-582. doi:10.17763/haer.68.4.5wv1034973g22q48

DeMello, M. (2000). *Bodies of Inscription: A cultural history of the modern tattoo community.* Durham, NC: Duke University Press.

Dostoyevsky, F. (1968). *Crime and punishment* (S. Monas, Trans.). New York, NY: Signet Classics.

Ellison, R. (1995). *Invisible man.* New York, NY: Vintage International. (Original published in 1952).

Fairclough, N. (2003). *Analyzing discourse: Textual analysis for social research.* New York, NY: Routledge.

Fanon, F. (1963). *The wretched of the earth.* New York, NY: Grove Press.

Foucault, M. (1977/1979). *Discipline and punish: The birth of the prison.* New York, NY: Vintage Books.

Galindo, D. L., & González, M. D. (Eds.). (1999). *Speaking Chicana: Voice, power, and identity* Tucson, AZ: University of Arizona Press.

Gaspar de Alba, A. (1998). *Chicano art inside/outside the master's house: Cultural politics and the CARA exhibition.* Austin, TX: University of Texas Press.

Gates, H. L., Jr. (1987). *Figures in Black: Words, signs, and the "racial" self*. New York, NY: Oxford University Press.

Gee, J. (1991a). What is literacy? In C. Mitchell & K. Weiler (Eds.), *Rewriting literacy: Culture and the discourse of the other* (pp. 3-11). Westport, CT: Bergin & Garvey.

Gee, J. (2003). New people in new worlds: Networks, the new capitalism and schools. In B. Cope & M. Kalantzis (Eds.), *Multiliteracies: Literacy learning and the designs of social futures* (pp. 43-68). New York, NY: Routledge.

Goffman, E. (1959). *The presentation of self in everyday life*. New York, NY: Doubleday.

González, G. (1999). Segregation and the education of Mexican children, 1900-1940. In J. F. Moreno (Ed.), *The elusive quest for education: 150 years of Chicano/Chicana education* (pp. 53-76). Cambridge, MA: Harvard Educational Review.

Gonzalez, J. C., & Immekus, J. C. (2013). Experiences of central California Latino male youth: Recollecting despair and success in barrios and schools. *Diaspora, Indigenous, and Minority Education, 7*, 180-197. doi:10.1080/15595692.2013.787063

Gregory, A., Skiba, R. J., & Noguera, P. A. (2010). The achievement gap and the discipline gap: Two sides of the same coin? *Educational Researcher, 39*(1), 59-68. doi:10.3102/0013189X09357621

Gustafson, M. (2000). The tattoo in the later Roman Empire and beyond. In J. Caplan (Ed.), *Written on the body: The tattoo in European and American history* (pp. 17-31). Princeton, NJ: Princeton University Press.

Heath, S. B. (1996). *Ways with words: Language, life, and work in communities and classrooms*. Cambridge, MA: Cambridge University Press.

hooks, b. (1990). Talking back. In G. Anzaldúa (Ed.), *Making face, making soul/Haciendo caras: Creative and critical perspectives by women of color* (pp. 207-211). San Francisco, CA: Aunt Lute Books.

hooks, b. (1994). *Teaching to transgress: Education as the practice of freedom*. New York, NY: Routledge.

Hurtado, A. (2003). Theory in the flesh: Toward an endarkened epistemology. *Qualitative Studies in Education, 16*(2), 215-225. doi:10.1080/0951839032000060617

Kirkland, D. E. (2009). The skin we ink: Tattoos, literacy, and a new English education. *English Education, 41*(4), 375-395. Retrieved from https://www.jstor.org/stable/40607891

Lorde, A. (1983). The master's tools will never dismantle the master's house. In C. Moraga & G. Anzaldúa (Eds.), *This bridge called my back: Writings by radical women of color* (pp. 98-101). Watertown, MA: Persephone Press.

Luttrell, W. (2009). Reflexive writing exercises. In W. Luttrell (Ed.), *Qualitative educational research: Reading in reflexive methodology and transformative practice* (pp. 469-480). New York, NY: Routledge.

MacQuarrie, C. W. (2000). Insular Celtic tattooing: History, myth and metaphor. In J. Caplan (Ed.), *Written on the body: The tattoo in European and American history* (pp. 32-45). Princeton, NJ: Princeton University Press.

Marshall, C., & Rossman, G. B. (2010). *Designing qualitative research* (5th ed.). Thousand Oaks, CA: Sage Publications.

Maxwell, J. A. (2009). Validity: How might you be wrong? In W. Luttrell (Ed.), *Qualitative educational research: Reading in reflexive methodology and transformative practice* (pp. 279-287). New York, NY: Routledge.

Moraga, C. (1983). *Loving in the war years: Lo que nunca pasó por sus labios.* Boston, MA: South End Press.

Moraga, C. (2011). *A Xicana codex of changing consciousness: Writings, 2000-2010.* London, UK: Duke University Press.

Noguera, P. (2003). Schools, prisons, and social implications of punishment: Rethinking disciplinary practices. *Theory Into Practice, 42*(4), 341-350. doi:10.1207/s15430421tip4204_12

Oesterreich, H. A., Sosa-Provencio, M. A., & Anatska, T. (2017). Mexican American male masquerades in the Institution as Bully. *Journal of Latinos and Education, 16*(3), 229-242. doi:10.1080/15348431.2016.1229616

Olguín, B. V. (1997). Tattoos, abjection, and the political unconscious: Toward a semiotics of the pinto visual vernacular. *Cultural Critique, 37*, 159-213. doi:10.2307/1354544

Riley, S., & Cahill, S. (2005). Managing meaning and belonging: Young women's negotiation of authenticity in body art. *Journal of Youth Studies, 8*(3), 261-279. doi:10.1080/13676260500261843

Rumberger, R. W., & Rodriguez, G. M. (2011). Chicano dropouts. In R. R. Valencia (Ed.), *Chicano school failure and success: Past, present, and future* (pp. 76-98). New York, NY: Routledge.

Sanders, C. R. (1989). *Customizing the body: The art and culture of tattooing.* Philadelphia, PA: Temple University Press.

Schildkrout, E. (2004). Inscribing the body. *Annual Review of Anthropology, 33*, 319-344. doi:10.1146/annurev.anthro.33.070203.143947

Senger, J. M., Villaruel, F., & Walker, A. A. N. (2004). *Lost opportunities: The reality of Latinos in the U.S. criminal justice system.* Washington, DC: National Council of La Raza.

Slattery, P. (2006). *Curriculum development in the postmodern era.* New York, NY: Routledge.

Sosa-Provencio, M. A. (2017). Curriculum of the Mestiza/o Body: Living and learning through a corporal language of resistance and (re)generation. *Diaspora Indigenous and Minority Education, 12*(2), 95-107. doi:10.1080/15595692.2017.1393798

Swindler, A. (1986). Culture in action: Symbols and strategies. *American Sociological Review, 7*(2), 273-286. doi:10.2307/2095521

Taliaferro-Baszile, D. (2010). In Ellisonian eyes, what is curriculum theory? In E. Malewski (Ed.), *Curriculum studies handbook—the next moment* (pp. 483-495). New York, NY: Routledge.

U.S. Census Bureau. (2016). *State and county quickfacts*. Retrieved from https://www.census.gov/quickfacts/fact/table/NM/IPE120216#viewtop

U.S. Department of Education, Office for Civil Rights. (2014). *Civil rights data collection: Data snapshot (school discipline)*. Retrieved from https://ocrdata.ed.gov/downloads/crdc-school-discipline-snapshot.pdf

U.S. Department of Labor, Bureau of Labor Statistics. (2015). *Educational attainment and occupation groups by race and ethnicity in 2014*. Retrieved from http://www.bls.gov/opub/ted/2015/educational-attainment-and-occupation-groups-by-race-and-ethnicity-in-2014.htm

Vera Sanchez, C. G., & Adams E. B. (2011). Sacrificed on the altar of public safety: The policing of Latino and African American youth. *Journal of Contemporary Criminal Justice, 27*(3), 322-341. doi:10.1177/1043986211412565

Villenas, S. (2009). The colonizer/colonized Chicana ethnographer: Identity, marginalization, and co-optation in the field. In W. Luttrell (Ed.), *Qualitative educational research: Reading in reflexive methodology and transformative practice* (pp. 345-362). New York, NY: Routledge.

Wagner, R. (1986). *Symbols that stand for themselves*. Chicago, IL: The University of Chicago Press.

Yarbro-Bejarano, Y. (1998). Laying it bare: The queer/colored body in photography by Laura Aguilar. In C. Trujillo (Ed.), *Living Chicana theory* (pp. 227-305). Berkley, CA: Third Woman Press.

Ybarra-Frausto, T. (1991). Rasquachísmo: A Chicano sensibility. In R. Griswold del Castillo (Ed.), CARAS: *Chicano art: Resistance to affirmation*, 1965-1985 (pp. 152-162). Los Angeles, CA: University of California.

Notes

1. Participants self-identify across *Mexican*, *Mexican-American*, and *Hispanic*. In contending with this, we gravitate toward *Mexicano*, which bears particular cultural and historical significance in this region as a land-bound identity of Indigenous, Spanish, and African ancestry formed within Spain's 16th century conquest of Mexico and current-day Southwest (Acuña, 1988; Gomez, 2006 Menchaca, 2002).

Where *Mestiza/o* is utilized, it is done to name the hybridized reality of a People who transcend man-made divisions of citizenship along the U.S./Mexico Border. Besides the italicized introduction of *Mexicana/o*, we do not italicize so as not to alienate it from other identity signifiers including Black, White, Hispanic, and Latina/o.

2. Participants elected to use their initials in lieu of pseudonyms.

CHAPTER 10

PRAGMATIC ACTS OF THE TALKING DRUM IN PRE-COLONIAL YORUBA WARFARE AND PEACE INITIATIVE

Waheed A. Bamigbade

Introduction

Using a functionalist, pragmatic account, this chapter proposes that there is more to drumming than entertainment. Talking drumming is a major global-cultural peculiarity of the Yoruba, and no major events such as ceremonies and festivals are complete without the involvement of the talking drum. In certain circumstances, however, drum-beats do not prompt one to dance or to feel, but to act—where dancing is not part of the actions required—or to send a message of action, rather than to solely entertain. This is when the talking drum is actually used to engage in a discourse, to communicate and demand compliance to its directives and/or suggestions. Although not all the drums can produce a speech or a discourse, the Yoruba talking drum has been used for centuries to produce human communication that is clearly understood by people who are talented enough to "hear" or decode or interpret its valuable messages in various contexts, including war and peace situations. This present chapter is thus a cultural linguistic perspective that shows the discourse or linguistic practices of a people through cultural artifacts such as the talking drum. The questions this chapter seeks to answer are three: What is the role of the talking drum in the pre-colonial Yoruba context of war and peace? What are the specific pragmatic acts that are performed by the Yoruba talking drum in this aforementioned context? And finally, what is the significance of the pragmatic acts performed?

Traditional drumming practice cuts across ethnic groups in Nigeria and indeed Africa. However, the talking drum has a unique role among the Yoruba of the present-day southwestern Nigeria, having been claimed to have originated from the pre-colonial Oyo (Olajide, 2011, para. 5), one of the ancient cities in Nigeria. In his article, Olajide posits that "it is one of the cultural instruments that has endured and survived many generations" (ibid., para. 6). The drum, in varying sizes and names depending on ethnicity, is a very important aspect of the African cultural life, cutting across all strata, including the spiritual and the mundane. Rituals, festivals, cultural, social, and professional celebrations usually feature the use of the drum to make the whole event interesting, entertaining, ceremonial, and inviting. The talking drum, according to Olajide (2011), is one of the drums linked to royalty, and "plays a significant role in the dissemination of information by traditional rulers to their subjects" (para. 3). In his words, "[t]he drum is thought to mimic language by closely imitating the rhythm and intonation of the spoken word, that is, the talking drum speaks in tones that are adopted with leather cords that run the length of the drum's body" (Olajide, 2011, para. 6). In addition, the drum is useful in sending long-distance signals and messages to people, especially to indicate the commencement of a festival or ritual, wake up the king (by the royal drummers), warn of an impending danger, or to announce the arrival of an important visitor.

Traditional drumming practice is said to be a lineage vocation among the Yoruba, and can only be taken up as a profession by a member of the *Ayan* compound, based on a belief that the descendants possess the innate skills through a deity known as *Ayan*, the god of the drum. This usually reflects in the names of children born to the drummer's family to which the prefix: *Ayan* is added: *Ayandele, Ayantunde, Ayanwale, Ayangbemi, Ayanniyi, Ayankojo, Ayanwola, Ayanronke, Ayanbiyi, Ayanbunmi, Ayankemi*, etc., are examples of such names. Such professional families are prominent in Oyo-Alaafin and Oke-Ogun in Oyo State, Erin-Osun and Ede in Osun State, as well as some communities in Ogun State, all in Nigeria.

The use of the drum in peace and conflict is however replete with strategic linguistic value and significance with separate purposes for each event. Whereas in a war situation, it aims to ensure total victory, to elicit courage, bravery and strength, to prevent loss, and to invite gallantry by its message while prosecuting the war, in negotiating peace, the talking drum seeks to ensure an end to a war, and invite peaceful co-existence, love, care, family cordiality, preaching virtuous moral conduct, hope, help, support, and neighbourliness. This paper therefore explores in some detail, using authentic locutions, the use of the talking drum, and seeks to identify the specific pragmatic acts performed by the talking drum in war and peace situations during the pre-colonial period among the Yoruba in the present-day Nigeria. This is to shed more light on the importance of the talking drum in the Yoruba socio-cultural life, and to show that the talking drum is a significant part of war and peace negotiation in the pre-colonial Yoruba life.

War and Conflict

There is a consensus among scholars that conflict is a central fact of life and is thus inevitable in human society, and that societies and organizations are best understood as arenas of conflicting interests (Abraham, 1982; Collins, 1975). There have been different types of war in human history. According to Goodman (2017)...

> [w]ars have been a part of human history for thousands of years, becoming increasingly destructive with industrialization and subsequent advances in technology. Typically, a war is fought by a country, or a group of countries, against an opposing country with the aim of achieving an objective through the use of force. Wars can also be fought within a country, however, in the form of a civil war, or in a revolutionary war. ("What is war?," para. 4)

From the above, we can argue that the civil wars prosecuted in the pre-colonial Yoruba period are entirely in line with human nature and the exegesis of the time.

Scholars of war and conflict have also identified the various causes of war and conflict, ranging from politics or power struggle, to economic, egocentric, sociological, expansionist, and ethnocentric factors. For instance, Goodman (2017) lists eight reasons for war, namely economic gain, territorial gain, religion, nationalism, revenge, civil war, revolutionary war, and defensive/preemptive war (Goodman, 2017), which are entirely applicable to pre-colonial wars and conflict in Africa. Ethnicity is closely related to nationalism. Ezenwoko and Osagie (2014) simply categorize conflicts in pre-colonial Igbo society of Nigeria into three: inter-personal, intra-community, and inter-community (p. 135). Regarding the impact of war, the Consultation Document of the Department for International Development of the British Government records as follows:

> [t]he effects of war cut across all levels of the economy down to the level of the household. War has a direct and immediate economic impact through the physical disruption it creates, denying access to land, key resources or markets. Some of the effects of conflict are less tangible. Nor is the impact of war limited to the area of conflict. (DFID Consultation document, 2001, p. 11)

This explains the central need for peace initiatives and negotiation towards forestalling conflicts. The African talking drum has been playing critical role in this endeavour as will be shown in our data below.

Theoretical Perspectives

The theoretical framework for this present work is not the speech acts of Austin and Searle, but the pragmatic acts, or pragmeme, of Mey (2001). There is the need to centralize the role, not only of the interpreter, but also of the language user who Mey (2001) places "in the center of attention" (p. 5) in the essentially communicative matrix of pragmatics as shown in Figure 10.1.

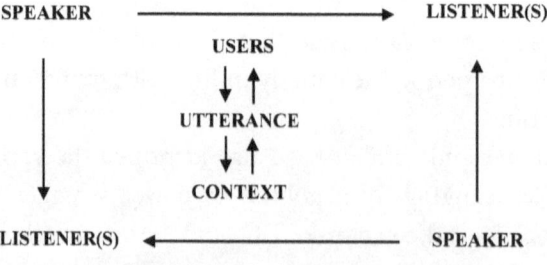

Figure 10.1 Matrix of pragmatics.

The matrix in Figure 10.1 places users, utterance, and context at the heart and core of pragmatics. Users (speakers and listeners) produce Utterances within the boundary of Context. Users determine Context and vice versa, but both Users and Utterances are Context-constrained. In the matrix, turn-taking leads to role-exchange which ensures that there is only one Speaker at any time, and Listener(s) seems to be passive but in fact actively listening and communicative, otherwise they would not be able to take their turn sensibly. The communication could be horizontal (between users of similar status), or vertical (between users of different status). According to Mey (2001), "the users are of paramount interest, inasmuch as they represent the driving force behind the linguistic enterprise, both in its theoretical (grammar-oriented) and practical (usage-bound) aspect" (p. 30). Furthermore, it is noted that:

> pragmatic acts are so called because, they base themselves on language as constrained by the situation, not as defined by syntactic rules or by semantic selections and conceptual restrictions. Pragmatic acts are situation-derived and situation constrained; in the final analysis, they are determined by the broader social context in which they happen, and they realise their goals in the conditions placed upon human action by that context. (p. 228)

Pragmatic acting therefore is more of a product of the social context in which they are produced, where such social context applies to all human activities in the society. According to Mey (ibid.), all the pragmatic acts that human beings can potentially perform can neither be listed nor be subjected to certain principles and rules, as, according to Mey (ibid.), such rules tell us nothing about the outcome of a conversation, such as its success or failure. Mey (ibid.) therefore replaces the notions of principle and rule with the notion of "constraints", which "represents the wider structure of society", and is based upon "the relationships of dependency and hegemony that exist in any actual speech situation", and therefore "guarantees the outcome of any pragmatic acting" (p. 228). Mey (2006) describes speech acts as "situated speech and pragmatic acts", arguing that "no speech act is complete, or even possible, without, and outside of, its proper situational conditions" (p. 57). Context, or social context, is therefore the criterion that distinguishes a sentence from an utterance. It is the category that enables successful interpretation of a pragmatic act.

Applying pragmatic act theory to the socio-cultural phenomenon of the talking drum is by no means out of place; rather it falls within the purview of pragmatic research. Morris's assertion (as cited in Fasold, 1990) that Pragmatics concerns "everything human in the communication process, psychological, biological, and sociological", correlates with Fasold's view that "...any aspect whatsoever of linguistic interaction (is) a legitimate topic for pragmatic research" (p. 176; also see Verschueren, 1987). Language use, in Mey's (2001) point of view is "whatever happens when users are 'doing things' in and with language" (p. 6). It therefore seems apt when Verschueren (1999) characterises pragmatics as "a general cognitive, social, and cultural perspective on linguistic phenomena in relation to their usage in forms of behaviour" (p. 7), also underscoring the role and importance of the user of language and the context of use. For instance, Allan (2010) has tried to expand the notion of pragmatic acts to include other things done with language such as a speaker's referring, intentionality, and a listener's understanding and interpretation of an utterance (p. 2929). Every speaker intends to produce a certain effect or act by means of an utterance, and this is perhaps why Mey (2001) implores us to see language as an activity, and not necessarily rely on the actual use of a performative verb since pragmatic acts can be performed without such verbs (p. 54). According to Green (2014) in the online Stanford Encyclopedia of Philosophy, "a given communicative act may be analysed into two components: force and content. While semantics studies the contents of communicative acts, pragmatics studies their force" (Speech acts: The Independence of Force and Content, para. 4).

Levinson (1983) distinguishes between sentence and utterance, describing the former as "an abstract theoretical entity defined within a theory of grammar", simply put, a "linguistic expression," and the latter as "the issuance of a sentence, a sentence-analogue, or sentence-fragment, in an actual context;" in other words, "their use in context, on concrete occasions for particular purposes" but admits of certain empirical obscurity in "the relation between an utterance and a corresponding sentence" (pp. 18, 242). Harris (1951) defines an utterance as "any stretch of talk, by one person, before and after which there is a silence on behalf of that person" (p. 14), and this definition, according to Levinson (1983, p. 19) is adopted by Lyons (1977, p. 26). It is in this sense that we use the term "speech" in this present paper to describe what is communicated by the talking drum by the drummer. Utterance and speech both connote a sense of human oral vocal sounds received by hearing. Speech is defined as "spoken language, especially as distinct from the written language" (Microsoft Encarta, 2009). The drum might not be human, but it is being controlled by the human, and so speech, not sound, produced by the drum, is human.

Context, or social context according to Mey (2001), is the criterion that distinguishes a sentence from an utterance (p. 6). Thus, Lyons (1977) lists six features of context of utterance, namely, knowledge of (1) role and status, where role covers both role in the speech event, as speaker or addressee, and social role, and status covers notions of relative social standing; (2) spatial and temporal location; (3) formality level; (4) the medium, roughly the code or style appropriate to a channel, such as the distinction between written and spoken varieties of a language; (5) appropriate subject matter; and (6) appropriate province, or domain determining the register of a language (Lyons, 1977, p. 574; Levinson, 1983, p. 23). Levinson (ibid.) describes the notion of context as "understood to cover the identities of participants, the temporal and spatial parameters of the speech event, and the beliefs, knowledge and intentions of the participants in that speech event, and no doubt much besides" (p. 5). In this context, according to Mey (2001), "the users are of paramount interest, inasmuch as they represent the driving force behind the linguistic enterprise, both in its theoretical (grammar-oriented) and practical (usage-bound) aspect" (p. 30). The work of a pragmatist is not complete without inference-making which is what shows the pragmatist understanding of an utterance. Inference is necessary to evidently connect what is uttered to the context of utterance or speech event, especially such that cannot be captured in a simple syntactic or semantic rule. This is where the phenomenon of implicature comes in. According to Bilmes (1986):

> in everyday talk, we often convey propositions that are not explicit in our utterances but are merely implied by them. Sometimes we are able to draw such inferences only by referring what has been explicitly said to some conversational principle. (p. 27)

From the foregoing, pragmatics seems to be the right domain to cater for what goes on in the activities of the talking drum as a cultural linguistic strategy, and a component, of the Yoruba civil war and peace initiative. In other words, "if we want a fuller, deeper and generally more reasonable account of human language behaviour" (Mey, 2001, p. 12), pragmatics is the right theory that can be employed to expose what the talking drum is used and meant to do or achieve, on the addressee in these particular socio-cultural contexts of use.

Data Collection

With the help of some research assistants, I contacted over two dozen traditional drummers in their homes in two southwestern states in Nigeria, namely Osun State and Oyo State, to collect what drummers used to say with the talking drums during war and peace. Those found were not the actual people who have participated with their talking drums in wars during the pre-colonial Yoruba warfare, but they have listened to stories and reports passed down from generations to generations of their parents who actually participated with their talking drums in battles and peace initiatives. The drummers contacted were also interviewed regarding the role and significance of the talking drum during the Yoruba pre-colonial warfare and peace initiatives. They acknowledged that traditional drummers usually accompany soldiers to battle fronts, not only to entertain them, keep them company and encourage them, but also to communicate useful information to them before, during, and after the battle through the talking drum. They were then requested to provide samples of some of what they usually say with their talking drums at such occasions of prosecuting war and bringing back and sustaining peace. This way, a total of 67 speeches were gathered, out of which 46 were selected after excluding non-substantive ones and repetitions, compiled into a list, translated into English, and categorized into context of war (31 locutions in all) and context of peace (15 locutions in all). Two (2) more drum speeches were sourced from the epic movie, *Jógunómi*, and presented as Appendix 10B. The context of war locutions was sub-categorized into pre-battle, during-battle, and post-battle. These are presented in Appendices 10A and 10C.

Jógúnómí ("Allow War to Come to an End"), an epic Yoruba movie written by Anike Obot, is one of the pre-colonial Yoruba war movies seen for the purpose of enriching this present paper. It tells stories of the civil wars and slavery among the pre-colonial Yoruba communities of Ibadan, Ile-Ife, Ijebu, Ijesha, Ekiti, among others. In the battles fought in the film, the talking drum plays significant roles along with the combatant soldiers, from the beginning to the end.

Also, complementary to our methodology was our meeting with a Yoruba elder, a traditional Chief in the Timi of Ede palace in Osun State, Nigeria, and a veteran Yoruba movie actor who has also participated in several Yoruba epic movies including *Jógúnómí*, Chief Adedeji Aderemi, popularly known as *Olofa-Ina* ("One with the Flaming Arrow"). This interaction on the role and discourse of the talking drum in pre-colonial Yoruba war and peace initiatives was quite illuminating.

All the speeches collected are in poetic dialogues, and so were presented and translated in lines separated with a coma to prevent a line being read into another, except run-on lines. Some Yoruba words such as *Sango*, the Yoruba god of iron, *Iroko* and *Araba*, two of the biggest tree species in Africa, and *alakara*, one who sells a local kind of fried bean cake, were left un-translated to retain the original, while well-known common nouns such as dogs and tiger were translated. The translation mode adopted was mostly connotative rather than literal so as not to lose the meaning of the utterances to literal interpretation.

In the analysis, the pragmatic acts are discussed and situated within the socio-cultural context of utterance that produced them. Two specific pragmatic acts, namely inciting (in the context of war), and calling to peace (in the context of peace) are selected for detailed discussion.

Analysis of Findings and Discussion

Appendices 10A and 10C represent findings from our data. The tables show the talking drum locutions in Yoruba and English, as well as the pragmatic acts performed by each. The analysis of the findings and discussion are presented in this section.

In the analysis and discussion that follow, it is important to reiterate that finding a one-to-one correspondence between the words of the utterance and the particular speech act performed by the drum speeches is not within the purview of this present paper, and so we shall not dwell on speech act verbs or on performatives as classified by either Austin or Searle, but rather on pragmatic acts as originated by Mey (2001), inherent and performed by the speeches or locutions of the talking drum in the appendices (p. xxx). Thus, in this present analysis and discussion, we shall adopt Mey's (2016) suggestion that "a correct pragmatic interpretation…should take into account both the circumstances of use and the way this use has developed" (p. 4).

The speeches are presented in lines and stanzas because talking drum locution is generally poetic. This is not unconnected to the fact that the words or the speech of the talking drum are essentially poetic. From the data, we realize that one utterance is equivalent to one line, and one speech is equivalent to one stanza, where, especially, the first and second utterances for most of the drum speeches are repetitions. So, like poems, the drum utterances are presented in lines in the appendices, each set of utterances thus representing a verse in a long, dramatic, musical poetry.

In the Appendix tables, language is being actively used, and for purposes that go beyond syntactico-semantic explanations (Enfield, 1998; Hanks, 1996; Mey, 2001, p. 228). The talking drum has produced utterances in a context that is as rich, emotionally charged, and stimulating as the utterances it gave rise to, and so our data is replete with pragmatic acts that are themselves as appropriate and context-produced as the context is fertile and weighty. Thus, in our data, we have situation-bound utterances (Kecskes, 2010) as they are not only situation-constrained, but are also situation-constructed (p. 2891). It is important to add that most of the soldiers are usually professional hunters who are already used to the language of the talking drum. Associations of professional hunters meet for merry-making supported with poetic renditions that are accompanied with drumming and dancing, especially the talking drum, and to worship "*Ogun*" the god of iron.

Pragmatic Acts in the Context of Peace

When it is time for peace and conflict resolution, the talking drum performs the pragmatic acts of calling to peace, ceasefire, cooperation, re-union, brotherhood, love and unity; repudiating terrorism, violence and aggression; exhorting to patience and fairness to all; resisting bad influence; and calling attention to the evil of war and hostility. This call is usually an appeal to the conscience of both parties to come to their senses and abandon violence and aggression. It is therefore a support system and complementary strategy to any other peace initiative that might be underway to bring an end to the violence. Whether parties accept the call is another thing entirely, however, when it appears they do, it usually marks the end of aggression and hostility, and the success of the peace initiative. The peace efforts continue where hostility is yet to end.

Pragmatic Acts at the Pre-battle Stage

At the pre-battle stage, the talking drum performs the pragmatic acts of inciting, goading, hero-worshipping of their war commanders and soldiers, arousing, empowering, instigating and provoking combatant soldiers to war and aggression, while indicting, terrorizing, warning, abusing, accusing, intimidating, defying, insulting, challenging, and coercing enemy soldiers to combat, to be defensive, and to humiliation and finally to submission. In W9: "/Let it become war if it must/Let it become a fight if it must/ If it becomes a quarrel, or it becomes a fight, what can anybody's father do about it/ Lagbaja destroy them altogether/The initiates and the ignorant, destroy them/," we have the pragmatic acts of intimidating, inciting, terrorizing, challenging, and provoking. Also in W7: "/Let's just forget about such friendship/Let's just forget about such friendship/ Friendship of today that turns to fighting tomorrow/Let's just forget about such friendship/" we have the pragmatic acts of accusing, abusing, and intimidating. All these are just preliminary rivalries and aggressions. These acts are meant to inject their soldiers with a dose of confidence, courage, and provocation necessary to face a battle and to scare the enemy soldiers to surrender, perhaps they (the enemy soldiers) could hear them from their own location. There is no doubt that the sound of drums could go very far.

Pragmatic Acts during the Battle

While the battle rages on (dur-batl stage), the talking drum performs the pragmatic acts of resisting, defying, intimidating, hero-worshipping, chest-beating, self-praising, terrorizing, blood thirsting, celebrating victory, jeering, mocking, reporting victory, and cautioning. For instance, in W26: "/But you said you are powerful/ But you said you are powerful/ You that fell down weakly upon a mere slap from us/ But you said you are powerful/," we have the pragmatic acts of jeering, mocking, and intimidating; while in W17: "/Attack him, fight him/ Attack him, fight him/ If you dont attack him then you are a bastard/ Attack him, fight him/," we have the pragmatic acts of provoking and instigating. These are acts calculated to snatch victory and scare the enemy soldiers. When they praise their commanders to high heaven, the tendency is for him to fight harder to merit the praises. Through these acts, they use the talking drum to empower their soldiers with confidence, while the soldiers enjoy the support and fight harder so as to continue to merit the support.

Pragmatic Acts at the Post-Battle Stage

At the post-battle stage, the pragmatic acts are Hero worshipping, celebrating and asserting victory, humiliating, mocking, and abusing the enemy soldiers. For instance, in W30: "/What else does he want to say/ What else does he want to say/ A person beheaded still trying to say something/ What else does he want to say/," we have the pragmatic acts of humiliating, mocking, celebrating and asserting victory. With these acts, they praise the gallant soldiers and deride the vanquished soldiers.

Implications of the Acts

All these acts amount to psychological warfare already waged, or being waged, by the talking drum on behalf of the combatant soldiers. This appears cowardly (from the comfort of their hiding place and protection by their soldiers, and with the conventional immunity not to be touched by enemy soldiers but which can be broken anyway), but it is usually rather effective. According to Mey (2001), this technique of the pragmatic acts of persuasion to submission or acceptance of defeat, which is the overall goal of the talking drum, borders primarily on the unsaid rather than on the said (p. 210). For instance, when the talking drum communicates insults, abuse and warning to the enemy soldier, on one hand, as well as defiance and chest-beating on the other, the enemy soldier(s) is being persuaded to think twice, embrace defeat, or expect the worst. Victory, thus, is linguistically negotiated, both in war and in peace. This necessitates a focus on the pragmatic acts of "inciting" and "calling for peace" in more detail.

The Pragmatic Act of Inciting
To incite is to stir up feelings and provoke to action, usually of a violent nature. The overall expectation of the community engaged in battle is for their army to be victorious; the drum thus has a duty of not just to entertain but to help their soldiers win. One legitimate way of executing such help is to incite them to fight, with the intention and assurance of victory. To felicitously perform the pragmatic act of inciting, the felicity conditions include a context of mutual aggression between two parties; the speaker, in our case the talking drum, must be supporting one of the two parties; the party being supported by the speaker must be ready and be in a position to attack the other party; and finally the speaker must be asking or commanding their own party to hit or attack the other party, using all linguistic means, direct or indirect, to convey the instruction, such as "Attack him, fight him" (direct) in W17, and "/It's today we shall know/ It's today we shall know/ Whether they are our father whether we are their father/ It's today we shall know/" (indirect) in W14.

Scholars have constantly reminded us that "more is involved in what one communicates than what one literally says" (Green, 2014). Mey (2001) quotes Kurzon as follows: "any utterance may constitute an act of incitement if the circumstances are appropriate to allow for such an interpretation" (p. 28). Kuzon (1998) earlier assumed that "the act of incitement is a perlocutionary act" (p. 571), but later agrees that "what is of concern to pragmatics is the illocutionary act with the speaker's purpose as an integral part, while the actual effect on the hearer is not a necessary condition" (p. 571). To incite further, speaker would say derogatory, insulting and humiliating things about the other party who is seen as an enemy already marked for destruction.

To the speaker, their own party is an angel, while the other party is a devil that must not be allowed to live or rise. We can simply categorize this as hate speech, which alongside other forms of hate speech is a crime in most laws of the world. But in battle, it is a required strategy for victory, euphemistically termed propaganda, and it is capable of demoralizing the enemy soldiers, and has been used successfully in most modern wars.

The Pragmatic Act of Calling to Peace
Out of over a dozen meaning of the word "call", only one meets the context of the pragmeme of calling for peace: a request for something to happen. To call for peace is to appeal to two opposing parties for patience, unity, cooperation, love, and an end to hostility, terrorism and aggression. To felicitously do this, the context must be such that the evil of aggression is no more in doubt, the speaker is convinced this is the right call, and the targets of appeal are on the path to remorse (in other words, they may be or may not be entirely remorseful, and the call is to make them become entirely remorseful and build on the entirely remorseful ones). In our data, this is never in short supply, and this call is being done directly, as in P8: "/Fighting is bad/ Fighting is bad/ Don't let's face each other in a fight/ Fighting is bad/,"and indirectly through appeal to the sense of humanity of the warring camps especially the elders and the war generals: "/Don't ever be harsh/ Don't ever be wicked/ A wicked elder can never have followers/ Don't be wicked/" (P11); and by foregrounding the painful effect of war: "/It has consumed children and kindred/ It has consumed children and kindred/ The conflict and war of this land/ It has consumed children and kindred/" (P14). As a result of this call, the warring parties are expected to sheath their sword.

What we have in the context of war and peace is situated speech acts, and thus a speech event, where only certain utterances are affordable, expected, and acceptable (Mey, 2001, p. 219). For instance, it would be unacceptable for a talking drum to utter and perform the pragmatic acts of accusing his own soldier of cowardice, or insulting him as irresponsible while the battle rages, or telling the listener, where peace is being negotiated, that peace and love is not only an aberration but in fact a sign of cowardice.

Exploring the Discursive Language of the Acts in Context

In the war speeches, the dominant imagery is of war, aggression, accusations, incitement and provocation, while in the peace speeches it is that of peace, patience, fairplay, unity, and love for one another. This is also not unconnected to the context of utterance which is war and aggression on the one hand, and the call for peace on the other. We have such verbal imagery as in W24: "/Hit him with a rod!/Before he escapes into the buka/ Hit him with a rod!/." The mental picture invented in this imagery is that of aggression, and we can see how one or two soldiers are chasing another person, perhaps an enemy soldier, before escaping into a deserted buka (or cafeteria) and getting out at the back. According to Reeves (1965), "if there are to be ideas in a poem, it is better that they should be apprehended through concrete and sensuously realized imagery," for poetry should be "more physical than intellectual" (p. 179). In P15: "/It's enough!/ It's enough!/ Malicious people leave me alone/ It's enough!/," we also have the physical imagery of an aggressor holding back the speaker, either physically or psychologically, from waving the olive branch. So, we see him refusing the entreaties of this warmonger, and breaking loose from his grip, and stepping forward to embrace the peace.

The manipulative use of metaphor, analogy, parallelism, and verbal repetition is quite plenty in the data. As an aspect of imagery, metaphor presents certain mental picture that helps to connect the equation in the concrete images and the reality on ground in an appropriate context of usage. For instance, in W11: "/You are the one to blame/ You are the one to blame/ You who hold the whip and flog no one/ You are the one to blame/," there is a direct connection between a powerful leader who has the authority and the whip to discipline errant, recalcitrant individuals, but then refuses to do so even when certain individuals are being flagrantly disobedient and defying his authority, thinking perhaps they could overcome his authority. The talking drum therefore blames the leader for refusing to wield such powers, as that is perhaps the cause of the present aggression and overstepping of bounds.

Also in P12 in the line: "/Only cool water drops from the fish's mouth/," there is an analogy between the water that comes out of the mouth of the living fish in the ocean, and the words that should come out of the mouth of a leader. As the water from the mouth of a live fish is expected to be cool, so also are the words that should drop from the mouth of a leader expected to exude peace and love. Also, we have a strong metaphorical analogy in P10: "/Don't be angry/Don't be angry/It is the patient elder that has plenty of children/Don't be angry/" where a warring party is made to see the benefit of being patient, peaceful, and accommodating in happy followership, thereby arousing the mentorship quality in the elders towards the children. It is a direct comparison of a peaceful warlord with the patient elder and the expected benefits accruing to them.

Cases of repetition abound in almost every speech in both the contexts of war and peace. According to Leech (1969), repetition refers to the exact copying of some previous part of a text. For instance, in P15, we have the clause "It's enough" repeated three times in one speech: "/It's enough!/It's enough!/ Malicious people leave me alone/ It's enough!/." This is the pattern of repetition in most of the speeches in our data. Repetition is a fundamental artistic device of poetic intensification (p. 78), a means of beautifying thoughts, making it aesthetically pleasing (Egudu, 2007, p. 65), and helping to evoke lyricism, rhythm, and eloquence, suggesting spontaneity and exuberance (Leech, 1969, p. 79). It thus helps to provide a combination of auditory pleasure and an urgent illocutionary force each time a repetition, better described as a refrain, is encountered.

Parallelism refers to structural pattern of reoccurrence of two or more elements in a poem. In W10, we have cases of syntactic parallelism: "/ You people reject all our entreaties to peace/ And spun all our appeals to dialogue/" where we have a Verbal ("reject" and "spun") + Complement ("all our entreaties to peace" and "all our appeals to dialogue") kind of parallelism; and in: "/It is what they do that gets them uneasy/ It is their actions that get them scared/" (W10)where we have a Subject ("It" and "It") + Verbal ("is" and "is") + Complement "what they do...." and "their actions...." kind of parallelism. As in repetition, parallelism helps to capture attention by appealing to listener's emotion through the rhythmic lyricism it generates. Both repetition and parallelism therefore help towards a quick and smooth uptake of the pragmatic act of the speeches.

For a casual observer, the drummers are involved in a great performance; but for a pragmatist, they are using the talking drum speech to elicit certain pragmatic psychological empowerment for the soldiers, battlefield re-ordering and re-alignment, namely, aggressively communicating ruthless instructions, courage, cautions, bravery, and solidarity, all of which are geared towards achieving victory for the soldiers. Thus, we say that the talking drum is essentially manipulative of the addressees, namely their own soldiers on one hand, and the enemy combatant on the other. The manipulation is both ways: while their own soldiers are manipulated into continuous aggression, for instance in W16: "/Attack him, fight him/ If you dont attack him I'll get away from your back/ Attack him, fight him/," and "/Attack him, fight him/ If you dont attack him then you are a bastard/ Attack him, fight him/" (W17); the enemy soldiers are manipulated into surrendering their might and accepting defeat as we see for instance, in W12: "/Maybe God would make it possible/ That someone would say something beyond the capacity of his own father's mouth/ Maybe God would make it possible/" where the pragmatic acts of inciting and provoking are at play in the former case, intimidating in the latter case, and manipulating in both.

It therefore seems clear that the talking drum war speech is bi-directionally focused: to the drummers' soldiers and to the enemy combatants. Also, we are able to show that victory is linguistically negotiated. The war drum discourse consists of the pragmatic acts of eliciting attack from their own soldiers, initiating rebellion, encouraging aggression, praising the soldiers' bravery, extolling the military prowess and the spiritual powers of commanding officers and soldiers, thus acting as a fight-on signal to the drummers' brave soldiers. The pragmatic acts of coercing, threatening, accusing, abusing, scaring, and indicting are addressed to enemy combatants and hostile communities. It performs the pragmatic acts of inciting their own soldiers/combatants to attack like angry and ferocious bulldogs, while soliciting surrender from the enemy camp. On the other hand, the talking drum locution in peace situation seems to perform the pragmatic acts of calling and appealing for calm, encouraging conflict resolution, peace accord, and unity, indicting aggression and the aggressors, inviting cooperation from both sides involved in the conflicts, and playing down centrifugal sentiments. Peace comes easier with drumming, which also has an entertainment side to its performance. It is remarkable to find out that the discursive language of most of these drum speeches is not presented in denotative dictions, but is rather demonstrated in picturesque, palpable metaphors and lyrical refrains which help to send pungent messages with a strong emotional impact on the addressees.

Conclusion

In conclusion, the talking drum war speech is bi-directionally focused: to the drummers' soldiers and to the enemy combatants. Also, we are able to show that both war and peace, and the victory or defeat that comes with either of them, are linguistically but carefully negotiated while the acts are situation-constrained. We also see a manipulative use of language as a veritable strategy for victory. Finally, we are able to show that most of the discursive language used in achieving the pragmatic acts are essentially metaphorical, and this helps to enrich the import of the acts.

The role of the talking drum has been shown to be crucial in the context of pre-colonial Yoruba war and peace. This also goes to confirm the fact that in Africa, drumming is not only about entertainment, as both the serious-minded, violent, and emotion-laden encounters such as the context of war, as well as the relaxed, relieved, and happy situation such as the context of peace, employ the talking drum as the tool of communication. This shows the talking drum as a veritable part of the African life.

The place of context of utterance in pragmatic acts theory and the way situations constrain the acts have been demonstrated in our analysis and discussion. The acts were performed within the appropriate contexts of war and peace situations, and this enables a successful interpretation of the locutions from where the pragmatic acts are derived. It affirms further that without a context of utterance, no meaningful interpretation is possible.

As a culture based discourse, the talking drum provides a cultural in-house avenue for confidential discourse that can be exploited for exclusive communication, especially where one intends to exclude some people from such communication exploiting their inability to understand the message of the talking drum, and for a culture-centric intelligence security service among the Yoruba and other users worldwide, such as in building solidarity, providing security surveillance, or fighting terrorism.

References
Abraham, M. F. (1982). *Modern sociological theory*. Oxford, UK: Oxford University Press.
Allan, K. (2010). Referring as a pragmatic act. *Journal of Pragmatics, 42*(11), 2919-2931. doi:10.1016/j.pragma.2010.06.017
Collins, R. (1975). *Conflict sociology*. New York, NY: Academic Press.
Department for International Development. (2001, March). *The causes of conflict in Africa*. Retrieved from http://webarchive.nationalarchives.gov.uk
Egudu, R. N. (2007). *The study of poetry*. Ibadan, Nigeria: University Press PLC.
Enfield, N. (1998). On the indispensability of semantics: Defining the "vacuous." In A. Boguslawski & J. L. Mey (Eds.), *E pluribus una: A Festschrift for Anna Wierzbicka* (pp. 285-304). Odense, Denmark: Odense University Press.
Ezenwoko, F. A., & Osagie, J. I. (2014). Conflict and conflict resolution in pre-colonial Igbo society of Nigeria. *Journal of Studies in Social Sciences, 9*(1), 135-158.
Fasold, R. (1990). *The sociolinguistics of language*. Oxford, UK: Blackwell.
Goodman, P. (2017). *The 8 main reasons for war*. Retrieved from https://owlcation.com/social-sciences/The-Main-Reasons-For-War
Green, M. (2014). Speech acts. In *The Stanford Encyclopedia of Philosophy*. Retrieved from https://plato.stanford.edu/entries/speech-acts/
Hanks, W. F. (1996). Language form and communicative practices. In J. Gumperz & S. C. Levinson (Eds.), *Rethinking linguistic relativity* (pp. 232-270). Cambridge, UK: Cambridge University Press.
Harris, Z. (1951). *Methods in structural linguistics*. Chicago, IL: University of Chicago Press.
Kecskes, I. (2010). Situation-bound utterances as pragmatic acts. *Journal of Pragmatics, 42*, 2889-2897.
Kurzon, D. (1998). The speech act status of incitement: Perlocutionary acts revisited. *Journal of Pragmatics, 29*(5), 571-596.
Levinson, S.C. (1983). *Pragmatics*. Cambridge, UK: Cambridge University Press.
Mey, J. L. (2001). *Pragmatics: An introduction*. Oxford, UK: Blackwell Publishing.
Mey, J. L. (2006). Pragmatics: Overview. In K. Brown (Ed.), *Encyclopedia of language and linguistics* (2nd ed., pp. 51-62). Oxford, UK: Elsevier.
Mey, J. L. (2016). Sunt verba rerum: The pragmatic life of words. *SpringerPlus, 5*(1653), 1-11. doi:10.1186/s40064-016-3269-z

Olajide, A. E. (2011, December 31). The Yoruba talking drum. *Nigerian Guardian Newspaper Online.* Retrieved from http://www.ngrguardiannews.com/index.php?option=com_content&view=article&id=72305:the-yoruba-talking-drum&catid=74:arts&Itemid=683

Reeves, J. (1965). *Understanding poetry.* London, UK: Heinemann.

Searle, J.R. (1979). *Expression and meaning.* Cambridge, UK: Cambridge University Press.

Verschueren, J. (1987). Pragmatics as a theory of linguistic adaptation. In *Working Document No.1.* Antwerp, Belgium: International Pragmatics Association.

Verschueren, J. (1999). *Understanding pragmatics.* London, UK: Arnold.

Appendix 10A

Talking Drum Locutions in the Pre-Battle, During-Battle and Post-Battle Contexts and the Pragmatic Acts Performed by Each

SN	Speech in Yoruba	English Translation	Context	Pragmatic Act
W1	A o de'bi ti a fe de, A o de'bi ti a fe de, E baa t'enu b'epe, k'ee t'enu b'ase, A o de'bi ti a fe de.	We shall reach our destination We shall reach our destination Even if you use spiritual power to curse us and talk to us We shall reach our destination	Pre-Bt	Defying
W2	A si maa k'abuku A si maa k'abuku B'omo kekere ba jo'raa re l'oju a si maa k'abuku	And he would keep getting into trouble And he would keep getting into trouble A young lad that is arrogant and self-conceited ...he would keep getting into trouble	Pre-Bt	Warning, Inciting
W3	A wi wi wi e le o ni gbo, A fo fo fo e le o ni gba, Agbe'lu sile a tun f'enu wi, Apoti alakara kabiawu, Ohun ti won se ni n fu won l'ara, Iwa ti won wu ni n ba won l'eru, Amu'ni si wi a mu'ni siso, Amu'ni f'okele bo'mu ni baba won.	You people reject all our entreaties to peace, And spun all our appeals to dialogue We put down our drums and spoke with our mouth To hell with the box of the akara seller It is what they do that gets them uneasy It is their actions that get them scared They are real trouble makers and confusers, They make you mis-talk and put morsel into your own nose, they and their fathers	Pre-Bt	Warning, accusing, abusing, insulting, Inciting, Indicting
W4	Agbada o gbona, l'agbado o ta Awa o f'ori ba'le f'enikan o.	Only when the frying pan does not heat up, that maize grains in it are not roasted, we shall never bow for anyone	Pre-Bt	Defying, Resisting, Challenging, Inciting
W5	T'ogunt'ogun l'o n rin, T'ogunt'ogun l'o n rin, asiwaju ogun ko gbodo keyin ogun, t'ogunt'ogun l'o n rin.	Always war-like in his strides Always war-like in his strides A war general must never lag behind in battle Always war-like in his strides	Pre-Bt	PraisingHeroism, Hero-worshipping
W6	Enu won l'efa enu won l'eje ao b'elenu meji se're mo.	They are the sayers of this they are the sayers of that so we have nothing to do with an hypocrite again	Pre-Bt	Accusing, Indicting

W7	Ka kuku p'ore yen ti, Ka kuku p'ore yen ti, ore t'aase l'oni t'odi'ja l'ola, ka kuku p'ore yen ti.	Let's just forget about such friendship Let's just forget about such friendship Friendship of today that turns to fighting tomorrow, Let's just forget about such friendship	Pre-Bt	Accusing, Indicting, castigating
W8	Bii ti'gi nla ko, bii ti'gi nla ko Bi Sango ba p'Araba, to tun fa Iroko ya, bii ti'gi nla ko	Never like the Big Tree Never like the Big Tree If *Sango* killed *Araba* and destroyed *Iroko* Never like the Big Tree	Pre-Bt	Intimidating, Challenging, Defying, Bluff calling
W9	B'ole d'ogun k'od'ogun, B'ole dija kodi'ja, t'oba di'ja, t'oba di'binu, kini baba enikan le se, Lagbaja pa won po at'awo at'ogberi pa won po	Let it become war if it must, Let it become a fight if it must If it becomes a quarel, or it becomes a fight, what can anybody's father do about it Lagbaja destroy them altogether, The initiates and the ignorant, destroy them	Pre-Bt	Inciting, Terrorizing, Challenging, Provoking
W10	Ilee won naa nuun ni, ilee won naa nuun ni, ile abere wo bi ile ekute, ilee won naa nuun ni	That is their house over there That is their house over there Such a tiny house like that of the house rat That is their house over there	Pre-Bt	Intimidating, Humiliating, Abusing, Indicting
W11	Iwo l'ari bawi, Iwo l'ari bawi iwo too m'ore lowo t'oofi na'nikan, iwo l'ari bawi.	You are the one to blame, You are the one to blame, you who hold the whip and flog no one You are the one to blame	Pre-Bt	Humiliating
W12	Boya Olorun a see, Boya Olorun a see, Enikan a soro to j'enu baba e lo, Boya Olorun a see.	Maybe God would make it possible Maybe God would make it possible That someone would say something beyond the capacity of his own father's mouth Maybe God would make it possible	Pre-Bt	Intimidating, Humiliating, Terrorizing, Challenging, Provoking
W13	Oju ogun la n lo, ero oja pa'ra mo Oju ogun la n lo, ero oja pa'ra mo.	On our way to the warfront, market people disappear On our way to the warfront, market people disappear	Pre-Bt	Arousing, Teleguiding, Terrorizing

W14	Oni la o mo, oni la o mo, B'awon ni babaa wa, B'awa ni babaa won oni la o mo.	It's today we shall know It's today we shall know Whether they are our father whether we are their father It's today we shall know	Pre-Bt	Arousing, Humiliating, Challenging, Provoking, Inciting
W15	Oro yi o ni le wo, oro yi o ni le wo, k'as'aja mo'le k'as'ekun mo'le, k'a wa mu'ru ekun k'a fi l'aja l'owo, oro yi o ni le wo.	This issue will not be easy This issue will not be easy To tie down the dog and tie down the tiger and then place the tiger's tail in the hands of the dog This issue will not be easy	Pre-Bt	Defying, Challenging
W16	Digboluu, koluu, digboluu, koluu, T'ooba digboluu, un o pada l'eyin e, digboluu, koluu.	Attack him, fight him Attack him, fight him If you dont attack him i'll get away from your back Attack him, fight him	Dur-Bt	Inciting, Arousing, Instigating, Provoking, empowering
W17	Digboluu, koluu, digboluu, koluu, T'ooba digboluu, babaa re ko lo bi o digboluu, koluu.	Attack him, fight him Attack him, fight him If you dont attack him then you are a bastard Attack him, fight him	Dur-Bt	Inciting, Provoking, Instigating, Empowering
W18	G'esin ni kese, G'esin ni kese, b'o de'nuun baba won bio d'okanan won, g'esin ni kese.	Move on with the horse Move on with the horse Whether their grandfathers like it or not Move on with the horse	Dur-Bt	Inciting, Abusing, Instigating
W19	Ibi taa wi l'aa de i, ibi taa wi l'aa de i, k'a ma gbodo so'ro k'a ma gbodo s'enu wuye, ibi taa wi l'aa de i	Here is the point of decision Here is the point of decision We must never talk, we must never say anything Here is the point of decision	Dur-Bt	Instigating, Asserting
W20	Ijagun lo, ijagun lo Ijagun lo, ijagun lo	Go on with the fight, go on with the battle Go on with the fight, go on with the battle	Dur-Bt	Instigating, Inciting, Encouraging
W21	Awa o ni le gba, Awa o ni le gba, E o le keru kee keruu wa lo Awa o ni le gba, Tori boro ba se bi oro yoo se bi owe, awa o ni le gba	We shall never accept We shall never accept You can never cart away our people and property We shall never accept For if the issue comes up later there will be aspersions and insults, We shall never accept	Dur-Bt	Resisting, Defying

W22	Ko mo'gi ko mo'nikan, ko mo'gi ko mo'nikan, Af'oju ajanaku omo Balogun Ko mo'gi ko mo'nikan	He recognizes neither tree nor any human He recognizes neither tree nor any human Except the face of the Elephant the son of Balogun He recognizes neither tree nor any human	Dur-Bt	Intimidating, Warning, Hero worshipping, Instigating
W23	Ogun o ko wa ri, Ogun o ko wa ri, omo Ibadan kii se'ru enikan, Ogun o ko wa ri.	War has never ravaged us before War has never ravaged us before Ibadan people is no slave to anyone War has never ravaged us before	Dur-Bt	Chest-beating, Self-praising, Encouraging, Inciting
W24	Jan-an n ponpo, jan-an n ponpo, k'oto bere k'oto wo buka, janan n ponpo.	Hit him with a rod, hit him with a rod, Before he escapes into the bukateria Hit him with a rod	Dur-Bt	Inciting, Instigating, terrorizing, Blood thirsting
W25	Owo t'agadagodo won, Owo t'agadagodo won, Alawo ekun, alawo Agiliti, Owo t'agadagodo won.	Now we've got hold of their talisman Now we've got hold of their talisman One with Leopard skin, one with the skin of *Agiliti* Now we've got hold of their talisman	Dur-Bt	Celebrating victory, Jeering, Mocking
W26	Se b'oo looloogun ni Se b'oo looloogun ni Iwo taa gba l'eti to n subu yege Seb'oo loo loogun ni	But you said you are powerful But you said you are powerful You that fell down weakly upon a mere slap from us But you said you are powerful	Dur-Bt	Reporting victory, Mocking, Jeering, Humiliating
W27	Soso meji ko gbodo f'oju k'oju Soso meji ko gbodo f'oju k'oju	Two fireballs must never see eye to eye Two firebrands must never see eye to eye	Dur-Bt	Provoking, Instigaing
W28	W'eyin re wo, Lagbaja w'eyin re wo, Boo l'omo ogun boo l'omo ogun, W'eyin re wo	Check your back Lagbaja check your back Whether you have soldiers or not Check your back	Dur-Bt	Cautioning
W29	Ogun to se bee se o Ogun to se bee se o Nitori ogun la n se kondu Kondu kondu, Ogun to se bee se o	War is so much worth it War is so much worth it It is because of war that we grow proud and arrogant War is so much worth it	Pst-Bt	Hero worshipping, Celebrating victory
W30	Ki lo tun ku ti o so, Ki lo tun ku ti o so, Eni t'aa be l'ori ti n je'nu wuye, Ki lo tun ku ti o so.	What else does he want to say What else does he want to say A person beheaded still trying to say something What else does he want to say	Pst-Bt	Humiliating, Mocking, Asserting victory

| W31 | Lagbaja iwo ni baba won, Iwo ni baba won, B'eni kan n fon'nu firi t'o n fon'nu firi bi aja gbeegun, Iwo ni baba won. | Lagbaja you are their uncontestable father, You are their uncontestable father, Even if anybody throws their mouth around like a bone-eating dog, You are their uncontestable father | Pst-Bt | Hero worshipping, Celebrating and Asserting victory, Mocking, Abusing |

Appendix 10B

Talking Drum Locutions Sourced from Jógunómí and the Pragmatic Acts Performed by Each

SN	Speech in Yoruba	English Translation	Context	Pragmatic Act
W32	Àátìigbó Jógunómí, omo Ládèéké, àátìigbó, Kápérúu baba ení ní n réníije, Àátìigbó	What a big affront! Jógunómí, husband of Ládèéké, what a big affront, To say that one's father's age mate is the one oppressing one, What a big affront!	Pre-Bt	Defying
W33	Àgbàrá òjò kòlóhun ò ní'lé wó, onílé ni ò ní gbà fun	Flowing rain water does not mind pulling down the house, it is the house owner that would not allow it.	Pre-Bt	Warning, Inciting

Appendix 10C

Locutions in the Context of Peace and the Pragmatic Acts Performed by Each

SN	Speech in Yoruba	Speech Translated to English	Pragmatic Act
P1	Asiwaju ogun, so'gun ro, apadaba, sogun ro, Ogun l'otun ogun l'osi, so'gun ro Asiwaju so'gun ro, apadaba, so'gun ro.	War Commander, end this war, Apadaba, end this war, War in the right, war in the left, end this war, War Commander, end this war Apadaba, end this war ("Apadaba" is name of a war commander in a particular war in history)	Cautioning, Calling to Ceasefire
P2	Awa l'a wa ri 'ra wa o Awa l'a wa ri 'ra wa Ologini r'omo Ekun Awa l'awa ri 'ra wa.	Eventually we have seen one another Now we have seen one another The cat has seen the tiger's kid Eventually we have seen one another	Re-Union

P3	Awa o f'ogun ni'le yi o d'okeere, tefetefe o d'okeere. A o ni r'ogun mo ni'le yi o d'okeere, tefetefe o d'okeere	We don't want war again in this land, away with it! Far far away, away with it! May we never see war again in this land, away with it! Far far away, away with it!	Repudiating war
P4	Eere l'a o maa se Eere l'a o maa se Awa o jaa mo o e Eere l'a o maa se.	We shall only engage in friendly games We shall only engage in friendly games We are no more fighting We shall only engage in friendly games	Calling to Peace and Friendship
P5	E fa'ra yin mo'ra E fa'ra yin mo'ra ko gbodo baje, at'omo egbon at'omo aburo, e fa'ra yin mo'ra, ija o d'ola.	Embrace yourselves Embrace yourselves It must not spoil, nephews and cousins Embrace yourselves, conflicts bring no wealth	Calling to Peace, Unity and Brotherhood
P6	E je ka fi'fe lo E je ka fi'fe lo Oju ogun ko dabi oju oja oba E je ka fi'fe lo	Let us live together in peace Let us live together in peace The battlefield is not like the oba's market Let's walk in love	Calling to Love, Cautioning against war
P7	Gbogbo ile ni e ki Gbogbo ile ni e ki Eni ti o dagbalagba yoo ni suuru Gbogbo ile ni e ki	Make sure you greet everyone Make sure you greet everyone One who wants to become an elder would have to be very patient, Make sure you greet everyone	Exhorting to fairness to all, and to patience
P8	Ija o dara Ija o dara E ma je a d'oju ija ko 'ra wa Ija o dara	Fighting is bad, Fighting is bad, Don't let's face each other in a fight Fighting is bad	Repudiating Aggression
P9	Ija yi pari Ija yi pari E sinmi ariwo pelu agbaja Ija yi pari	The fight has ended, The fight has ended, Let's stop all agitations and clamours The fight has ended,	Ending quarrelling
P10	Ma bi'nu, ma bi'nu, agba ti o binu l'omo re n po, ma binu.	Don't be angry Don't be angry It is the patient elder that has plenty of children Don't be angry	Appealing for peace
P11	Ma roro o, ma roro o, agba t'o roro kii ko'yan jo, ma roro o.	Don't ever be harsh Don't ever be wicked A wicked elder can never have followers Don't be wicked	Repudiating Terrorism

P12	Omi tutu nii t'enu eja bo, oro tutu ni o t'enu mi jade	Only cool water drops from the fish's mouth So shall only cool words come out of my mouth/so shall my speech be cool	Promising peace and to say only (what is) good.
P13	O to ge, Ija ti to ge, Efowo sowopo, Kale ni lo siwaju O to ge, Ija ti to ge	Now it's enough Fighting is enough Cooperate with one another for progress It's enough Fighting is enough	Calling for unity and development
P14	T'eru t'omo l'o ti ko lo T'eru t'omo l'o ti ko lo Irukerudo, itaporogan ile yi T'eru t'omo l'o ti ko lo	It has consumed children and kindred It has consumed children and kindred The conflict and war of this land It has consumed children and kindred	Opening eyes to the evil of war
P15	O to ge! O to ge! K'enimoni pada leyin mi, O to ge!	It's enough! It's enough! Malicious people leave me alone It's enough!	Resisting bad influence to violence

CHAPTER 11

THE ROLES OF LANGUAGE USE IN THE ELUSIVE PEACE OF THE NIGERIAN SOCIAL AND POLITICAL LANDSCAPES

Babatunji H. Adepoju

Introduction

Nigeria is a country in West Africa. By the 14th century, through trade relations Nigeria had already established contact with speakers of English. It was by 1807, after the abolition of slave trade, that the presence of the British was more prominent. Lagos, a coastal city, was bombarded by Britain between 1851 and 1861 and was made into a British colony. Nigeria became a protectorate of Britain in 1901 and remained a colony until its independence in 1960. Nigeria is a territory which is naturally divided by the rivers Niger and Benue into North, South West, and South East regions. The North and South East are comprised of people of diverse cultures and languages. The fact that the people in the various regions speak and use different indigenous languages tends to keep them somewhat separated. However, in 1914, the colonial master under Sir Lord Lugard amalgamated both northern and southern protectorates and named the region Nigeria (Niger Area) after River Niger. From then on until the present day, this arrangement has been seen as a forced marriage. There have been accusations and counter accusations about which region holds Nigeria back in the journey to political and economic prosperity.

This was made worse after the 1990s with the advent of the computer, the Internet, and mobile telecommunications. A large number of the population now has access to the Internet to express personal views (in English or

Pidgin), that usually run counter to the opinion of people from other regions. As of 2018, religious and political opinion leaders, legal luminaries, human rights watch dogs, high profile military officers, and concerned citizens all agree that never in history has Nigeria been so polarised along religious and ethnic division as today. As an example, the Governor of Plateau State Simon Lalong stated that "the social media was filled with hate utterances that incite and set the stages for mayhem and rancour" (Nan, 2017, para. 1). In a culturally plural society such as Nigeria, it is commonplace for people to use disparaging language in describing one another, especially in political and religious contexts which are inevitably framed within the bounds of ethnicity. Consequently, finger-pointing is a very common phenomenon in Nigerian polity, both in conventional and new forms of media. The usual pattern is for incumbent regimes to insist on the sanctity of Nigerian unity, while those in the opposition call for restructuring of the federation. To be sure, the areas of national disagreement usually have to do with accusations and counter-accusations of corruption. Corruption is regarded as the main cause of the parlous state of Nigerian infrastructure. It appears that for as long as democratic deficit persists in Nigeria and for as long as mutual ethno-religious distrust remains, divisive language use will continue to feature not only in the mediasphere but also in interpersonal relations. It is in light of the above conflicts that I explore language use as the cause of the absence of peace in Nigeria in social, political, religious, ethnic, governmental, cultural, and linguistic apparatuses.

The Political and Linguistic Landscapes of Nigeria
Nigeria is divided into six geopolitical zones: North East, North West, North Central, South East, South West, and South South. Each geopolitical zone has states, local governments, and senatorial districts demarcated for administrative convenience. On the whole, Nigeria has 36 states, one Federal Capital Territory (FCT), 774 Local Government Areas (as recognised by the Constitution), Local Government Development Areas (LCDA; as created by states seeking to correct the perceived anomaly of the military delineation of the country), 109 Senatorial Districts and 306 Federal Constituencies.

As a multicultural and multilingual society, Nigeria has 521 indigenous languages spoken within her borders, according to *Ethnologue*, an online database (Daramola, 2006; Taiwo, 2012, p. 3). Nigeria is seen as comprising three regions and consequently three major languages: the Hausa language to the North, the Igbo (Ibo) language to the South East, and the Yoruba language to the South West. This compression is a source of worry and protest by individuals and groups whose language and culture have been made to merge with others. It needs to be observed here that it is not the official position that a language should dominate another. Nonetheless, it certainly reflects the power play among the major ethnic blocs. It is only in the South West that only one language, Yoruba, is available for the indigenous people. The North, which is generally thought to be Hausa, actually has more than 250 separate languages spoken by people of diverse cultures. There is no doubt that the Fulani hegemony holds sway in the North. By such compression, the Igbo are made to inundate the Ijaw, Urhobo, Itsekiri and more than 250 other ethnic nationalities. Other prominent languages in Nigeria are Tiv, Fulfude, Efik, Kanuri, Nupe, Ebira, Igala, Edo, and Idoma.

The mutual distrust among the three major ethnic nationalities can be regarded as a kind of triangulation in which there are always verbal attacks from one to the other two. The triangulation among the three major ethnic nationalities—Hausa, Yoruba, and Igbo—and the direction of their verbal attacks look to a large extent like what is seen in Figure 11.1.

Figure 11.1 The triangulation of face attack expressions in Nigeria.

The arrows indicate the direction of words that are negatively deployed towards the other group in a sort of power play scenario. By implication, neutral words become pejorative even though they would normally identify particular groups with regard to their occupations, preferred foods, diction and pronunciation, among others, as explained later in this chapter.

Contact with English in the colonial and post-colonial eras altered the linguistic landscape of Nigeria. According to Awonusi (2004), "Nigeria's Cycles of Linguistic History" in relation to English are divided into the earliest incursion (1400-1842), the era of missionary adventurism (1843-1914), and independence and experimentation (1915-1990; pp. 46-59). There is no Nigerian language that can be termed as lingua franca that could serve as a unifying national language for political purposes. In the early days of various societies in Nigeria, trade and commercial activities were done by barter, although this was not the result of paucity of language. Rather, linguistic and cultural restrictions made inter-ethnic interactions difficult, thereby aiding the spread of English as a prestige language in the country. English then provided a common linguistic tool for inter-ethnic communication. Pre-independence, during, and toward the end of the British rule in Nigeria (1950s), different ethnic affiliations already had English-speaking individuals to present their front. Post-independence, owing to the spread of Christianity, growth in education, and the increase in the number of Nigerians in the government, exposure and usage of English grew tremendously.

Commenting on the processes of naturalisation of English in Nigeria, Banjo (1996) states: "... having fully naturalised, the language would be on its way to becoming an indigenous language in the country, and one which, in time, might well assume the status of the mother tongue of some Nigerians" (p. 149). This, perhaps, is the state of the English language in Nigeria today. English is now a tool of communication for classroom instructions, science and technology, media, law, government policies, and much more. The position of the English language in these areas corroborates what Banjo (1996) foresaw as "the status of official language and Lingua Franca", which will thus put "an end to the contest between the three major indigenous languages" (p. 149). Indeed, English has bridged the linguistic gap in Nigeria.

The Place of Pidgin in the Nigerian Linguistic Landscape

Adamu, the current Minister of Education in Nigeria, said the country had about 65 million to 75 million illiterates ("Illiteracy Rate," 2017). This fraction of the population can neither read nor speak communicable English, which often is the yardstick for measuring literacy in Nigeria. However, this set of people is able to relate, interrelate, and participate in national discourse. Many of them can use the phone and social media using pidgin which may not require serious linguistic prescriptions.

The relevance of Nigerian Pidgin to this work is that it is most often the medium of interaction not only in face to face encounters but also on social media. The emergence of Pidgin in Nigeria has far-reaching effects on the development of English in the country (Onuigbo & Eyisi, 2009, p. 115). Irrespective of their educational level, Nigerians find Pidgin as a spontaneous linguistic development that fills a particular communicative gap, although some purists see its use as resulting from a sort of linguistic laziness. Basically, Pidgin is a product of contact between English and different Nigerian languages; depending on the region of use, the vocabulary of English is usually mixed with that of the indigenous language. Generally, in Nigeria, Pidgin is used informally even in the university environment. It bridges gaps in relationships as it does away with the formal "finer structural details or inflectional niceties and concord requirements that go with the polished performance of the high social class" (Onuigbo & Eyisi, 2009, p. 117). This form of communication has adversely affected the growth of indigenous languages in Nigeria to a large extent.

Methodological Framework

In order to track responses of Nigerians to national socio-political issues, the research requires fieldwork, especially media monitoring, which is a process of observing and recording the content of media sources on a continuing basis (CyberAlert, 2010; Snjezana, 2003). It involves monitoring the output of print, online, and broadcast media. Media monitoring is appropriate for this study because technological advancement has taken discourses beyond traditional media, such as newspapers and magazines. It now encompasses social media which involve phones, computers, and the internet—all of which emerged as veritable communication technologies just less than twenty years ago in Nigeria. Since the advent of the internet in Nigeria, reactions to national issues have taken forms that would not be accommodated in conventional media. Online newspapers as well as Facebook and Whatsapp messages are sources of my data.

My interest in divisive expressions was ignited late in 2007 when friends started sharing telephone SMS that are laden with segregation and hatred. There was enough material there to sustain my curiosity and analysis for ten years till in 2016 when International Society for Language Studies provided a platform in the form of a conference dedicated to the theme "Discourse and Peace." For a period of ten years, I jotted hundreds of expressions capable of breaching the peace in Nigeria. Through purposive sampling, however, the less offensive expressions are analysed here. There are many that are not "printable" and so are not fit to be documented and propagated for upcoming generations.

In Nigeria today, individuals who, for one reason or another, do not have access to comment directly on television, radio, newspaper, or newsmagazines can type messages, record their voices, or take pictures and post them on Whatsapp or Facebook. As at December 2017, reportedly 98,391,456 Nigerians had an online presence, 17,000,000 of whom had their own Facebook profiles (Internet World Stats, 2018). Considering these figures, posted messages could reach fifty million Nigerians in just 48 hours. From web sources such as *Linda Ikeji's Blog, Premium Times, Sahara Reporters, Nigeria News App* and *News Now Nigerian News* I extracted a diverse range of readers' comments.

Theoretical Considerations of Speech Act Theory and Pragmatics
Language usage may imply much deeper meanings than what is openly stated. Pragmatics is the study of the implications of an utterance beyond its surface meaning. It is the study of language usage in relation to the context, in which it occurs, be it a particular situation or a culture as a whole. This differs from semantics, which studies the primary use of language independent of context. Pragmatics is concerned with the domain of additional meaning. In the study of meaning, semantics deals with the literal meaning an individual

has garnered from the knowledge of the language. However, the speaker's agenda, which is hinted at in the utterance, is the concern of pragmatics.

In order to analyse the comments of Nigerians on issues of national interest, context is of utmost importance, and therefore pragmatics is an appropriate and excellent tool for it. More than simply weaving words or encoding and transmitting messages, we employ language principally as a tool to do things (Finegan, 2004, p. 294). What we make language do are speech acts relevant to speech events. Finegan reiterates that we accomplish a great deal each day by verbal acts. These are of diverse types— complimenting, condemning, advising, attacking, cautioning, seeking and supplying information, insulting, abusing, and so forth. These actions performed with language are called speech acts. Speech Act Theory was introduced by J. L. Austin between 1952 and 1954. Austin (1962) explains that "the uttering of a sentence is, or is a part of, the doing of an action" (pp. 5-6). It is also called "performative" action, however, Searle (1978) replaced the term "performative" with the notion of "Speech Act" (p. 22). A speaker's utterance generally involves three diverse acts: locution, illocution, and perlocution. Locution concerns the utterance of an individual or a group of individuals as a reaction to the happenings within the environment; illocution focuses on the intentions of the speaker in making such an utterance and perlocution deals with the consequences of the utterance on the listener/addressee. These three acts are apt in that they are relevant to the discussion of the roles languages perform in the elusive peace in Nigerian socioeconomic, political, and tribal life.

Data Presentation and Analysis
Reinterpretation of Abbreviations to Denounce Persons and Groups

Mostly created for convenience, abbreviations are short forms or contractions of words or phrases. Abbreviations could come in three forms—acronyms, initialisms, and truncations. National leaders in Nigeria generally have their names abbreviated either in admiration or denunciation, such as: OBJ—Ọbásanjo; GEJ—Goodluck Èbélè Jonathan; IBB—Ibrahim Bàdàmósí Bàbángídá; MKO—Moshood Kashimawo Oláwálé; PMB—President Mohammad Bùhárí. However, some have their name expanded or enlarged.

For example, General Sánní Àbáchà's name ABACHA has been reduced to an acronym and then expanded to: ABACHA—After Babangida Another Criminal Has Arrived. The pragmatic implication is obvious here; both Àbáchà and the former head of state, Babangida, have been deemed as criminals. There is a number of such examples:

BUHARI—Brought Unnecessary Hardship Among Reasonable Igbos: The newly elected president of Nigeria seems to have in place harsh economic policies, which the government attributes to the previous regime mishandling the economy. Certain sections of the country appear unconvinced about the government's excuses and thus the name of the president is enlarged as we have it.

HAUSA—House Animals Using Seat of Authority: It is very often the case that the Hausas are compared to animals as they raise cows on commercial basis. This observation is definitely not from within the community, but a description from the outside. Hausa is a name of a group of people and not an acronym. However, some individuals creatively found a demeaning and offensive description of what the letters represent.

IBADAN—Ibo Boys Are Dangerous at Night: As it will be seen in the enlargement of IBO, the Igbo (Ibo) are often perceived and accused of criminal activities. Ibadan, situated in Nigeria's southwest, is a purely Yoruba society and the third largest city in Africa. However, the word Ibadan is expanded solely to attack a rival region in Nigeria.

IBO—I Before Others: Tannen (1992) calls this "First me, then me" (p. 259). A variation of this is 'I, me and myself'. The Ibo (Igbo) are often seen as selfish and greedy. Such personality traits are, especially in African societies, frowned upon and condemned as antisocial and definitely not worthy of self-pride. However, whenever it is convenient, members of the group use the description for themselves.

IMO—Igbos Must Overcome: This is an expression of self-determination of a nation that sees itself as marginalised and repressed. The world "overcome" implies a situation of enslavement, suffering, and bondage. It presupposes accusations towards a group or an institution positioned in power that is oppressive. "Igbo must overcome" suggests hope and encouragement. However, from the non-Igbo, IMO is "Igbos Must Obey". This suggests repression.

KOBO—Kill Obásanjó Before Others: The kóbò is Nigeria's lower currency denomination. It is not an abbreviation but a word. Nonetheless, kóbò is enlarged by the Ìgbò and by political rivals of the former president Obásanjó to express how much hatred they have for him. In the political circuit, Obásanjó is considered to be an unforgiving punisher of his enemies. Yoruba version of this is "Kill Ojukwu Before Others" to attack the Igbos.

NAIRA— Never Allow Igbos Rule Again / Never Allow Idiots Rule Again: This is an expression of dismissal against a people that are perceived to be capable of mischief and other social vices. This refers back to the fact that Nigeria's first military coup (January 1966) appeared to have been Igbo-orchestrated. That junta lasted only six months.

In Table 11.1, I analyse some abbreviations as used conventionally in Nigeria, with pragmatic applications revealing the illocutionary act and the perlocutionary force.

Table 11.1
Abbreviations (as Locutionary Force) Showing Pragmatic Reconfigurations to Provoke Perlocutionary Force

No.	Abbreviations	Conventional Meaning	Pragmatic Application
1	ABN	Association of Better Nigerians	Association of Bastard Nigerians
2	APC	All Progressive Congress	All Promises Cancelled Association of Protected Criminals Association of Past Criminals All Present Criminals
3	PDP	Peoples Democratic Party	People Deceiving People People Destroying Places Papa Deceiving Pickin

4	MTN	Multinational Telecommunication Nigeria	Maintaining Total Nonsense; Mobile Telecommunicathief Network; Most Thiefing Network; Mumu Telling Nonsense; MadnessTormenting Nigerians; Empty Network; Mobile Thieves in Nigeria; Many Thieves in Nigeria
5	NEPA	National Electric Power Authority	Never Expect Power Again (Always)
6	NYSC	National Youth Service Corp	Now Your Struggles Continue Now Your Sufferings Continue
7	PHCN	Power Holden Company of Nigeria	Please Hold Candle Now Problem Has Changed Name
8	MFM	Mountain of Fire and Miracles	Mumu Follow Mumu Mumu Follow Mugu
9	MMM	MavrodianMondial Moneybox (Ponzi scheme)	*MogbeMokuModaran **Mole Mo ba Mo gbapada

*Mogbé (I am lost) Mokú (I am dead) Mo dáràn (I am in trouble)
**Mo le (I pursue it) Mo ba (I overtake it) Mo gbapada (I recover it)

Morphological Reformulations for Face Attack

In addition to abbreviations and expansions, often references are made to persons and groups of persons through morpho-pragmatic processes that belittle the addressees' status and personality, as seen in Table 11.2.

Table 11.2
Morphological Reconsideration of Expressions to Attack Persons, Places and Processes

	Datum	Target lexemes	Morphological process	Pragmatic implication
1	AbubakarShecow	Shekau	Blending Shekau+cow	Brutish Animal
2	arithMAGIC	Arithmetic	Arithmetic+Magic	Fraudulence
3	Asshole Rock	Aso Rock/Villa	Replacement (Aso)	Unpleasantness
4	Bagluck/Badluck Jonathan	Goodluck	Replacement (Good)	Evil

5	Biafraud/ Biafraudulent/ Biafraudians Supportors	Biafra	Blending (Biafra+ Fraudulent)	Fraudulence/ Deceitfulness
6	Bingo [local dog] (Dino) Melaye	Dino	Replacement	Mannerless
7	Bokohari	Buhari	Book+buhari	Avoidance/ violence
8	Buafraud Intelligent Agency (DSS)	Buhari	Blending (Buhari + Fraud)	Untrust- worthiness
9	Buharam	Buhari	Buhari+haram	Violence
10	Buharinomics	Economics	Buhari+economics	Uninformed
11	Executhieves	Executives	Executive+ thieves	Banditry
12	Fayoinsane	Fayose	Fayose+insane	Madness
13	Fayoshame	Fayose	Fayose+shame	Ignominy
14	Foolanis	Fulani	Fool+Fulanis	Stupidity
15	Judisharing	Judiciary	Judiciary+sharing	Dishonesty
16	Legislathieves	Legislatives	Legislature+ thieves	Crookedness/ criminality
17	Malamocracy	Democracy	Malam+ democracy	Idiocy
18	Obassajor	Obasanjo	Respelling	Non recognition
19	Poli-tricksters	Politicians	Politician+trickster	Cheat/Deceit
20	Sharia Reporters	Sahara Reporters	Respelling/ replacement	Parochialism/ Bigotry
21	SinnatorBuruji	Senator	Sin+senator	Lawbreaking
22	Thiefnubu	Tinubu	Thief+Tinubu	Crookedness
23	Undistinguished Sinnators	Distinguished Senators	Respelling	Disrepute/ dishonour
24	Yemi Oshibaje (Osibajo)	Osibajo	Respelling	Degrading
25	Zoogeria	Nigeria	Zoo+Nigeria	Jungle/Barbarism

Discriminatory and Pejorative Application of Nomenclatures

Illocutionary acts are non-linguistic acts performed through a linguistic or locutionary act (Osisanwo, 2003, p. 58). In our context, illocutionary acts carry out a number of intentions or functions, especially attacking, insulting, deriding, denigrating, belittling, and demeaning. They have an effect on the addressee, who is then further pushed to act or react. This effect is the perlocutionary act. In this case, increase in the level of hatred, distrust, or the desire to harm another is perlocutionary.

Two more terms are important here: presupposition and implicature. Presuppositions, as the word suggests, are the speaker's basic assumptions about the hearer, even when either or both parties are not particularly conscious of them. Pragmatic presuppositions are contextual assumptions or things taken for granted as part of the background of the information. Implicature refers to that which can be understood from what is said even when it is not explicitly stated. It is what is implied, suggested, or meant differently from what the speaker or writer has overtly explicated. The following name-calling devices illustrate presupposition and implicature:

Aboki: Aboki literally means "friend" in Hausa language. It is in itself inoffensive. However, the word has over time acquired a pejorative status outside its native use. "Aboki" is used in a way that connotes stupidity, foolishness, and senselessness. It was originally reinterpreted to refer to any individual of Hausa descent, who may have engaged in offensive behaviour, but the word was later used for the Hausa people as a whole as an attack on their reasoning capacity. In Nigeria "Aboki" also now refers to any individual anywhere in the world, irrespective of tribe or race, who acts without knowing the appropriate way to do something. Some notable Hausa companies and institutions have adapted the word "Aboki" to wear out the negativity as a result of overuse (Brothers, 1992, p. 457). This has not yielded the desired result.

Agatu: The "Agatu" are a tribe in the Northern part of Nigeria. They are farmers but many of them travel out of their region to settle in western Nigeria or elsewhere. They work as farm hands and are quite dexterous at this. How this innocuous label managed to become pejorative is unknown. "Agatu" now connotes, in certain contexts, a person full of energy but with little brain. A person who is called an *agatu* feels the pain for a long time. The pragmatic implication is that the *àgàtú* are human beings of lesser quality.

Bàrìbá: Much like the Àgàtú, the Bàrìbá are natives of northern Nigeria. They are notable for the profession of guarding or securing towns, cities, and properties. They are deemed to be merciless, as they refuse to compromise in their duties. This presupposes diligence and dedication to duty, whereas those who have had unpleasant experiences with Bàrìbá as security guards on night duty will always have a different tale to tell. The negative reference to Bàrìbá as ominous and dangerous fellows is quite a reversal of the old sense of trust that they earned for keeping people and property safe.

Bèérébè: This is a name given to the Yoruba by the Hausa in the north. Bèèrèbè is a clipped word from the reduplication of the word bèèrè (ask/inquire). The Yoruba repeat the word - bèèrèbèèrè- for emphasis, for example to say, "I have asked (bèèrè) after you several times." The repetition suggests care and concern for the welfare of another. However, the Hausa, who are unfamiliar with this, distort the word to bèèrèbè. Overtime, an originally positive word has been changed by the non-native to deride the manner in which the Yoruba speak.

Ègùn: This is a group of people at the Nigeria-Benin Republic border. Ègùn is also their language. To designate their "foreign" and "unpopular" language, the word Ègùn is now used to describe a person who is incoherent. The word has acquired this negative connotation, and the context in which it is used does much to determine the level of its offensiveness (Buckley, 1992, p. 468).

Ìkòbòkóbò: This is a Yoruba coinage which means a language that is incomprehensible or not understood. It generally refers to the Igbo language. The Igbo people are aware that they are referred to as Ìkòbòkóbó. In retaliation, they call the Yoruba Ńgbàtí. They are usages of mutual discrimination.

Málà: "Mala" is clipped from "Mallam," which means a Muslim cleric or scholar. Outside of its original meaning, the word Mala negatively refers to the Hausas. In this pejorative context, it is synonymous with Àbókí. The words are used to abuse Hausas and non-Hausas alike and carry undeniably painful implications.

Nna: "Nna" is a discourse marker in the Igbo language. It is usually applied to attract the attention of an addressee. However, the Yoruba use it as Ọmọ Nna (a child of Nna) to refer to the Igbo people as those "not belonging to us".

Òkóró: This is onomatopoeic. The Yoruba call the Igbo Òkóró. This is supposed to refer to the strength and rugged nature of an Igbo man or woman. The Igbo are, however, criticized for their ability to withstand stress, an attribute that is otherwise commendable.

Tápà: The Tápà, like the Àgàtú, are from northern Nigeria. They share attributes and condemnations for their industry and language, much more so for being in the minority and for settling outside their traditional domain. Their language, which is a part of their identity, has become for them an object of ridicule.

Yánmírín: This is an appellation given to the Igbo by the Hausas. Other ethnic groups in the country feel that the Hausa oligarchy sees non-Hausas as nobodies. They expect everyone to speak the Hausa language and practise Islam. Igbo people do neither and are hence dismissed as (A)yanmirin in addition to Kaferi (non-believers).

Insult and Hatred-Laden Expressions
The data is replete with attacks on individuals. Social media users in Nigeria doubt that President Goodluck Ebele Jonathan has earned a Ph.D. They claim not to know any of his school friends nor his external examiner. It is not uncommon to find a comment ridiculing *"Badluck"* who has no school mates. To win election in 2011 President Jonathan identified with poor people of Nigeria and claimed that he too had no shoes to wear while he was growing up. This has earned him "Mr. Footprints" as a nickname. Such examples pervade social media. Rev. Fr. Mbaka is criticized for his "stomach prophesy" that only "kwashiorkor Christianity can listen to." Senator Bola Ahmed Tinubu, who comes from a prominent Lagos family, is reformulated as "Tinuburuku," a word in Yoruba that connotes evil. Muslim leaders Saraki and Buhari are called "saint" and "pope" respectively. Lai Mohammed is called Lai Lie or Liar Mohammed. Governor of Ekiti State Peter Ayodele Fayose is ridiculed as idiot of Fayoinsane, Fraudyose, Father

Cheeseballs, Fayoshame, "omo mama onipampers" (whose mother wears pampers). There are countless such examples, not only against individuals, but against institutions, race, region, tribes, and traditions.

Denial/Rejection of State
Every state or nation in the world expects from the citizens their loyalty and a pledge of this loyalty from time to time. Entrenched in the constitution are the national anthem to be sung and the pledge to be recited most especially at official functions. The Nigerian constitution declares "Though tribes and tongues may differ, in brotherhood we stand." However, to such nationalistic claims of unity in diversity, it is not uncommon to find comments, such as this: "In brotherhood kó in Nollywood ni. Keep lying to yourself. Nigeria is not united now and it will never be." Similar sentiments are expressed in an extended statement below, a passionate rejection of the expected loyalty to the Nigerian state, a strong condemnation of a group of people. The original National Pledge of Nigeria is restructured as follows:

> I pledge Nigeria is not my country, how can I be faithful, loyal and honest to an expired country? To be a Nigerian is not by force, I don't defend her unity, I don't uphold her honor and glory, so BREAK it God. ("Trump Meeting," 2018, para. 17)

Such declarations are made in the spirit of confrontation with institutions and instruments of governance in the country. The verbal attack has the potential toward perlocutionary action against people and the whole country. After all, verbal war precedes guns and grenades.

Intersection of Peace and Language

Those who use denigrating words and expressions are largely aware that words have more than one meaning, and so they often explore and test this opportunity. People betray their opinions, social attitudes, and ideologies through their choice of words. In addition to it, variations in the manner, tone, and context affect the meaning of an utterance. Language users are, therefore, deliberate in their use of certain expressions to hurt, ridicule, and attack the interlocutor or addressee. This happens despite being aware of a sense of respect they should have for others' personality, dignity, honour, and right to live. Even in disagreement socio-cultural norms demand politeness and appropriateness in the choice of words.

Clearly, language is a double-edged sword, used to hurt or love, cause conflict or build peace. More often than not, the Nigerian socio-political landscape embodies the former purpose. This is particularly so when people comment on national matters using abusive language to describe not only the country's public and political officers but also fellow Nigerians. Words, therefore, become weapons to harm one another. As the Yoruba say, "the sheep does not say it would not be friends with the goat, but the goat knows its mother did not give birth to children with black skin." It presupposes that we know where we belong and where we do not. On the other side of this, Mother Teresa observed, "If we have no peace, it is because we have forgotten that we belong to each other." There is no peace in Nigeria because many parts do not see themselves as part of the whole, as belonging together in a conglomeration.

Data analysis for this study shows that in the Nigerian context verbal attacks are not so much about religion as about ethnicity and political partisanship. Peace has therefore been elusive in the country as one ethnic group or political party is often presented as either the problem or the solution. These beliefs and views are transferred from one generation to another. Hateful and indecent words and labels are like arrows shot at one's enemy. Whether the impact is felt or not is largely dependent on, for instance, the worldview or background of the interlocutors and context of utterance.

There is no doubt that verbal war precedes gun and grenade war. Many a time, intra and inter-tribal wars are provoked because people have not learnt to manage words. It is often said that Nigerian democracy has tribal marks; the current agitation for the emergence of a Biafra nation out of the Nigerian federation has encouraged other agitations for, say, an Odùduwà Republic, a Delta Republic, a Middle Belt Republic, or even, for that matter, an Islamic State. In the light of these conflicts, therefore, it might be difficult, if not impossible, to achieve unity or even peaceful negotiations when verbal attacks continue to be fostered on social media as well as the conventional media. It is recommended therefore that, along with freedom of expression, language awareness should be included on a fundamental level into the country's education policy. The study of language and its effects on interpersonal relationships should be part of the school curriculum, so that children may learn community and peace building early.

References
Adeniyi, O. (2017). *Against the run of play.* Yaba, Nigeria: Prestige Books.
Adepoju, B. H. (2014). An analysis of grapho-phonological infelicities in Nigerian political discourse. *Lagos Notes and Records: A Journal of the Faculty of Arts, 20*(1), 35–50.
Adepoju, B. H. (2016a). Euphemism as politeness strategy in language change. *Papers in English and Linguistics, 17*(3&4), 54–70. doi:10.4000/lexis.355
Adepoju, B. H. (2016b). Ebola and humour: A reconstruction of paralinguistic greetings in Nigeria. *Ijagun Journal of English & Literature, 1*(1), 1–17.
Awonusi, S. (2004). Cycles of linguistic history: The development of English in Nigeria. In A. B. K. Dadzie & S. Awonusi (Eds.), *Nigerian English, influences and characteristics* (pp. 46-69). Lagos, Nigeria: Concept Publications.
Banjo, A. (1996). *Making a virtue of necessity: An overview of the English language in Nigeria.* Ibadan, Nigeria: Ibadan University Press.
Begeron, J., & Vachon, M. A. (2008). The effects of humour usage by financial advisors in sales encounters. *International Journal of Bank Marketing, 26*(6), 376–398. https://doi.org/10.1108/02652320810902424
Brothers, J. (1992). What "dirty words" really mean. In G. Goshgarian (Ed.), *Exploring language* (6th edition, pp. 455-459). New York, NY: Harper Collins.
Clouse, R. W., & Spurgeon, K. L. (1995). Corporate analysis of humour. P*sychology: A Quarterly Journal of Human Behavior, 32*(3– 4), 1–24.
CyberAlert. (2010). Media monitoring. Retrieved from https://www.cyberalert.com
Emeka-Nwobia, N. U. (2008). Language as a tool of discrimination against women. *Journal of Nigerian Languages and Culture, 10*(2), 267–272.
Finegan, E. (2004). *Language: Its structure and use (4th edition).* Boston, MA: Thomson Wadsworth.
Goshgarian, G. (Ed.). (1992). *Exploring language* (6th edition). New York, NY: Harper Collins.
Illiteracy rate in Nigeria alarming – FG. (2017, September 21). *Vanguard.* Retrieved from https://www.vanguardngr.com/2017/09/illiteracy-rate-nigeria-alarming-fg
Internet World Stats. (2018). *Usage and population statistics.* Retrieved from https://www.internetworldstats.com/africa.htm

Lee, Y-P., & Kleiner, B. H. (2005). How to use humour for stress management. *Management Research News, 28*(11/12), 179–186. https://doi.org/10.1108/01409170510785372

Meyer, J. C. (1990). Ronald Regan and humor: A politician's velvet weapon. *Communication Studies, 41*, 76–88. https://doi.org/10.1080/10510979009368289

Nairaland. (2016). *Some funny Nigerian abbreviations*. Retrieved from https://www.nairaland.com/2574460/funny-meaning-most-abbreviation-nigeria

Nan. (2017, September 21). Social media promoting hate speeches, insecurity – Lalong. Retrieved from https://guardian.ng/news/social-media-promoting-hate-speeches-insecurity-lalong/

Onuigbo, S., & Eyisi, J. (2009). *English language in Nigeria: Issues and developments*. Calabar, Nigeria: Paclen.

Romero, E. J., & Cruthirds, K. W. (2006). The use of humor in the workplace. *The Academy of Management Perspectives, 20*(2), 58–69. https://doi.org/10.5465/amp.2006.20591005

Snjezana, M. (2003). *Media monitoring manual*. London, UK: Media Diversity Institute Publications.

Taiwo, R. (2012). *Language and mobile telecommunication in Nigeria: SMS as a digital lingual-cultural expression*. Ile-Ife, Nigeria: OAU Press.

Tannen, D. (1992). "I'll explain it to you": Lecturing and listening. In G. Goshgarian (Ed.), *Exploring a language* (Sixth Ed., pp. 257-271). New York, NY: HarperCollins.

Trump meeting: Biafra, herdsmen killings, stepping down in 2019 top Nigerians wishlist. (2018). *The Herald*. Retrieved from https://www.herald.ng/trump-meeting-biafra-herdsmen-killings-stepping-down-in-2019-top-nigerians-wishlist

Waelateh, B. (2003). *A speech act analysis of advertising headlines in the Bangkok Post* (Unpublished master's thesis). Prince of Songkla University, Chang Wat Songkhla, Thailand.

CHAPTER 12

INVESTIGATING LANGUAGE POLITICS BEFORE AND AFTER THE 2016 U. S. ELECTION

Nicole King, Jackie Ridley, and Esther Yoon

Introduction

Gomes de Matos (2000) issued a plea to educational stakeholders to promote the intersection of language and peace and to share the message that "communicating well means communicating for the well-being of humankind" (p. 343). These statements were contained within a larger piece regarding the importance of humanizing political discourse, especially related to issues of conflict, and likely the result of decades of academic discourse and theoretical development in the areas of aggression (Galtung, 1964), critical pedagogy (Freire, 1970), and the politics of English as a world language (Kachru, 1986). Since this proclamation, many researchers have contributed to the scholarship in peace linguistics (Crystal, 2004; Friedrich, 2007, 2013; Morgan & Vandrick, 2009), peace education (Bar-Tal & Rosen, 2009; Olowo, 2016; Salomon, 2004), critical peace education (Bajaj, 2008; 2015b; Wenden, 2014), and critical peace linguistics (Wenden, 2007). As yet, critical synthesis of the ideas and findings within these disciplines has not been compiled and disseminated to classroom practitioners.

Perhaps this is because the role of teachers in the scaffolding of development in students to use language to communicate both peacefully and about peace has not been uniformly established. Thus, it is critical for a compilation of the theories and empirical support to be developed. The literature pertaining to peace linguistics, peace education, critical pedagogy, and other related disciplines spans the globe in contexts of thoughts, theory, and research. However, in order for the presence and role of peace education and peace linguistics to be investigated empirically, it is necessary to explore these constructs within a specific local context (Bajaj, 2015a, 2015b).

Given the recent socio-political change in the United States with Trump's election on November 8, 2016, an important, insightful, and imperative opportunity has occurred to pursue an exploration of peace and the multitude of factors which mediate students' perceived access to symbolic, physical, and linguistic peace. Understanding the election amplified pre-existing racial, ethnic, linguistic and social strains, these strains notably in language education have taken different forms of oppression. The hostile English-only movement is sweeping across the country, creating an atmosphere that demeans cultural and linguistic diversity; further, high stakes assessment constrains educators and students by pushing forward print text-based learning, devaluing the rich oral cultures of storytelling. These new policies continue to privilege monolingual English speakers and disadvantage multilinguals. Furthermore, the framing of language as "have it or have not" and view of diversity as deficit impacts school culture. As statements like "build a wall" between the US and Mexico or a Democratic word-play slogan "love trumps hate" in response to hate speeches have penetrated the discourse in classrooms in the United States, the search for peace in education and the role of language in the promotion of peace in a variety of educational settings in the United States has reached a critical crux of importance.

Whether it was used to humorize the current political and social situation or to bring serious questions and answers, these recreated statements in classrooms represent students' responses to various forms of nationalism, xenophobia and resistance against them. Unfortunately, these forms of oppression and struggle are fueling ideologies, which in turn are fueling policies both nationally and locally, the impact of which is magnified in the language education classroom. Students' access to languages of their choice, including heritage languages, are being impacted by how they are positioned through others, across a variety of educational contexts.

Globalization and language as power continue to shape language curriculum all over the world, either embracing or denying the tragic histories of imperialism and colonialism. In the United States, the consequences of the genocide of Native Americans, slavery, Japanese concentration camps, the Black Lives Matter movement, the Muslim travel ban and many more tragedies shaped and continue to shape the US today. Based on the results of a Southern Poverty Law Center (2016) report, the fear and anxiety in the schools in the United States is at a precipice, and educators require access to the theoretical and practical tools necessary to imbue in students a desire to peacefully engage with their peers, regardless of perceived difference. Lombardo and Polonko (2015) beautifully construct a powerful rationale for the importance of research in peace education and peace linguistics to occur in educational contexts: "Our childhood is a part of our lives forever even if we try to forget. We may not be physically living it longer, but it does stay in our minds through our entire life" (p. 192). The experiences of children in a variety of school settings are being shaped right now, and how they are positioned in and through language will mediate how they view the world. The opportunity to illuminate how teachers and students use language is here.

Because of the lasting influences and critical development which occurs during childhood and young adulthood, we sought to investigate the following questions during this change in socio-political equilibrium in the United States, across three different learning contexts in K-16 education:

1. How do students view their language choices and rights to use language before and after the 2016 election?
   a. What languages do students think they have the right to use?
   b. How does this language positioning impact them emotionally and socially?
2. How do students feel others (namely, the media, politicians, teachers, etc.) have positioned them through language during this time period?
   a. How has this positioning impacted their understanding of their linguistic identity?
   b. How has this positioning impacted their language rights?
   We used these guiding questions to explore how students in a second grade French immersion classroom, in an after-school program for recent immigrants, and in an EAP course at a Midwestern university to guide our classroom-based qualitative investigation of language rights and politics through the lenses of peace education, peace linguistics, and critical pedagogy.

Literature Review

Peace Education

In 1964, Johan Galtung contributed a seminal work to the first volume of the *Journal of Peace Research* in which he explored the "structural theory of aggression" (p. 95). The crux of this theory is that aggression is only a possible resultant in cultures where aggression is viewed as a typical response and in which there is unsolvable disequilibrium of resources across groups of people. In many cases, the aggression which results is one with negative consequences. However the implications of this theory are not entirely reflective of dystopian consequences of inequality. Two important caveats are discussed and provide the necessary impetus for the importance and significance of both peace education and peace linguistics. First, it is possible for aggression to be circumvented through "multi-dimensional change" (p. 113); thus there is great potential power and impact in the critical examination of how social policies, progress, and resulting distribution of wealth impact each group of people inter- and intra-culturally within a society. This factor speaks to implications related to macro-level considerations, including language ideologies and language policies (c.f. Kubota & Miller, 2017).

However, a second caveat provides the foundation requisite for the development of peace education (Bar-Tal & Rosen, 2009; Olowo, 2016; Salomon, 2004), peace linguistics (Friedrich, 2007, 2013), and critical peace education (Bajaj, 2015a, 2015b). In the final words of Galtung's (1964) seminal piece, he posits the potential for the positive aspects of aggression to develop once methods of conflict management and transformation are developed within a society. It is in these words which the path forward for peace education and its derivations could begin. Researchers and practitioners have the opportunity to explore how language could be used as a conflict transformation strategy (c.f. Bajaj, 2015b) in classroom interactions and in spaces of language and cultural contact.

Friedrich (2013) provides a necessary distinction between peace education and peace linguistics; she defines peace linguistics as "communicating peacefully" and peace education as "communicating about peace" (p. 75). This clear dichotomy is helpful in developing an understanding of the divergent though related goals of each of the two frameworks of thought and pedagogy. The components of peace education have been increasingly explored in research (Danesh, 2006; Olowo, 2016; Salomon, 2004), and across studies a consensus of the constituents of peace education has developed. Most specifically, Bajaj (2015b) provides five clear principles for teachers employing peace education:

1. raising consciousness through dialogue,
2. imagining nonviolent alternatives,
3. providing specific modes of empowerment,
4. transformative action,
5. reflection and re-engagement. (p. 161)

A further extension of peace education, specifically direct peace education, has been identified by Cann (2012). By extending notions of critical pedagogy (Bajaj, 2008; Freire, 1970), this framework acknowledges "the social reproduction function of societal institutions and the structural forces of poverty, racism, sexism and heterosexism" (Cann, 2012, p. 219). A clear construct which presides within this subset of peace education is a critical stance of inquiry towards societal systems. In order for peace education to occur, researchers and practitioners must situate themselves within both the macro and micro levels of context. Each level of context assists in the composition of the other; thus, change is possible through both micro and macro level actions. While the current study places emphasis on local uses of language to construct peaceful interactions, it also places credence in the use of contextualized language to transform and mediate policy and ideology.

Critical Pedagogy

Six years after Galtung (1964) proposed a structural theory of aggression and provided two possible caveats therein, Freire (1970) proposed a new pedagogy designed to address the structural inequalities between the "topdogs" and the "underdogs" discussed by Galtung (1964). Within the two stages of the "pedagogy of the oppressed" (Freire, 1970, p. 54), Freire provides the necessary requirements to ensure that change is "multidimensional" (Galtung, 1964, p. 113) and that "alternative methods of conflict management [are] better developed" (pp. 113-114). This localized critical pedagogy focuses on the disequilibrium of access to resources across groups of people and the joint effort of both groups to solve the disequilibrium in the pursuit of social justice solutions. Freire calls upon each community of people to name instances of injustice, in order for transformation to occur; from his pedagogical stance, there is great power in using language to describe lived experiences within the world. For critical pedagogy to be effective, communities must work in collaboration towards awareness, action, and transformation of resources and justice. Solutions will not arise from dependence of the oppressed on the oppressor (Freire, 1970); the success of effective critical pedagogy is contingent upon agency and efficacy in both groups. Critical pedagogy is a grounded, communal exercise towards justice for all.

Peace Linguistics

Situated at the intersection of peace studies and language studies, peace linguistics inquires how language, including language ideologies and policies, works for or against the pursuit of peace at local and global levels. In the *Dictionary for Linguistics and Phonetics*, Crystal (2008) defines peace linguistics as:

> a term reflecting the climate of opinion which emerged during the 1990s among many linguists and language teachers, in which linguistic principles, methods, findings and applications were seen as a means of promoting peace and human rights at a global level. (p. 355)

More of a concept than a discipline, peace linguistics is concerned with the relationship between language, communication, education, and peace (Friedrich, 2007; Gomes de Matos, 2000).

While considered a descendent of peace studies, in her discussion of teaching languages for peace, Friedrich (2013) distinguishes between the study of peace through language and peace linguistics. In the study and education of peace through language, language is the vehicle for communicating pedagogies, practices, and policies that contribute to peace. In the field of peace linguistics, language is both the medium and the content of study. Peace linguistics goes beyond communicating about peace to the study of how language can be used to communicate peacefully (Friedrich, 2013; Gomes de Matos, 2000).

As evident in the definition and description above, the field of peace linguistics emphasizes the role of language in constructing peaceful political discourse (Gomes de Matos, 2000). Within this discipline, researchers and scholars aim "to bring a linguistic solution to specific issues in the area of peace research, defense of human rights and the promotion of education for democracy" (Crystal, 2004, p. 24). Peace linguistics holds that language is more than just a mean of communication; rather, it is a "principle of social action" (Wenden, 2007, p. 164), and can play a part in the creation of war and the restoration of peace (Friedrich, 2007). Peace linguistics thus has the potential to address how language scholars and researchers can stop hegemonic forces of cultural homogenization and instead foster linguistic and cultural heterogeneity across the world.

Because language is both the content and the vehicle of instruction, peace linguistics is particularly relevant to the language learning classroom. Critical awareness of language is a fundamental element in language education that promotes democracy (Wenden, 2007) and peace linguistics addresses how teachers can encourage language use that promotes an appreciation of linguistic diversity (Friedrich, 2013). This critical, democratizing, and asset-based perspective is especially important if teachers are to view their multilingual students in terms of resources rather than deficits (Morgan & Vandrick, 2009). In sum, a language curriculum integrated with peace linguistics not only addresses language learning and peace education, but it also creates an inclusive and just classroom environment in which the full cultural and linguistic repertoires of linguistically diverse students are valued and supported.

Theoretical Framework

We approach this study employing a critical peace education theoretical framework, operating at the intersection of critical pedagogy and peace education. This intersectionality informs our inquiry into peace linguistics, which aims to shed light on structural oppressions and inequalities, and to explore local meanings, misunderstandings and experiences of peace (Bajaj, 2004, 2008). It is through language in which conflict management skills and "conflict transformation skills" (Bajaj, 2015b, p. 153) are enacted and contextualized. A study to promote and to mediate peace is only possible through an awareness of contextualized language use and localized beliefs

In this study, we aim to address the interplay of language, power, and politics (Kachru, 1986) in a transformative yet critical approach and explore the cultivation of agency to raise consciousness for transformative modes of behavior (Bajaj, 2008, 2015a, 2015b) and language use (Friedrich, 2007, 2013). Using this theoretical intersection, we seek to illuminate how language as the conduit for social change impacts students' language experiences and rights in classrooms. Our classroom research combines the affordances of peace linguistics, critical peace education, and critical pedagogy. This lens allows us to explore the relationship between language use and social action and how in and through language we are able to explore the concepts of communication, education, and peace at the classroom level (Wenden, 2007). Peace linguistics maintains our focus on the power of the languaging (Becker, 1988, 1991) practices of the teacher and students with whom we have the pleasure to work. Critical pedagogy focuses our attention to the connection between teacher and student agency within specific structural contexts. Further, critical pedagogy provide a lens to look at the work of the languaging of the teachers and students as Subjects, never objects (Freire, 1970), in how they interact with each other and the world. The social nature of critical pedagogy allows us to see the "conscientizacao" between the teachers and students as they think critically together (Freire, 1970). Finally, critical peace education combines the views of language as the medium and mode of social action and the awareness of agency within structure together.

Critical peace education is foregrounded in Giroux (1983), who explored how teachers and students engage in individual and coalitional agency to resist structures of domination. Students and teachers work together in solidarity to create contexts in which all people are positioned as knowledgeable and equal. These ideas are combined together in Bajaj's (2015b) classroom components of critical peace education: "critical thinking and analysis, empathy and solidarity, individual and coalitional agency, participatory and democratic engagement, education and communication strategies, conflict transformation skills, and ongoing reflective practice" (pp. 162-163). With equal focus on language, transformation, and collective efforts we have explored how students perceived language rights have been mediated by the 2016 US election, the media, and by the community in which they interact.

Methodology
Research Settings
This multi-site study collected data from three settings within the same mid-sized Midwestern city. Data was collected from each site by a one author: a French immersion school (Nicole), a grant-funded ESL afterschool program (Jackie), and an undergraduate English for academic purposes (EAP) writing class (Esther). Each site was chosen by the respective author because of her research interests in the linguistic and cultural diversity of the setting and how these demographics influenced and were influenced by the particularities of language teaching and learning at the site. Upon selection of the individual research sites and throughout the process of data collection, the authors collaborated and reflected throughout the process of data analysis. Analysis focused on how participants across sites viewed language, language sights, language choices, and positioning in and through language in their daily lived experiences.

French immersion school: École des Arbres. The first location in this study, a second-grade classroom in a public, Title-I French immersion school, École des Arbres[1]. This setting included twenty-one, primarily native-English speaking students who are learning French as an additional language through content-based, dual language instruction; thirteen of these students provided consent and assent to participate in this particular study. The model of language immersion provided 100% instruction in French in kindergarten, 90% in first grade, 80% in second grade, and followed this gradual model until 50% of instruction was given in French in fifth and sixth grade. The classroom teacher is from Tunisia and is multilingual in French, Arabic, and English, as are a few of the students. In addition to being multilingual, the class is also ethnically diverse, and the students represented a wide range of socioeconomic statuses and cultural backgrounds. Participant information for the students and teacher is displayed in Table 12.1. I (Nicole) obtained access to this research site through a research and curriculum partnership between the school and a local university. Over time, my positioning as participant observer evolved into a classroom assistant, as I became more familiar with the teacher, students, and the routines and language practices within the classroom.

Table 12.1
Participants at French Immersion School: École des Arbres

Name (Pseudonym)	Sex* M/F	Grade	Languages Spoken*
M. Brahim	M	Teacher	French, Arabic, English
DJ	M	2	English, French
Marie	F	2	English, French
Jared	M	2	English, French
Jordan	M	2	English, French
Stan	M	2	French, Arabic, English, Japanese
Belinda	F	2	English, French
Lola	F	2	English, French
Rhumba	M	2	English, French
Tricia	F	2	English, French
Kelly	F	2	English, French
Jenna	F	2	English, French
Tara	F	2	English, French
Corey	M	2	English, French

École des Arbres has recently celebrated its thirtieth year of teaching French and English to students in the Midwest. Prior to its advent, district level stakeholders decided to visit some of the schools in Louisiana because of interest in the Council for the Development of French in Louisiana (CODOFIL), a program which allows students to experience instruction through language immersion in French and in English. Further, the stakeholders were impressed by the international teachers in Louisiana, and they decided to create a similar experience for students in this Midwestern city by recruiting international teachers to provide instruction. There are 114 French immersion programs in the U.S. (Center for Applied Linguistics, 2011). Out of a total of 448 language immersion programs in the U.S., there are a total of 100 language immersion programs in the Midwest (Center for Applied Linguistics, 2011).

ESL afterschool program. The second site in this study is a grant-funded ESL afterschool program at a local public elementary school. This setting is unique from other afterschool programs in that it admits exclusively refugee and immigrants in second through fifth grade who are learning English as an additional language. Admission to the program is determined by performance on state-mandated standardized tests; the students who demonstrate the "highest need" for additional support in their English language development, based on their test scores, are given priority for enrollment. The forty students and eight staff at this site represent over a dozen different home countries and languages, and the children featured in this study are primarily from Latin America, Southeast Asia, and Northern Africa. Twenty eight students consented to participate in this study and eighteen students assented to interviews. Pertinent information about the student participants who were interviewed is included below in Table 12.2. I (Jackie) gained access to the site through serving as a volunteer English tutor, a position I continued once this study and data collection began.

Table 12.2
Student Research Participants at the ESL Afterschool Program

Student Name (Self-selected Pseudonym)	Sex* M/F	Grade	Languages Spoken*	Country of Origin / Ethnicity *	Years in ESL program
Jasmine	F	2	Somali, English, some Arabic	Somalia	1
Emily	F	2	Spanish, English	Dominican Republic	1
Ice Queen	F	2	Nepali, English	Nepal	1
Rosie	F	2	Spanish, English,	El Salvador	1

Julie	F	2	Nepali, English, Hindi	Nepal	1
Emma	F	3	Arabic, English	Iraq / Syrian	2.5
Diamond	F	3	Spanish, English	Mexico	2
Amber	F	3	Nepali, English, Hindi	Nepal	2
Olivia	F	3	Nepali, English, Hindi	Nepal	2
Brendan	M	3	Nepali, English, Hindi	Nepal	1.5
Christiano Rinaldo	M	3	Nepali, English	Nepal	1.5
Storm Girl	F	3	Nepali, English, Hindi	Nepal	.5
Leopard Lady	F	4	Nepali, English, some Hindi	Nepal	3
Lion King	F	4	Somali, English	Somalia	3
Raj	M	4	Nepali, Hindi, English	Nepal	2
Captain Bad Hair Cut	M	4	Swahili, Burundi (Kirundi), Kinyarwanda, English, some French	Kenya / Burundi	2.5
Fantasy Girl	F	5	Nepali, English, Hindi	Nepal	4
Diamond Hunter 101	M	5	Spanish, English	Mexico	.5

Undergraduate EAP writing class. The third research site included in this study is an undergraduate English for Academic Purposes (EAP) writing course at a large public university (see Table 12.3). This writing course focuses on skills and topics pertinent to writing in U.S. higher education classroom contexts, such as source-based writing and the concept of intellectual property. Student enrollment in this particular class was mandated by university policy that requires incoming multilingual students with test scores below a certain benchmark to take foundational English writing courses. Students within the class had varying levels of experience and comfort with English, both for academic and for social purposes. There were approximately sixty students from three different countries enrolled in the class. I (Esther) gained access to this course as an instructor in previous semesters. While I was an instructor, I recruited participants to meet outside of class in the following semesters.

Table 12.3
Participants at Undergraduate EAP Writing Course

Student Name (Pseudonym)	Sex M/F	Grade	Languages Spoken*	Country of Origin / Ethnicity *	Academic Background
Ben	M	Freshmen	Mandarin Chinese, English	China	Computer Science & Engineering
Jojo	F	Freshmen	Mandarin Chinese, English	China	Mathematics
Yuan	F	Transfer Sophomore	Mandarin Chinese, English	China	Mathematics & Economics
Zhen	M	Freshmen	Mandarin Chinese, English	China	Business

Data Collection and Analysis
This study adopted a qualitative methodological approach to investigate the research questions with regards to politics, language politics, and language rights in the wake of the 2016 US presidential election. Across research sites, data comprised of three main sources: audio recordings of open-ended interviews and key events, participant observations recorded as field notes, and artefact collection (e.g., student work products). An open-ended interview protocol was employed in interviewing participants, and every effort was made by the researchers to make interviews feel like informal conversations in which participant interests and responses guided the direction of the interview. Informed consent procedures were utilized throughout the process of data collection and analysis. Participants and the parents of school-aged participants consented to the process of data

collection; in addition, school-aged participants providing ongoing assent during interviews and collection of artefacts.

Field notes and audio recordings were reviewed within twenty-four hours of their initial documentation, and recordings with rich points relevant to the research question were transcribed in part or in whole within a week of their original recording to ensure they were rendered as accurately as possible. Each researcher initially coded and analyzed transcriptions and field notes from her respective site. During this ongoing process, descriptive coding procedures were utilized. Examples of codes noted across settings included language use, positioning, media, family or peer influences, and affect related to answering interview questions or present in classroom interactions concerning language use. Additional data from field notes, student work products, and member check-ins was also utilized to triangulate participant claims. The three researchers met on a weekly basis to talk through findings as salient themes and patterns began to emerge. These meetings and processes guided the development of the findings explored in the following section.

Findings

In this section, findings from each of the specific field sites will be discussed in detail under the field site heading. Overall, themes related to language use, language positioning, bi/multilingualism, and opportunities to language peacefully were noted across sites. However, given the distinct nature of each site, how each of these themes manifested among participants varied. Within this section, pseudonyms for each of the participants, including the teachers and research sites are utilized. Findings which demonstrated concurrence across sites will be discussed at the conclusion of this section.

French immersion school: École des Arbres

During the 2016-2017 school year, I (Nicole) collected and analyzed data through participant observation, audio recorded interviews, artefact collection, and extensive field notes. As I reviewed and revisited the data, I noticed that several themes appeared salient across observations, interviews, and artifact collection. M. Brahim and his students maintain and promote a positive view of bi/multilingualism, with an awareness of how this view is not universal across contexts and language policies. In addition, M. Brahim's actions mediate how the students respond to monolingual language ideologies and policies and have allowed a sense of agency among the students to develop in how they view language rights and language use. The complexity of thoughts surrounding language, language use, and language rights held by seven and eight year old students is notable and worthy of continued investigation. A preliminary overview of findings at this site follows.

Of the twenty-one students within the French immersion second grade classroom, thirteen students and the teacher provided both consent and assent in order to take part in this study of language rights and language politics. Across all participants, a theme of pride in being bilingual was noted. For instance, Marie discussed how her mother attended École des Arbres in elementary school and how she too has a goal of teaching her younger brother as well as her father how to speak French. Jared and Jordan each discussed how they were "bilingual" or "bilingue", and each demonstrated a preference for utilizing French over English during instruction; their words and actions convey an interest and a sense of belonging within the French immersion space. Stan, a multilingual speaker, stated that he is able to speak "three and a half languages," the languages being French, English, Arabic, and Japanese. Across informal student interviews and field notes documenting whole group and small group interactions, each of the students either implicitly or explicitly displayed a positive bilingual identity. For many of the students, this positive bilingual identity and bilingual language usage also translated beyond the school environment.

During a semi-structured interview with the teacher, M. Brahim, he noted that the students enjoy utilizing French outside of the school setting. For example, students showcased their French abilities at birthday parties to demonstrate their unique strengths as multilingual speakers. Interviewing the students informally and in an unstructured manner allowed for triangulation of this finding. The students did in fact utilize French outside of the school setting, and two students (Belinda and Lola) reported that their parents were surprised by how fast they were learning and able to use French. All students and the teacher discussed how the parents viewed French knowledge and French use in a positive manner.

However the students also displayed an awareness that even though being bilingual is a positive attribute within the local context of the classroom and within their family communications, this view of bilingualism is not universally held. The students often conveyed a distrust and a sense of anxiety regarding President Trump. While some students simply expressed their thoughts on President Trump and his impact on French language rights and language use as "bad" or "he doesn't like it," one student provided a more nuanced theory. Rumba's theory is that "he [President Trump] wants to stop French, because he can't speak it." Using member check-ins across non-sequential days of observation and interviews, this participant belief was triangulated. This theory is poignant considering the monolingual nature of President Trump. Thus even though his theory may serve as a coping mechanism for an eight-year old in order to reconcile how his accomplished linguistic capabilities could be denigrated by a person of power, it may also provide insight into the development and preservation of monolingual ideologies and enacted policies.

Finally Rhumba's insight into the perpetuation of monolingualism which is occurring within the current U.S Administration may not have become articulated without the teacher's, M. Brahim's, embodiment of Bajaj's (2015b) components of critical peace education. These components include "critical thinking and analysis, empathy and solidarity, individual and coalitional advocacy, participatory and democratic engagement, education and communication strategies, conflict transformation skills, [and] ongoing reflective practice" (pp. 162-163). Each morning, M. Brahim began the students' day with an "ethical discussion" while the students finished their breakfasts and while he waited for all of the students' buses to arrive. Topics of discussion include walking away from a physical altercation and animal testing (e.g., for medical reasons). He refered to the classroom as "our community", and eventually all of the students appropriated this term and identified together as a "community." For the end of the year project, the students created individual multimodal presentations on "How to Make the World a Better Place", and the students selected topics such as recycling, composting, welcoming immigrants and refugees, and charity. M. Brahim then arranged for the entire school to go through a gallery walk of all of the presentations. This activity provides the students with the benefit of developing a multimodal, multilingual composer identity for a large audience. The inclusive, thoughtful activities engender the components of critical peace education and allow for language to be used to "communicate peacefully" (Freidrich, 2013, p. 75) about peace and about all topics which impact the "community." He helped to engender the medium necessary for his students "to exist, humanly, ...to name the world, to change it" (Freire, 1970, p. 88). In M. Brahim's classroom students use language to critique and to transform their lived experiences.

ESL Afterschool Program
With regards to the first research question (How do students view their language choices and rights to use language before and after the 2016 election? What languages do students think they have the right to use, and how does this make them feel?), confidence in and awareness of their multilingual repertoires was a common theme student responses at the ESL afterschool program. Students from different linguistic and cultural backgrounds heartily asserted they had the right to speak whatever language they wanted, whenever they wanted, and they were quick to list all the languages they speak and the different spaces and places they use these languages. For example, when I (Jackie) asked Mobutu, a refugee from Burundi, what languages he speaks, he confidently named over a half dozen languages; included in this list was Nepali and Spanish, two languages Mobutu explained he was learning socially from his friends at school while on the playground and on the bus. Olivia and Julie, two refugees from Nepal, both explicitly outlined where they used the many different languages in their linguistic repertoires, detailing how they use Nepali at home with their family, English at school and in the community, and Hindi for religious holidays and celebrations.

Similarly, when asked the question "who owns English," the most frequent response was utter disbelief and even outright rejection of the questions premise. For instance, Rosie reacted in a way that exemplifies a typical response: "No one owns English, Mrs. Jackie," the third grade student from El Salvador replied, shaking her head, "you can't own English–English is for everyone!" Amber, a third-grade student from Nepal, thoughtfully explained how she believed everyone should feel they have the "right" to speak English, and English "shouldn't only belong to one person." These responses are emblematic of the asset based perspective and inclusive language ideology that was a common theme in students' expressed feelings on this topic.

However, when discussing the second question (How do students feel others have positioned them in and through language during this time period, and how has this impacted their understanding of their linguistic identity and language rights?), the hope and optimism that marked their previous responses faded, and students expressed fear, insecurity, and uncertainty, especially in connection to Trump as president. Their fears were based in a combination of facts and abstractions of facts: Rosie, the same student who laughed at the suggestion that someone could own English, fervently insisted, "Trump's going to send all the Spanish people to El Salvador and make them slaves." Olivia reported how she heard Donald Trump "doesn't like people from other cultures," and "he only wants English speaking people to stay in America." In the wake of the announcement of the proposed travel and refugee ban, Raj, a refugee background student from North Africa shrugged his shoulders and quietly wondered aloud: "When I first came to America I was so excited. Now with the new president here... I feel like... why am I even here if he's just going to send me back?" These examples are just a few of the statements that embodied students' anxiety with regards to their positionality and security.

Preliminary data analysis for the refugee and immigrant students at the ESL afterschool program has thus revealed participants were able to hold multiple, mutually exclusive, and often conflicting beliefs about their linguistic rights and identities. On one hand, students would repeat and recite these internalized American narratives about inclusiveness and diversity—multilingualism is good, I can speak whatever language I want, no one owns English, among others. However, they are also attempting to deal with the rise of exclusionary and xenophobic language ideologies and policies, which they perceive as a threat to their personal and familial security, let alone their linguistic rights and language use.

So far, it is unclear if these young participants are unable to recognize the discrepancies in these conflicting views, if they hold them completely separately and thus do not see them in contention, or if this response is a sophisticated coping mechanism these children have developed to help them navigate the current, hostile political climate. It is possible these hybrid identities allow students to deal with the insecurity of the present times while simultaneously maintaining optimism and hope for their future in this country as multilingual speakers.

Undergraduate EAP Writing Course
This EAP writing course is a required course at a large public university for international students who achieved a certain range of scores on their entrance composition exam mandated by the university. The course is comprised of students from mostly China, Malaysia and Indonesia with varying levels of experience and comfort with English. Out of fifty-four students from three different countries, four students consented to participate in the study so far and two students, both from China, participated in the semi-structured interview during the recent cycle of the study. Through the interview, artifact collection and analysis memos, interesting patterns emerged. The Chinese undergraduate students demonstrated conscious language decisions and dynamic positionalities.

The participants showed a strong awareness of their language use. For example, Zhen repeatedly expressed how he is very conscious when he speaks Chinese. He discussed how "Chinese is personal," as in he uses Chinese in his close social circle. Explaining why he is "careful" speaking Chinese and how Chinese is context-specific for him, Zhen discussed he feels isolated when speaking Chinese. Yuan discussed how she consciously uses English the majority of the time. She stated how she thinks it is "better for [her] to communicate in English with others" because she is "here […] in America."

While continuously engaging in their conscious decision of language use, the participants positioned themselves in dynamic ways. Zhen expressed that his floormates and other classmates showed interest in Asian students and Asian education systems. Zhen took this opportunity and positioned himself, feeling "proud" that he is able to discuss about his background. While Zhen bridged the general cultural differences, Yuan explained how she likes to discuss the complexities and specific cultural differences of international students and even amongst Chinese international students from different regions of China. She pushed back against stereotypes like "Chinese are good at math" or "Chinese are always the silent group" and the racial slurs she encountered as a Chinese international student. She felt strongly to position herself not only inform like Zhen with his friends, but also to "change their impress[ion] on [her and other Chinese students]."

Zhen and Yuan positioned themselves as bridges and informants in relation to others. However, they also appeared conflicted with regards to positioning after the 2016 election. Zhen expressed he feels "proud" to inform others about his Chinese culture and about the experiences of other "Asian students." He added he doesn't feel the impact of the U.S. election on campus, saying "people are nice here [...] they don't judge Asians." Yuan similarly stated that she feels comfortable on campus. While feeling this way, however, the participants were also very aware of and consciously decided where, when and with whom they spoke Chinese on campus. This ambivalence was present and continued as Zhen and Yuan discussed language rights. Unanimously the participants stated that anyone who speaks the language owns the language. Despite this performance-oriented approach to language rights, both Zhen and Yuan referred those who speak English as "them," "Americans," and "native speakers," creating a boundary between themselves and those who speak English as their first language. This positionality reveals that though the participants speak English and say that they have language rights, they do not actually feel they own English. Though conflicting and dynamic, these very views on language rights and the perceived detached impact of the U.S. election may serve as a coping mechanism for these participants.

Preliminary Findings Across Contexts

Across the three different research sites, we found multilingual students' perceptions of their language rights and reactions to positioning in and through language depended on (1) age and life stage, (2) perceived security of residency, and (3) relationships and positionality within families and communities. The following discussion reflects our preliminary findings based on the initial round of data collection and analysis.

Age and Life Stage

Perhaps not surprisingly, preliminary findings indicate that participants' perceptions of their linguistic rights and their reactions to positioning in and through language corresponded with age and life stage. For example, the students at École des Arbres and at the ESL afterschool program expressed similar sentiments surrounding their linguistic rights and language use: They are aware of their multilingualism and talk readily and with pride about the different languages they know and use. For example, at the French immersion school, Stan said "*J'aime parler avec deux langues* (I like to speak with two languages)," when asked what he liked about learning French. Similar to Stan, Jared and Jordan preferred to speak in French during instructional moments, and Jared frequently translanguaged (García, 2009, 2011) during instruction. For instance, he would ask, "Is it *montrer* (show) time?" prior to holding up his small white board to show his answers. At the ESL afterschool program, several Nepali students discussed how they were learning Spanish from some of their friends: On this topic, Leopard Lady, a fourth-grade student from Nepal excitedly shared: "I love learning Spanish! My friends teach it to me on the playground and on the bus. When I get to high school, I want to take Spanish class." Across both of these sites, the students demonstrated awareness and pride in bi/multilingualism during both formal and informal instructional moments.

Additionally, students at both elementary school sites shared similar notions of confusion, fear, and uncertainty when discussing how they as multilingual speakers were positioned in and through language throughout the election process, and how this made them feel. At the French immersion school, Jordan frequently said President Trump is "bad" or "he [President Trump] doesn't like it [French]." This sentiment was consistent across participants, however, Rhumba also voiced and revoiced (O'Connor & Michaels, 1993, 1996) a theory that "he [President Trump] wants to stop French, because he can't speak it." At the ESL afterschool program, Olivia's quote discussed above ("[Trump] only wants English speaking people to stay in America") is representative of the confusion and hurt children expressed about their status as multilinguals in the U.S. Across each site, students signaled awareness of how they were being positioned and developed perspectives to guard their linguistic rights.

In contrast, the international undergraduate students displayed a different response to the election and surrounding political climate; unlike the elementary age participants whose responses covered a range of strong emotions from unyielding optimism to outright fear, the international college students in the undergraduate writing course expressed much more tempered and almost ambivalent reactions. Rather than fear and uncertainty, the undergraduates articulated their language rights and positioning through language as multilingual speakers in light of the election as a matter of fact. Yuan expressed multiple times that "who can speak it and can communicate efficiently owns the English language." Ben echoed that statement saying, "Anyone speaks English owns English." While these adult participants did not express the same optimism and pride as the younger participants, they also did not express the same levels insecurity and uncertainty. Zhen expressed he is frequently accesses media via Facebook and Weibo, a Chinese microblogging platform that functions like Facebook, and he explained "They [media] don't really talk about me." In sum, the responses of the adult participants seemed to be conflicting and reluctant acceptance versus the outrage and fear that was present in the younger participants.

Perceived Security of Residency
Participants' perceived security of residency also impacted their sense of their linguistic rights and language choices. Across the different research sites, multilingual speakers with different statuses of residency[2] demonstrated differing levels of security and/or insecurity. As the language and discourses surrounding multilingual speakers grew increasingly hostile, many of the refugee and immigrant-background participants featured in this study expressed insecurity about their future in the U.S. For example, Diamond Hunter 101, a fifth-grade student from Mexico, calmly talked about what his family would do if they were deported: "We will just go back to Mexico and live with my mom's mom for a while... but I'll miss it here." Similarly, many refugee students from Nepal and North Africa shared their concern over the possibility of aunts, uncles, cousins,

and grandparents being stopped from coming to America as a result of the proposed travel ban.

In contrast, participants with legal status as U.S. citizens or student visas voiced various perspectives in regards to their security, freedom, and language rights in the wake of the election. Student perceived security at École des Arbres varied by participant. Three students had previously moved to the US from other countries. Stan's family was originally from Jordan and Lebanon, and his father is Japanese; however, he grew up primarily in Canada, and he expressed great pride in being Canadian. Jordan and Rhumba's families are originally from Sierra Leone and Senegal, respectively. Jordan and Rhumba manifested the greatest anxiety when discussing the election and President Trump. Their view of President Trump and the election as "bad," compares distinctly from that of Marie, whose mother attended École des Arbres and who enjoys speaking French at home and teaching her brother. Jojo, a freshmen student from China studying Mathematics, used an analogy of a visa when explaining her ownership of English: "I think it's open to everyone no matter where do you come from, as long as you can speak the language. Just like, if you are eligible for your visa, then you can come here. I think same thing." Thus, it seems that the micro-positioning of each participant mediated their responses to the macro events of the election and the media.

Relationships and Positionality within Families and Communities
Finally, the participants' relationships and positionality within their families and communities mediated their perceptions of their language rights and their reactions to positioning in and through language. In contrast to the international undergraduate students who consumed news and media from friends and on their own, many of our school-age participants reported they learned important news about politics and current events through adult family members, such as parents or aunts and uncles. For example, Rosie, the student who insisted "Trump's going to send all the Spanish people to El Salvador and make them slaves," told me (Jackie) her grandmother heard it on the news. Children would often relay not only what the trusted family member said, but how the person reacted as well. Children who reported that

their parents were worried tended to be more worried themselves; in turn, children who displayed a general lack of concern were those whose family members were also dismissive of politics and current events. For example, Ice Queen, a second-grade student from Nepal, would end her reports about watching the news with the following refrain: "But it's okay, my dad says do not worry." Family, community, and teacher actions had the potential to mediate how children felt positioned by society.

At École des Arbres, M. Brahim used language to construct a classroom space in which students learn how to use language and to make language choices agentively. In this space, he promoted the positive aspects of bi/multilingualism, often wearing both a French and a US scarf to indicate to the students that either language is accepted in this classroom. Further, Stan and M. Brahim often spoke together in Arabic, as a way to promote inclusivity of all language choices. M. Brahim engaged in these choices as a way to position all languages and language users as knowledgeable and welcome. Further during daily "ethical discussions" with the students from 9:00-9:15, M. Brahim talked with the students about language, politics, borders, money, careers, healthy food choices, and so many other topics, as a way to promote critical thinking and reflexivity with his students. M. Brahim viewed these discussions as integral moments to teach tolerance and culture through language: "My main goal in the classroom is to expose my kids to as much tolerance as possible—to learn the concept of tolerance, via the learning of a language, because with language comes culture." By discussing the media, family life, and the communities of the students lived experiences, across languages, the students in M. Brahim's classroom positioned themselves as competent, language users, regardless of how others or the media attempted to position them.

As exemplified at École des Arbres, teachers also played a role in fostering confidence in students' confidence in their language rights and cultural diversity, helping them to form positive, agentive identities and despite the promotion of homogeneity and English-only ideologies at a national level. Alternatively, for the undergraduate students from China, their family relationships mediated them to focus on and highlight performance of language. Jojo was very focused on sounding and perfecting her English to be more "native-like." Yuan, wanting to find a job in the United States after graduation, responded to "the new policy about visa" by saying "I will try speak more ... [to] improve my English [and] I think it's useful. I think it's good for me." As most of the students are the generation of "One-Child Policy" and are away from their family to attend university in the United States, this performance-oriented positioning impacted how they viewed their language rights. The different relational contexts of these multilingual students, therefore, influenced how they view and use language.

Implications and Future Directions

As we have shown, different age groups, sense of residency and positionings of the participants contributed to how the K-16 participants perceived their language rights and the impact of the 2016 U.S. election. As teachers and teacher educators, there is a pressing call to promote peace and discuss language use and rights in different language learning environments by being models of peace and non-violence. We concur with this call and posit that it should extend to all teachers in different classroom spaces. Teachers should recognize opportunities to promote advocacy efforts big or small, because all efforts have significance in constructing spaces for peace. We also note the importance of transformation in both language use and behaviors; critical peace transformations should "find alternative modes of engagement, ways of dealing with the world that encompass bodily and affective modes" (Appleby & Pennycook, 2017, p. 257) that extends outwards, so that students may exercise and maintain agencies beyond the classroom. Classrooms and communities across K-16 contexts that are safe and inclusive spaces, such as M. Brahim's classroom, foster the cultivation of agency and critical abilities to engage in dialogues and actions that promote peace. Students in these classroom spaces develop conflict transformation skills, agentive stances, and communication skills (Bajaj, 2015b) which extend beyond the walls of the classroom and into how these students view and describe the world around them. These experiences are especially salient in for multilingual children, as the events of childhood mediate a person's development throughout their lived experiences (Lombardo & Polonko, 2015).

As the study continues data collection through the Fall 2018 Midterm Elections, the analysis will further examine similarities and differences in formal and informal education contexts across age, language and culture groups, opening the door for more research on the interplay of language, politics and power. According to Crystal (2008), peace linguistics "emphasizes the value of language diversity and multilingualism, both internationally and intranationally, and asserts the need to foster language attitudes which respect the dignity of individual speakers and speech communities" (p. 355). To this end, our study seeks to provide a contextualized application of this conscious-raising approach to language education in the U.S. in the time of Trump.

Conclusion

In this politically, socially, and linguistically turbulent time, classroom-based research into the experiences of multilingual users is requisite to enhancing understanding of the potential to language peacefully with others and for the purpose of change. The current, multi-sited, qualitative study explored how multilingual speakers from a variety of cultural and linguistic backgrounds and in a variety of educational settings have come to understand language rights, language use, and language politics. Our preliminary analysis indicated that multilingual students' view of language rights is mediated by their ages, length of stay in the US, perceived sense of security, positioning by the media, and by family and community action and involvement. We also found that teacher actions, in the case of M. Brahim have the potential to transform student educational experiences and language use. Micro interactions have the possibility to supersede macro-level policies and ideologies.

Given the plausibility of teacher action to mediate student positioning through language, continued research into peace education and peace linguistics conducted within a variety of classroom settings is warranted. As this study continues to the mid-term elections in 2018, we look forward to illuminating in what ways teachers are able to impact student language identities and perceived language rights.

References

Appleby, R., & Pennycook, A. (2017). Swimming with sharks, ecological feminism and posthuman language politics, *Critical Inquiry in Language Studies, 14*(2-3), 239-261. doi:10.1080/15427587.2017.1279545

Bajaj, M. (2004). Human rights education and student self-conception in the Dominican Republic. *Journal of Peace Education, 1*(1), 21–36.

Bajaj, M. 2008. Critical peace education. In M. Bajaj (Ed.) *Encyclopedia of Peace Education* (pp. 135-146). Charlotte, NC: Information Age Publishing.

Bajaj, M. (2015a). Human rights education: Imaginative possibilities for creating change. *Teacher College Record, 117*, 1–9.

Bajaj, M. (2015b). "Pedagogies of resistance" and critical peace education praxis. *Journal of Peace Education, 12*(2), 154–166. doi:10.1080/17400201.2014.991914

Bar-Tal, D., & Rosen, Y. (2009). Peace education in societies involved in intractable conflicts: Direct and indirect models. *Review of Educational Research, 79*(2), 557–575. doi:10.3102/0034654308330969

Becker, A. L. (1988). Language in particular: A lecture. In D. Tannen (Ed.), *Linguistics in context* (pp. 17-35). Norwood, NJ: Ablex.

Becker, A. L. (1991). Language and languaging. *Language & Communication, 11*(1/2), 33-35.

Cann, C. N. (2012). Harvesting social change: a peace education program in three acts. *Journal of Peace Education, 9*(3), 211–223. doi:10.1080/17400201.2012.668493

Center for Applied Linguistics. (2011). *Directory of foreign language immersion programs in U.S. schools*. Retrieved from http://webapp.cal.org/Immersion/

Crystal, D. (2004, May). *Creating a world of language*. Paper presented at the 10th Linguapax Congress, Barcelona, Spain.

Crystal, D. (2008). *A dictionary of linguistics and phonetics*. Malden, MA: Blackwell.

Danesh, H. B. (2006). Towards an integrative theory of peace education. *Journal of Peace, 3*(1), 55–78. doi:10.1080/17400200500532151

Friedrich, P. (2007). English for peace: Toward a framework of peace sociolinguistics. *World Englishes, 26*(1), 72–83. https://doi.org/10.1111/j.1467-971X.2007.00489.x

Friedrich, P. (2013). Teaching language for peace. In C. A. Chapelle (Ed.), *The encyclopedia of applied linguistics*. Malden, MA: Blackwell. doi:10.1002/9781405198431.wbeal1163

Freire, P. (1970). *Pedagogy of the oppressed (30th Anniversary ed.)*. New York, NY: Continuum.

Galtung, J. (1964). A structural theory of aggression. *Journal of Peace Research, 1*(2), 95–119. doi:10.1177/002234336400100203

García, O. (2009). *Bilingual education in the 21st century: A global perspective.* Malden, MA: Wiley-Blackwell.

García, O. (2011). Educating New York's bilingual children: constructing a future from the past. *International Journal of Bilingual Education and Bilingualism, 14*(2), 133-153. doi:10.1080/13670050.2010.539670

Giroux, H. (1983). *Theory and resistance in education: A pedagogy for the opposition.* Westport, CT: Bergin & Garvey.

Gomes de Matos, F. (2000). Harmonizing and humanizing political discourse : The contribution of peace linguists. P*eace and Conflict: Journal of Peace Psychology, 6*(4), 339–344.

Kachru, B. B. (1986). The power and politics of English. *World Englishes, 5*(2), 121–140.

Kubota, R., & Miller, E. R. (2017). Re-examining and re-envisioning criticality in language studies: Theories and praxis. *Critical Inquiry in Language Studies, 14*(2-3), 129-157. doi:10.1080/15427587.2017.1290500

Kruger, F. (2012). The role of TESOL in educating for peace. *Journal of Peace Education, 9*(1), 17–30.

Lombardo, L. X., & Polonko, K. A. (2015). Peace education and childhood. *Journal of Peace Education, 12*(2), 182–203.

Morgan, B., & Vandrick, S. (2009). Imagining a peace curriculum: What second-language education brings to the table. *Peace & Change, 34*(4), 510–533.

O'Connor, M. C., & Michaels, S. (1993). Aligning academic task and participation status through revoicing: Analysis of a classroom discourse strategy. *Anthropology & Education Quarterly, 24*(4), 318-335.

O'Connor, M. C., & Michaels, S. (1996). Shifting participant frameworks: Orchestrating thinking practices in group discussion. In D. Hicks (Ed.). *Child discourse and social learning* (pp. 63-102). Cambridge, UK: Cambridge University Press.

Olowo, O. O. (2016). Effects of integrating peace education in the Nigeria education system. *Journal of Education and Practice, 7*(18), 9–14.

Salomon, G. (2004). Does peace education make a difference in the context of an intractable conflict? *Peace and Conflict: Journal of Peace Psychology, 10*(3), 257–274.

Southern Poverty Law Center. (2016). After election day: *The Trump effect: The impact of the 2016 presidential election on our nation's schools* [PDF]. Retrieved from https://www.splcenter.org/20161128/trump-effect-impact-2016-presidential-election-our-nations-schools

U.S. Department of Education, National Center for Education Statistics. (2017). *The condition of education 2017* (NCES 2017-144). Retrieved from https://nces.ed.gov/fastfacts/display.asp?id=16

Wenden, A. L. (2007). Educating for a critically literate civil society: Incorporating the linguistic perspective into peace education. *Journal of Peace Education, 4*(2), 163–180. doi:10.1080/17400200701523561

Wenden, A. L. (2014). Raising the bar for peace and sustainability educators: an educational response to the implementation gap. *Journal of Peace Education, 11*(3), 334–351. https://doi.org/10.1080/17400201.2014.954360

Notes

1. All names and places are pseudonyms.
2. Documentation and/or legal citizenship status of participants was not directly solicited by the researchers; rather, participants and the researchers had conversations more broadly about any fears or feelings students had as refugee or immigrant status.

CHAPTER 13

THE ROLE OF LANGUAGE IN THE WESTERN SAHARA CONFLICT BETWEEN ALGERIA AND MOROCCO

Kamal Belmihoub

Introduction

Algeria and Morocco have been embroiled in a conflict over the Western Sahara territory (see Figure 13.1 for territory's geographical location). The Polisario Front, a group fighting for the Western Sahara's independence from Morocco, engages in political efforts to gain independence. Algeria supports the Polisario, while Morocco accuses Algeria, which is home to a great deal of Saharan refugees, of interference in its internal affairs. Algeria claims that peoples, such as those of the Western Sahara, have the right for self-determination through a fair referendum. The potential of a referendum as a solution is, however, hampered by controversies surrounding its oversight and organization. In this context of conflict, English is employed as a weapon to communicate a political agenda to an international audience. This chapter sheds light on the job English does in government-backed online news written about the Western Sahara. Specifically, I examine the stance of journalists over the conflict to highlight the role of English as a weapon undermining peace. I also describe an alternative stance to such destructive discourse found in the language of UN resolutions about the conflict.

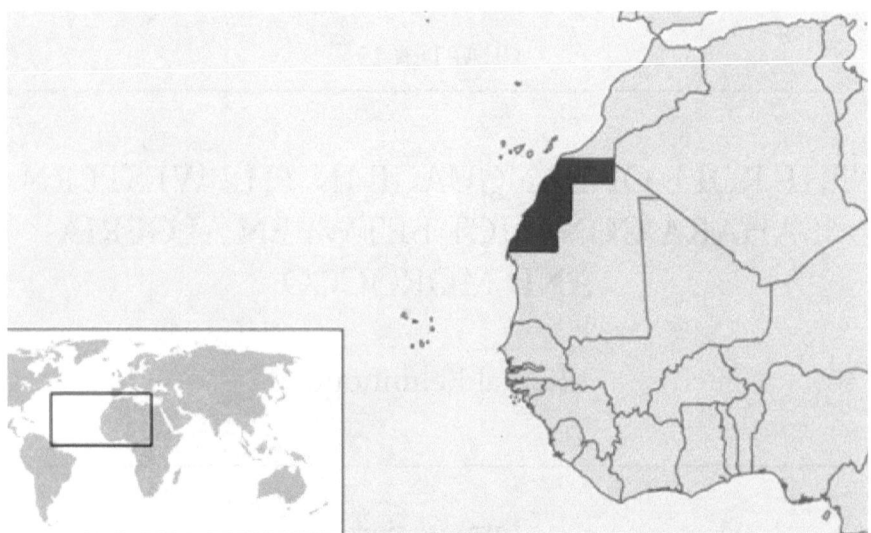

Figure 13.1 Map of the Western Sahara territory, in North Africa.

Motivation for the Study

This exploratory and interpretive descriptive study is motivated by various factors, including understanding the global sociopolitical roles of English (Friedrich, 2007). Analysis of online news texts reveals attitudes that English users, in this case Algerian and Moroccan journalists, have towards each other and their respective neighbors. The sociopolitical analysis of a conflict that continues to undermine unity among the highly culturally similar countries of the Maghreb highlights how language could contribute, possibly unconsciously, to the discord. In the same vein, another motive is understanding the potential of language use at the international level to foster peace instead of conflict (Friedrich, 2007). As Friedrich (2007) argues, peace can be fostered with and through language, and thus studying and understanding how language could undermine peace is important. Friedrich and de Matos (2016) add that:

> It is easy enough to observe that languages can sadly be employed as instruments of harm; a person can, for example, hurt with the words they choose or yet segregate and exclude those who share a different linguistic background. Thus, it seems intuitive to

us that we need to tip the scale in the opposite direction by reinforcing instead those humanizing uses of language, which help boost respect for human dignity and social inclusion. (p. 2)

Revealing how language is unnecessarily used to polarize in the context of the Western Saharan conflict highlights how language, used thoughtfully, could contribute to respect and improved relations between parties involved in the conflict. The chapter, as a result, puts forth alternative humanizing language that could be used, instead, to facilitate communication between the parties involved.

Examining how English is used in official online news in Algeria and Morocco highlights how English is used to communicate ideas on a regional issue to a global audience. As such, it fulfills a need for understanding the global role of expanding world Englishes in an effort to fill a gap identified in Berns (2005). The gap is that research on the Expanding Circle of world Englishes has been rare, especially in comparison to interest in the Inner and Outer Circles. The Middle East and North Africa region is particularly underrepresented in the research on world Englishes. This chapter focuses on two countries in the North Africa region.

Similar Corpus-Based Discourse Studies

This exploratory study builds on a great deal of previous corpus-based research that has been carried out on attitudes and ideologies in newspapers. Baker et al. (2008), for example, mix quantitative corpus analysis with qualitative critical discourse analysis in order to study the representation of refugees and immigrants in different kinds of newspapers in the UK. In addition, Freake, Gentil, and Sheyholislami (2011) used an English-French bilingual corpus, whereby texts from the public's description of their own views on Quebec, nationhood, and belonging, were investigated to demonstrate the role of language in building national identity. This study is a pioneer in utilizing a bilingual corpus and a Corpus Assisted Discourse Study approach. Tabassum et al. (2013) maintain that the media are influential in creating group identities. They conducted a discourse analysis of how a division between "We" and "They" can be detrimental in fostering division between groups. Similarly, according to Healy and Haberman (2015), Donald Trump, when running for US president used a great deal of "We" and "Them" to divide segments of white America on the one hand, and Mexicans and Muslims on the other.

Theoretical Framework

I employ a descriptive narrative approach to discuss the role of international journalistic language in conflict, particularly the Western Sahara conflict, using a bilingual English-French corpus and a Corpus Assisted Discourse Study (CADS) approach. A CADS framework merges insights from critical discourse analysis and corpus linguistics. This approach assists in understanding how language, through corpus linguistic tools such as frequency counts and Mutual Information (MI) scores, could foster conflict instead of helping to solve it. The critical discourse analysis component of the approach allows an investigation of the larger context, making sense of the corpus analysis results. Combining corpus tools with discourse analysis (CADS) has recently gained traction (Partington and Marchi, in press), heavily relying upon Halliday's view of language as "doing some job in some context" (as cited in Partington and Marchi, in press).

I chose to utilize a CADS approach for two main reasons. First, examining a large volume of authentic language highlights patterns of use. While these patterns are interesting for linguists in and of themselves, describing the impact of these patterns of language choices on a sociopolitical level is valuable to a larger audience. For example, attention to language features through corpus-based analysis might reveal a regular occurrence of terms with a negative connotation. Further analysis could demonstrate that the terms are used in connection to a phenomenon, a country, an entity, or a person, which is when the patterns could become meaningful in understanding how the language is used to convey meaning in particular contexts.

A useful concept utilized in this chapter is that of semantic prosody, also known as sentiment analysis. According to Hunston and Thompson (2000), semantic prosody refers to "the speaker or writer's attitude or stance towards, viewpoint or feeling about the entities and propositions that he or she is talking about" (as cited in Partington, 2004, p. 131). In other words, language users, when utilizing certain lexical items that carry built-in favorable or unfavorable evaluation, also carry these evaluations, whether they openly admit it or not. One technique used in this is to identify collocates of a given country and analyze their inherent evaluative meaning. Such a technique is not new as it is used in a study on the Arab Spring, whereby names of countries were searched in order to look at their immediate context for evaluative terms (as cited in Partington and Marchi, in press). An additional conceptual tool that could assist in the quest to identify any negative language conducive to conflict and explore its alternatives is discussed by LeBlanc (2016): "It is descriptiveness that makes it possible to create a space of openness. However, if the observation is clouded with language that is evaluative or judgmental, instead of being open to a conversation, the listener may become defensive" (p. 55). These tools are used in this chapter to explore the potential of language in the Algerian, Moroccan, and Western Saharan context to maintain conflict, and potential alternatives to such destructive language use.

This framework is implemented in this chapter by examining to what extent language employed by Algerian and Moroccan journalists is simply descriptive or clouded by judgment. That is, I describe the extent to which quarrelling Algerian and Moroccan journalists can be defensive. I also provide a selection of examples to illustrate descriptive language, from a UN corpus of diplomatic texts (University of Cambridge Faculty of Law, 2016), to contrast it with the judgmental language used in the corpus of government journalists with an agenda to promote about the conflict. The CADS framework and semantic prosody respectively provide a lens through which I examine patterns of language use and their evaluative meaning in context.

Corpus Building Process

News articles are selected from two different websites. Each website represents one of two countries in the Maghreb region. *Algeria Press Service (APS)* is Algeria's official news agency and *Maghreb Arab Press (MAP)* is Morocco's official news agency. The two countries stand out as two significant rivals in North Africa, preventing a linguistic, cultural, political, and economic union. The *MAP* articles are accessed through *Morocco World News (MWN)*, a supposedly independent website that publishes many of its articles in cooperation with *MAP*. *APS* is Algeria's government voice and unequivocally acknowledges this as they do not claim to be an independent journalistic voice. News texts from Reuters are also used to provide a neutral reference point.

Several factors are taken into account throughout the corpus design process to ensure trustworthiness. I added a subcorpus of French texts, comparing how English and French are used differently. Also, I collected a convenience sample of texts published during a three-month period (January-March 2015). The scope of the corpus is limited to this period due to the unusual flurry of news about the conflict at the time and to maintain a manageable consistent data set. Results in this chapter are employed for illustrative purposes only and future research could build a larger corpus for robust generalizable results. A small corpus of about 40,000 words was created to analyze the peace and humanizing potential of language, in this case English used for international communication. 40,000 words is the number of words published during the three-month period. Each news article written in English is short, approximately ranging between 200-300 words. Some of the articles written in French in the *APS* subcorpus tend to be longer and more detailed. All news articles are about the Western Sahara conflict.

Building the corpus involves visiting the page on each of the three websites that is dedicated to the Western Sahara issue. Starting from the uppermost articles at the top of the webpage, and the most recently published in the above-mentioned time period, I open, copy, and paste each one onto a .txt document including the title of the news article. This file format (i.e., .txt) is selected due to its compatibility with the concordance software utilized for the study. Files are then named, for example, "English Morocco," specifying the name of the country that published an article and the language of publication. These files are then uploaded to the concordance software called AntConc and analyzed.

Lexical items, specifically collocates of the terms "Algeria" and "Morocco" are examined for evaluative (positive, negative, or neutral) stance to reveal attitudes and ideologies about the Western Sahara issue. Pronouns and various collocates are examined in the texts (Tapia & Biber, 2014). Keyword analysis is carried out as well using the AntConc concordance software. The collocates feature on AntConc is utilized to allow for an analysis of collocations that can shed light on Algerians' attitudes toward Moroccans and vice versa, and attitudes toward various claims. Concordances and the larger context are reviewed for any patterns of words that reoccur (Partington & Marchi, in press). In other words, once collocates of "Algeria" and "Morocco" were identified, I qualitatively isolated terms with unfavorable semantic prosody based on how these terms were used in the concordance line, or within the context of the rest of the news article. Partington's definition of semantic prosody was used to aid in this qualitative analysis. Frequencies of "Algeria" in the Moroccan texts and "Morocco" in the Algerian texts were examined and interpreted in light of the nature of the conflict and what drives each country's views and ideologies. MI scores, also known as log likelihood, were examined. Lexical items with an MI score and a frequency of more than three is considered enough to be included in the results. The threshold of three is a commonly used benchmark (Staples, personal communication).

Using the semantic prosody framework, I include each collocate that has a frequency and MI score higher than the threshold of three. Both the frequency and MI scores are used to ensure that a certain term occurs enough times to be meaningful and at the same time it is associated more often with a particular collocate than another. Ideally, words with unfavorable prosody would not exist in news articles that claim freedom from bias. Thus, it is deemed essential to highlight these lexical items with an unfavorable prosody to illustrate patterns of biased language. The analysis of collocates of Algeria and Morocco were followed by a KWIC analysis to determine whether the collocates of the two countries are used negatively. Then, once these collocates of Algeria and Morocco in the three subcorpora are identified, a look at the concordance lines, and even the larger context is necessary in order to ensure that the word's semantic prosody actually reflects an unfavorable stance by the journalist toward the Other. In fact, a second coder has examined several collocates, and there was a 100-percent agreement that they indicate an unfavorable semantic prosody. A KWIC analysis is also used to examine some of the instances of "We" and "They," possibly revealing the use of these terms to divide between various sides of the conflict. This particular aspect of the study, which explored potential divisive language use, is qualitative since I did not rely on how often are the terms used, but simply how they are used to divide or not to divide. This data collection process is intended to identify examples of negative language use between two divided and conflicting parties and suggest examples of descriptive language use as an alternative to bridge the gap in communication using English as an international language.

Findings: Negative Language Use and a Proposed Alternative

In this section, the results of the collocate analysis of the terms Algeria and Morocco in the Algerian, Moroccan, UN, and Reuters subcorpora are presented, respectively.

Collocate Analysis: Collocates of Algeria in the Moroccan and Reuters Subcorpora

Table 13.1 below demonstrates that Moroccan journalists employ negative language toward Algerians, but Reuters do not. After the table's summary of findings, I elaborate on the results with extended excerpts from the corpus to highlight the negative tone in the journalists' voice. The excerpts are intended to contextualize the quantitative information in the tables.

Table 13.1
Examples of Lexical Items with Unfavorable Semantic Prosody, Their MI Scores, and Their Frequency Counts[1]

Subcorpus	Collocates of ALGERIA	Frequency	MI Score
APS	Not applicable	Not applicable	Not applicable
MAP and MWN	Schemes Reject Obstruct Blames Occupied Separatist/separatists Embezzled, embezzling, embezzle/ embezzlement Fraudulent	1 1 1 1 1 2 4/3 1	7.83 7.83 7.83 7.83 6.83 6.83 6.83/4.20 5.50
Reuters	No unfavorable collocates found	0	0

In the Moroccan *MAP* and *MWN*, the term *embezzlement* occurs thirty-seven times within the entire corpus, and three times within close range, that is within five words, to *Algeria*. Algeria rejects the accusation that they and the Polisario Front abuse/embezzle humanitarian aid, but the Moroccan press insists that embezzlement of international humanitarian aid by Algerian and Polisario official is rampant. In the Moroccan subcorpora of *MAP* and *MWN*, additional lexical items collocating with Algeria include *schemes, reject, obstruct, blames, occupied, separatist/separatists, embezzled/ embezzling/embezzle/embezzlement, fraudulent*. The MI score numbers range from 7.83 for *schemes* to 5.50 for *fraudulent. Occupied* is used, not in relation to the Western Sahara, but the Algerian Tindouf province, which Morocco believes to be theirs. As far as *separatist(s)*, it is employed when referring to Algeria's support of the Polisario Front, which governs the Western Sahara. *Embezzle* and *embezzlement* occur extremely frequently for a small corpus; the frequency is 40 times, and the MI score is 4.20. The following example demonstrates the deluge of unfavorable negative terms used to refer to Algeria and the Polisario Front, including *embezzle*:

The Moroccan diplomat pointed to the violation of UN resolutions by the Polisario and its mentor, Algeria, who continue to obstruct the conduct of a census of the population held in these camps so that they continue inflating the numbers to take advantage of international humanitarian aid that they embezzle. (MAP/MWN subcorpus)

In the Reuters subcorpus, terms such as *hurt* and *damaged* collocate with Algeria, but they are used to refer to Moroccan-Algerian relations and not Algeria alone. There do not seem to be any lexical items with negative evaluative prosody associated with "Algeria." In order to illustrate this finding is an example from the Reuters subcorpus: "Western Sahara has also drawn scrutiny as European and US authorities worry that *damaged* relations between Morocco and Algeria could hurt cooperation against Islamist militants who are active across the Maghreb." *Concern* is another item that occurs, but a closer look at the context shows that the African Union Commission chairwoman is concerned about *Morocco's* exploitation of natural resources in the Western Sahara, as can be seen here: "Zuma also expressed concern about the 'illegal exploitation of Western Sahara's natural resources.'"

Collocate Analysis: Collocates of Morocco in the Algerian and Reuters Subcorpora

Table 13.2 showcases how Algerian journalists also employ negative language toward Morocco. Unlike the tone of Reuters' journalists toward Algeria, this international news agency has a slightly negative tone toward Morocco despite efforts to report objectively.

Table 13.2
Examples of Lexical Items with Unfavorable Semantic Prosody, Their MI scores, and Their Frequency Counts

Subcorpus	Collocates of MOROCCO	Frequency	MI Score
APS	Victims Undermine Stall Recalcitrant Intimidation/ intimidations Torture Abuses Occupation/Occupied	4 2 1 1 3 5 1 3	7.76 7.35 7.35 7.35 7.35/6.35 6.35 6.35 3.95/4.54
MAP and MWN	Not applicable	Not applicable	Not applicable
Reuters	*Reluctant* *Pushes* *Pressuring* *Dismissed* *Counterproductive* *Controlled* *Annexed* *Violations*	1 1 2 2 1 2 2 3	6.20 6.20 6.20 6.62 6.20 6.20 6.20 5.79

In the Algerian English subcorpus, "Morocco" collocates with lexical items such as *victims, undermine, stall, recalcitrant, intimidation/intimidations, torture, abuses,* and *occupation. Occupation,* for instance, is a term that highly collocates with Morocco. It is worth noting here that this term is spelled the same but pronounced different in English and French, occurring a total of 23 times in both subcorpora, with an MI score of 5.53. The term does have the same meaning in both languages. An example in context of how this term is used is:

> Morocco's *occupation* is sustained through insidiously subduing the Saharawi people and their legitimate claims, said the Sahrawi official, underlining the daily human rights abuses, like arbitrary detention, torture, military trials for civilians, and restrictions on freedoms of movement and association. (APS English subcorpus)

Although some of the previous terms do not meet the criteria of having a higher than three frequency and MI score, I included them for two reasons. First, at least one of the scores is over three. Second, they are meaningful from a qualitative perspective, in that they reinforce how English terms are used negatively to convey how a certain side of the conflict is wrong and evil. The MI score of these items, indicating that they are likely to collocate with "Morocco," ranges between 7.76 for *victims* to 6.36 for *abuses*. "Victims" occurs a total of three times, meeting the threshold for significance. In the Algerian French *APS* subcorpus, *trompeuse* (liar) is a lexical item that is highly likely to co-occur with "Morocco;" its MI score is 8.08. *Provocatrice* (provocateur) and most frequently *occupé/occupation* collocate with "Morocco." Specifically, an example from the APS subcorpus to illustrate the use of the negative term *victim* is: "Nongovernmental human rights organisations [sic] (NGO) expressed their concern about the intimidations exerted in Morocco against torture *victims*." Looking at the larger discourse, beyond the term *victims* itself, it can be observed that there is a deluge of lexical items reflecting a negative stance by the Algerian journalists toward Morocco, including *intimidations*.

Collocates of Morocco in the Reuters subcorpus also reflect an unfavorable stance toward the country. Examples include *dismissed, counterproductive, controlled, annexed,* and *violations*. The latter occurred three times and its MI score is 5.79. It is worth noting that, upon closer examination, *violations* is employed as part of a quote or another entity accusing Morocco of these violations. The term occurs four times, with an MI score of 5.79. Reuters, thus, provides an example of possibly descriptive, judgment-free, reporting on the conflict. The following is an example to illustrate how this word reflects a negative stance by the user toward Morocco. Whether Reuters reporting this quote is an indication of their own bias or not is not clear.

> While Ban did not say it directly, U.N. officials and diplomats say that he would like the U.N. mission in Western Sahara to take on monitoring human rights violations in the territory, but Morocco, backed by France, has vigorously resisted the idea. (Reuters subcorpus)

Reuters itself does not seem to directly refer to Moroccan violations. The term *counterproductive* is also used in quotes in relation to Morocco's stance towards U.N. Human Rights Monitoring. One such example is the original quote in which the term is used: "'...For years France has enabled Morocco's counterproductive allergy to U.N. rights monitoring,' HRW's U.N. Director Philippe Bolopion wrote." This is yet another example of Reuters maintaining a level of distance from direct judgmental language. While choosing to report the quote might be interpreted as a biased move, it is not as strongly biased as directly referring to Moroccans as counterproductive.

While Reuters tend to maintain a larger distance from language use that reflects direct attacks, they do make choices at time to utilize terms with a negative prosody. In fact, the lexical item that is most likely to collocate with Morocco is *dismissed*; its MI score is 6.20, and it occurs twice in association with Morocco. *Controlled* is another example of one of the lexical items that Reuters uses. It is used four times, and the MI score is 6.20. Here is a context to illustrate it: "Morocco has *controlled* most of the Western Sahara since 1975...." The use of this item suggests that Reuters's stance about the issue is unfavorable towards Morocco.

Divisive Language: We and Them/They

To better understand how language can reflect divisive attitudes and conscious/unconscious bias, I review how the pronouns "We" and "They" are used in each subcorpus. The use of such pronouns could reveal that language is used by these government sites to create distance between the Maghreb countries instead of moving closer toward a resolution of the Western Sahara conflict. In the Algeria subcorpus "We" occurs four times, while it occurs seven times in the Moroccan subcorpus. It should be mentioned here that the Moroccan English subcorpus is larger than the Algerian one, but the aforementioned frequencies are from a three-month period, ensuring more or less a trustworthy comparability between the frequencies. In addition, these frequencies were normed to 100, and the result is .01 and .17 for "We" in the Algerian and Moroccan subcorpora respectively. Concerning "They," it occurs only twice (.005) when normed to 100 in the Algerian subcorpus, while it occurs six times (normed frequency: .015) in the Moroccan subcorpus. It is essential to note here that the previously-mentioned frequencies of "We" and "They" may not all be intended to be divisive and confrontational, but they provide insight into the subconscious attitudes of the press towards the other. An instance that illustrates such divisive attitudes between the two Maghreb countries is: "'At the same time, *we* are firm concerning the preservation of Morocco's territorial unity since this principle is non-negotiable like Morocco's sovereignty,' he said."

Another example, this time using "They" is: "*Ils* ont dénoncé ceux qui instrumentalisent cette polémique infondée pour priver les réfugiés sahraouis d'une aide humanitaire vitale…" ("They denounced those who exploit this unfounded controversy to deprive the Saharawi refugees of vital humanitarian aid…"). Various entities referred to in the Moroccan subcorpus, thus, seem to rely more on the division between "We" and "They" than Algeria during the three-month period in the English subcorpus. In the Algerian French subcorpus, both "We" and "They" are used twelve times each. Entities and individuals included in the Algerian subcorpus are, thus, not any less prone to divisive language.

Different Uses of English and French by Algeria and Morocco
Constructing this small corpus, although spanning only a three-month period, has revealed that Algeria seems to rely much more heavily on the French language to disseminate its views to a wider international audience than does Morocco. As shown in Figure 13.2, Algeria's French *APS* subcorpus is the largest. In the meantime, *Morocco World News* and *MAP* have published only *one* article in this three-month period in French. In addition, a closer analysis of the news articles' content demonstrates that those published in French by the Algerian press are longer and more detailed than those in English.

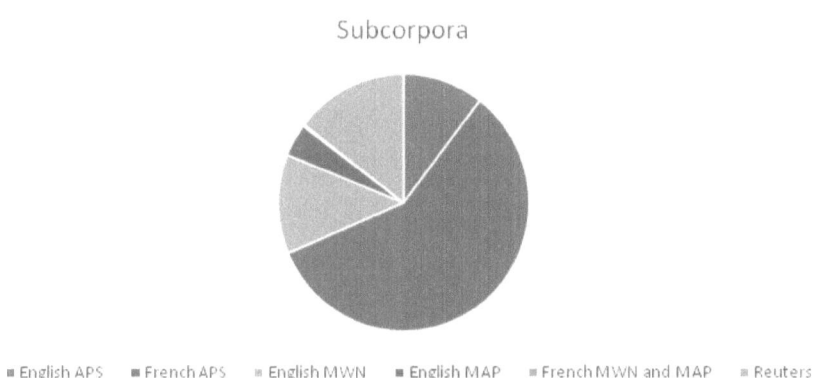

Figure 13.2 Proportion of texts for each language and news site.

UN Use of English over the Western Sahara Conflict

Alternatively, examining a non-journalistic source of language on the Western Sahara conflict adds a new dimension to the results. A small UN corpus was examined since this is an organization most interested in peace and is also involved in attempts to mediate between Algeria and Morocco to resolve the conflict. Analyzing language used in UN documents to discuss the conflict, descriptive language is favored over evaluative language with a negative prosody. I use this section as I have in previous ones, not to make generalizable claims, but simply to provide examples of neutral language that could serve as an alternative to the highly judgmental examples presented earlier in the chapter. Systematic research with a large corpus could be conducted in the future to elaborate on how a UN model of linguistic choices could be a model for dialogic communication for conflict-resolution in contexts of international communication.

As can be noticed in the italicized lexical items in the bulleted sentences below, the UN demonstrates how language could be used to discuss a conflict neutrally, without the negative evaluative language discussed earlier in the chapter.

- "So that a referendum may be organized without military constraints, Morocco *undertakes* to effect an appropriate, substantial and phased reduction of its troops in Western Sahara."

- "The neighbouring countries, Algeria and Mauritania, will do their utmost to *ensure* that the transitional arrangements and the results of the referendum are respected."
- "In this regard, the Governments of Algeria and Mauritania have *indicated their readiness to co-operate* with the Special Representative."

Notice the difference in the first sentence if, instead of "undertakes," the writer chose the verb "schemes." The latter word choice may suggest a malicious attempt to reduce troops for some ulterior motive. Due to fear and bias, Algerian and Moroccan journalists tend to deploy negative linguistic choices that reflect fear of the unknown. A UN-like approach that prioritizes the positive actions of the other party in the conflict could be more conducive to peaceful international communication. More research is essential to develop our understanding of the role of language in similar contexts of conflict and polarized communication as in the Western Sahara conflict.

Discussion

The above findings appear to illustrate how both Algeria and Morocco carry negative attitudes toward each other in their press coverage. The semantic prosody of terms associated with these two countries seems to reveal this negative stance as defined by Partington (2004). In addition, Algeria seems to rely much more on French, while Morocco on English to publish about the issue of the Western Sahara, at least during the three-month period examined in this study. Finally, the two Maghreb countries seem to sometimes use the pronouns "We" and "They" in a way that fosters division rather than bring the parties involved closer to a solution for the conflict.

Morocco World News (2015) claim that they "always strive for balance and freedom from bias." However, the above findings seem to suggest otherwise. That is, analysis of patterns of language use expose negative attitudesheld toward Algeria, the Polisario Front and entities that do not align with Morocco's official position on the Western Sahara conflict. *MWN* indicate in their "About Us" page that they "always guard against putting the reporter's opinion in a news story." However, the semantic prosody analysis of lexical items associated with Algeria in Moroccan texts unveiledhighly biased language. The *Algerian Press Service* and *Maghreb Arab Press*, the official press agencies, express a commitment to public service and providing quality information, but do not go as far as the *MWN* site in terms of expressing freedom from bias. In fact, Algeria goes a step further and describes the historical background tying the press agency to the government, implicitly acknowledging bias. Findings in this chapter have shown that *MWN's* "About Us" page claims to not align with their language choices in published news articles.

The wide gap between Morocco and Algeria in terms of their reliance on French could be explained by their differing colonial histories (Belmihoub, 2018; Benrabah, 1999). French is much more entrenched in Algeria. Algeria was a French department, an integral part of France, for 130 years. Morocco was only a protectorate of France, meaning that Moroccans had more autonomy than Algerians. Morocco could rely more on English because it is essential for its tourism industry. Tourism is Morocco's best asset for its economy. Algeria on the other hand has plenty of oil and gas and may not need English for the survival of its people. Also, Algeria went through a Black Decade, a civil war during which up to 200,000 people died. While Algeria was experiencing this dark period, Morocco was strengthening ties with the British Council and US academic and cultural programs. Algeria has only recently engaged more actively with the British Council and the US Department of State (Belmihoub, 2018; Benrabah, 1999). The different roles English and French seem to be playing in Algeria and Morocco contribute to Berns (2005) call for a more comprehensive sociolinguistic profile of English in the Expanding Circle.

It can be observed from the uses of the pronouns "We" and "They," that the Algerian and Moroccan press does not seem to see eye to eye. Although the presence of "They" and "We" does not necessarily imply group division, the aforementioned two cross-linguistic examples show the negative use of pronouns and the unfavorable semantic prosody of lexical items following them. Tabassum et al. (2013) found similar results in Pakistan, supporting the tendency of the polarized press in the two contexts to be divisive over conflicts.

The results above also have implications for Peace Sociolinguistics, a concept discussed by Friedrich (2007):

> a discipline engaged in investigating the place of peace through language in society, with the main charge of looking into peace (within and among languages), violence, education, activism, and the sociopolitical impact of language use on comprehensive peace and vice versa. (p. 76)

The above results support the notion that English and French on the Algerian side are not used by Moroccan and Algerian journalists to foster peace. The UN, however, does use descriptive language that could be modeled by anyone communicating about the conflict among the Algerian and Moroccan media.

These results demonstrate that Algeria and Morocco are still entangled in the Western Sahara conflict. In addition, the above results indicate that there is a need for peace-fostering education, especially among journalists in the Maghreb regions. Journalists could be educated on the impact of the language they use in maintaining an ongoing conflict rather than neutrally reporting or engaging in activist reporting that facilitates dialogue and understanding rather than division. Further, readers of the news sites should be aware of how language reflects biases in order not to be misled.

Conclusion

Regarding what might collocations reveal about the stance and attitude of the news agencies' writers on the issue of the Western Sahara, it is found that while Algerian and Moroccan journalists are biased against each other, Reuters seems to be slightly biased against Morocco only. In terms of the use of divisive pronouns "We" and "They," journalists from both countries engage in this divisive language in both English and, in the Algerian subcorpus, French. Regarding how English and French might be used differently, it is found that Morocco relies heavily on English, while Algeria relies more on French to share their views with the world on the conflict. The UN is shown to have used neutral language or language with a positive semantic prosody, modeling the kind of tone Algerian and Moroccan journalists could model to foster humanizing and respectful language that is conducive to peace.

The narrative in this chapter has also set out to raise awareness of the role English plays in international contexts. Berns's (2005) call for research on the functions of English in such underrepresented contexts as North Africa has been addressed by highlighting the sociopolitical role of English in communicating conflict stances to international audiences. This study is hoped to increase awareness of possible divisive functions of language, and urges curriculum developers in English and journalism schools to embrace linguistic peace education. It also calls for further corpus-based research on language use in conflict and peace studies.

References
Algeria Press Service. (2015). Sahrawi cause. Retrieved from http://www.aps.dz/en/world/tag/Sahrawi%20cause
Baker, P., Gabrielatos, C., Khosravinik, M., Krzyżanowski, M., McEnery, T., & Wodak, R. (2008). A useful methodological synergy? Combining critical discourse analysis and corpus linguistics to examine discourses of refugees and asylum seekers in the UK press. *Discourse & Society, 19*(3), 273-306. doi:https://doi.org/10.1177/0957926508088962
Belmihoub K. (2018). English in a multilingual Algeria. *World Englishes, 37*(2), 207-227. https://doi.org/10.1111/weng.12294
Benrabah, M. (1999). Langue et pouvoir en Algérie [Language and power in Algeria]. Paris, France: Séguier.
Berns, M. (2005). Expanding on the Expanding Circle: Where do WE go from here? *World Englishes, 24*(1), 85-93. https://doi.org/10.1111/j.0883-2919.2005.00389.x
Freake, R., Gentil, G., & Sheyholislami, J. (2011). A bilingual corpus-assisted discourse study of the construction of nationhood and belonging in Quebec. *Discourse & Society, 22*(1), 21-47. doi:abs/10.1177/0957926510382842
Friedrich, P. (2007). English for peace: Toward a framework of Peace Sociolinguistics. *World Englishes, 26*(1), 72-83. 10.1111/j.1467-971X.2007.00489.x
Friedrich, P., & de Matos, F. G. (Eds.). (2016). *English for diplomatic purposes*. Bristol, UK: Multilingual Matters.
LeBlanc, J. (2016). Compassionate English communication for diplomatic purposes. In P. Friedrich (Ed.), *English for diplomatic purposes* (pp. 42-74). Bristol, UK: Multilingual Matters.
Morocco World News. (2015a). Sahara issue. Retrieved from http://www.moroccoworldnews.com/category/sahara-issue/
Morocco World News. (2015b). About us. Retrieved from https://www.

moroccoworldnews.com/about-us/

Partington, A., & Marchi, A. (in press). Using corpora in discourse analysis.

Partington, A. (2004). "Utterly content in each other's company:" Semantic prosody and semantic preference. *International journal of corpus linguistics, 9*(1), 131-156. doi:10.1075/ijcl.9.1.07par

Tabassum, M., Shah, S. K., & Bilal, M. (2013). A critical discourse analysis of the left and right wing ideologies in Pakistani English newspaper editorials. *Journal of Education and Practice, 4*(13), 72-78.

Tapia, A. M., & Biber, D. (2014). Lexico-grammatical stance in Spanish news reportage: Socio-political influences on que-complement clauses and adverbials in Ecuadorian broadsheets. *Revista Española de Lingüística Aplicada, 27*(1), 208-237.doi:org/10.1075/resla.27.1.09gat

University of Cambridge Faculty of Law. (2016, December 7). Language of peace database launched at the United Nations. Retrieved from https://www.law.cam.ac.uk/press/news/2016/12/language-peace-database-launched-united-nations

Notes
1. A threshold of 3 Mutual Information score must be met for a term to be considered associated with ALGERIA or MOROCCO.

CHAPTER 14

WAGING WAR IN THE LANGUAGE OF PEACE:
The Use of Esperanto as the "Aggressor Language" by the U.S. Army

Timothy Reagan

Esperanto, by far the most successful of the international auxiliary language projects,[1] was created in the late 19th century by Ludwik Zamenhof not only as a way of facilitating communication between individuals and groups with different languages, but also as a means of fostering international harmony and brotherhood (see Duličenko, 1988; Eco, 1994; Garvía, 2015, pp. 103-111; Janton, 1993, pp. 35-37). Esperanto today has a significant number of speakers (estimates generally range from around 100,000 to perhaps 2,000,000),[2] most of whom share the language creator's commitment to peace and brotherhood (Forster, 1982; Large, 1985; Lins, 2000). Thus, it is somewhat ironic that one of the more interesting applications of Esperanto was its use in the 1950s and 1960s by the U.S. Army in training exercises, in which it functioned as the language of the enemy, identified only as the "Aggressor" (and hence making Esperanto the "aggressor language"; see Okrent, 2013; U.S. Department of the Army, 1962). In this chapter, we will briefly explore the creation of Esperanto, as well as its linguistic and extralinguistic aspects before examining this seemingly inappropriate historical case of Esperanto's use as a military "aggressor language."

The Creation of Esperanto

The necessity for speakers of different languages to communicate across linguistic boundaries has been with us, at the very least, for millennia. Most often, one group adopts the language of the other group, a *lingua franca* is used, or a pidgin language (which may or may not then develop into a creole language) emerges. We know, for instance, that Akkadian and later Aramaic were used widely throughout western Asia long after they had become largely extinct as daily vernacular languages (Beyer, 1986; Oppenheim, 2013); later, Latin and Koiné Greek were used throughout the Mediterranean world for centuries (see Adams, 2003; Horrocks, 2010). In the 17th and 18th centuries, there were a number of Enlightenment-inspired efforts to create artificial languages, initially for primarily philosophical rather than linguistic purposes,[3] and later, as attempts to resolve the social and political barriers created, or at least exacerbated, by linguistic diversity (see Eco, 1994; Janton, 1993, pp. 1-18). In 1990, Aleksandr Dulichenko identified some 900 international auxiliary languages, and by 2009, Detlev Blanke suggested that the number had risen to more than 1,000 efforts, which indicates the extent and continuing popularity of such projects (for a list of selected invented languages, see Table 14.1).[4]

Table 14.1
Selected Invented Languages

Selected Invented Languages		
Language	Creator	Date of Creation
Ars Signorum	Delgarno	1661
Universal Language	Newton	1661
Panglottie	Comenius	1665
Arte Combinatoria	Leibniz	1666
Ruski Jezik	Križanić	1666
Philosophical Language	Wilkins	1668
Lingua Filosofica Universale	Gigli	1818
Lingua Slavica Universalis	Herkel	1826
Langue Universelle	Grosselin	1836
Lengua Universal	Martinez	1852
Universal Language	Edmonds	1855
Volapük	Schleyer	1879
Néo-Latine	Courtonne	1884

Pasilingua	Steiner	1885
Nal Bino	Verheggen	1886
Balta	Dormoy	1887
Bopal	Streiff (de Max)	1887
Esperanto	Zamenhof	1887
Nuvo-Volapük	Kerchoffs	1887
Weltsprache	Eichhorn	1887
Lingua Franca Nova	Bernhard	1888
Spelin	Bauer	1888
Anglo-Franca	Henderson	1889
Nov Latin	Rosa	1890
Pure Saxon English	Molee	1890
Idiome Universel	Marini	1891
Dil	Lyakide	1893
Novilatiin	Beermann	1895
Veltparl	Nilson	1897
Idiom Neutral	Rosenberger	1902
Reform-Latein	Frölich	1902
Tutonish	Molee	1902
Latino Sine Flexione	Peano	1903
Antido I	De Saussure	1907
Ido	Beaufront and Couturat	1907
Weltdeutsch	Ostwald	1916
Glot	Pevich	1917
Interglossa	Hogben	1943
Mondial	Heimer	1943
Loglan	Brown	1960
Inglish (Basic English Improved)	Le Bretton	1972
Klingon	Okrand	1984
Láadan	Elgin	1984

By the nineteenth century, the second sort of undertaking had become the norm, and in the last quarter of the 19th century the first international auxiliary language to catch the attention of the public was Volapük (Garvía, 2015, pp. 21-33; Golden, 1997; Okrent, 2009, pp. 105-107). Volapük, proposed by Fr. Johann Martin Schleyer in 1879,[5] had within a decade held three conventions dedicated to the language (held in Friedrichshafen, Munich, and Paris). There were an estimated 283 Volapük clubs, 25 Volapük periodicals, more than three hundred Volapük textbooks, an Academy of Volapük, and claims that there were some 1,000,000 speakers of Volapük (Baugh & Cable, 2002). And yet, within only a few years, the entire Volapük movement was in disarray, with a rival Academy established and a large number of derived languages, such as Balta, Bopal, Dil, Idiom Neutral, Langu Universelle, Nal Bino, Obra, Spelin, Veltparl and Volapük Nulik, created and, for the most part, fairly quickly forgotten (Eco, 1994, p. 266).[6] Although there continue to be extremely small numbers of users of Volapük—Paul LaFarge estimated about 20 speakers of the language in 2000—it is essentially an interesting footnote in the history of international auxiliary languages.[7] The commitment to an effective auxiliary language remained, though, and the field was open for an alternative to Volapük, which soon emerged in the form of Esperanto.

Zamenhof, a Polish-Jewish ophthalmologist, first published the outline of Esperanto (originally called *la lingvo internacia*, the international language) in 1887 under the pseudonym "Dr. Esperanto" ("one who hopes"; Garvía, 2015, p. 65; Janton, 1993, pp. 41-43).[8] *The Unua libro* ("First Book", as it was later called), was initially published in Russian (as *Международный языкъ: Предисловіе и полный учебникъ*), and was quickly translated into Polish, French, and German, followed in the following year with English, Hebrew, and Yiddish versions (García, 2015, p. 65). This short, 40-page booklet was inspired by Zamenhof's own life experiences. Having grown up in Białystok, a multilingual, multiethnic, and multireligious city in what was then Russian-occupied Poland, Zamenhof had witnessed firsthand the tensions and conflicts between the Poles, Germans, Jews, and Russians who lived in Białystok. As he explained in a letter to his friend Nikolai Borovko,

> The place where I was born and spent my childhood gave the direction to all my future endeavors. In Białystok, the population consisted of four diverse elements: Russians, Poles, Germans and Jews; each spoke a different language and was hostile to the other

elements. In this town, more than anywhere else, an impressionable nature feels the heavy burden of linguistic differences and is convinced, at every step, that the diversity of languages is the only, or at least the main cause, that separates the human family and divides it into conflicting groups. I was brought up as an idealist; I was taught that all men were brothers, and meanwhile, in the street, in the square, everything at every step made me feel that men did not exist, only Russians, Poles, Germans, Jews and so on. This was always a great torment to my infant mind, although many people may smile at such an 'anguish for the world' in a child. Since, at that time, it seemed to me that grown-ups were omnipotent, I kept telling myself that, when I was grown up, I would certainly destroy this evil. (Zamenhof, 1948, vol. 1, pp. 343-344)

Zamenhof further noted that, "In such a town [one] feels more acutely than elsewhere the misery caused by language division and sees at every step that the diversity of languages is the first, or at least the most influential, basis for the separation of the human family into groups of enemies" (Zamenhof & Korjenkov, 2006, p. 33). His solution to the conflict between ethnic, national, and linguistic groups was the creation of a language that would be politically and ethnically "neutral"—that is, which would be "supranational" in the sense that it could be a common second language for speakers of other languages (Duličenko, 1988; Eco, 1994; Nuessel, 2000; Sikosek, 2006).[9] Such a language, Zamenhof believed, would need to be relatively easy to learn, and hence extremely regular morphosyntactically (Auld, 1988; Gledhill, 2000; Wells, 1978). The language which he created, Esperanto, did for the most part meet these standards, and while it does remain the most successful of the international auxiliary language projects (Duličenko, 1988; Garvía, 2015, pp. 159-164; Nuessel, 2000), it never fully met the expectations of either Zamenhof himself or most of its earliest advocates.

The Linguistic Characteristics of Esperanto

In terms of its structure, Esperanto is both remarkably simple and quite sophisticated—and it is both at the same time (see Kalocsay & Waringhien, 1985; Wells, 1978, pp. 15-26; Wood, 1987). The core of Esperanto grammar is provided in Zamenhof's "Sixteen Rules," which provide a basic scaffolding for the language (Janton, 1993, pp. 43-44). In a nutshell, Zamenhof's goal was to produce a language in which pronunciation, grammar, and orthography were absolutely regular, and while this is not completely true of Esperanto, the language is nevertheless remarkably regular.[10]

The phonology of Esperanto is the least studied aspect of the linguistics of Esperanto. One of the "Sixteen Rules" addresses the phonology of the language, albeit in somewhat informal terms: Rule 9 is that "every word is read aloud as it is written." As van Oostendorp (1999) notes,

> If we translate [this rule] into the terminology of modern phonology, we could say that phonological elements do not alternate or get deleted: the orthographic representation gives us underlying structure and surface structure at the same time. Underlying vowels and consonants stay the way they are in every phonological context. The rule (if seen as a rule guiding language planning, rather than a descriptive device) therefore had as an effect that Esperanto does not have any interesting phonological alternations. Its morphology is completely agglutinative: there is no allomorphy, no fusion, and there are no assimilation or dissimilation rules. We sometimes find some discussion in the literature . . . whether or not allophonic variation is permissible; e.g., whether or not (n) can be pronounced as a velar nasal in a word like *banko* 'bank'. Most of the discussion concerning this issue is prescriptive, rather than descriptive or theoretical, in nature. (p. 52)

In Esperanto, there are five vowels and two semivowels (which combine with vowels to produce six dipthongs), and 23 consonants (see Tables 14.2 and 14.3).

Table 14.2
Esperanto Consonants

		Bila-bial	Labio-Dental	Dent-al	Post-Alveo-lar	Palat-al	Velar	Glot-tal
Stop	Voiceless	/p/					/k/	
	Voiced	/b/					/g/	
Affri-cate	Voiceless				/tʃ/			
	Voiced				/dʒ/			
Frica-tive	Voiceless		/f/	/ts/	/ʃ/		/x/	/h/
	Voiced		/v/		/ʒ/			
Laterals					/l/			
Nasals		/m/		/n/				

| Ulvular Roll | | | | /r/ | | | |
| Semi-Vowels | /w/ | | | | /j/ | | |

Table 14.3
Esperanto Vowels

Esperanto Vowels		
	Front	Back
Close	i	u
Mid	ɛ	ɔ
Open	a	

Esperanto does have a variety of consonant clusters, which appear in forms up to three in initial positions (*strategio* "strategy", *splisi* "to splice") and up to four in medial positions (*instruisto* "teacher"). In final positions, consonant clusters do appear, but far less commonly (*cent* "hundred"). Focusing on the basic properties of the syllable in Esperanto, van Oostendorp (1999) observes that,

> The Esperanto syllable structure is of course very similar to that of Indo-European languages, more in particular to that of Romance and Germanic languages. This is not surprising, given the fact that most of the morphemes are borrowed from these languages. On the other hand, there is no system which has exactly the same system as Esperanto. The phonology of Italian comes close, but also this is still different. From a phonological point of view, Esperanto is an autonomous system. (p. 77)

The core vocabulary of Esperanto—900 root words—is defined by *Lingvo internacia*, published by Zamenhof in 1887. It appears to be largely Romance in nature, although there are also significant lexical contributions from Russian, German, Yiddish, and English.[11] In terms of its lexicon, Esperanto relies to a significant extent on a regular and extremely productive derivational morphology, based on a core group of radical stems (e.g., -*libr*-, -*patr*-, -*lingv*-, and so on; Eco, 1994, p. 328). Perhaps without realizing it himself, Zamenhof created a skeletal structure for Esperanto which allowed a complex set of morphological processes that makes it a far more agglutinative language than English (Jansen, 2016).[12] For example, one of the more intriguing aspects of Esperanto can be found in its use of affixes by adding various prefixes and suffixes, a huge vocabulary can be created from a remarkably small lexical base. For instance, using the base word patro ("father"), one can construct:

pat*rin*o	mother
*ge*patro*j*	parents
patr*ar*o	a group of fathers
patr*arin*o	a group of mothers
*ge*patr*ar*o	a group of parents
*gebo*patro*j*	in-laws
*bo*patro	father-in-law
*bo*patr*in*o	mother-in-law
*eksgebo*patro*j*	ex-in-laws
***eksbo**patro*	ex-father-in-law
***eksbo**patrino*	ex-mother-in-law

This productivity can be seen at least as powerfully in the case of verbs (see Nuessel, 2000, p. 46):

trinki	to drink
trink*igi*	to cause to drink
*ek*trinki	to begin to drink
trink*iĝi*	to be drunk[13]
trink*adi*	to continue to drink
*ek*trink*igi*	to cause (someone) to begin to drink
trink*iĝigi*	to make (someone) drink
trink*igadi*	to continue to cause to drink
trink*adigi*	to make (someone) continue to drink
trink*iĝadi*	to keep drinking

To be sure, this is something of an extreme example, and although all of these forms are certainly grammatically correct in Esperanto, many would not be commonly used by Esperantists. As Humphrey Tonkin has noted, "such transformations can be extended grammatically as far as we have lexemes to extend them; they are limited only by semantics and the ability of the audience to decode them. In practice, then, several of these combinations are rare" (Janton, 1993, p. 138).

Esperanto has a single definite article (la). All nouns in the singular end in –o, and all adjectives end in –a; the plural is formed by adding –j. There is also an objective case for nouns and adjectives, indicated by a terminal –n.

libro	book, a book (e.g., *La bona libro estas sur la tablo.* "The good book is on the table.")
libron	book, a book (e.g., *Mi havas bonan libron.* "I have a good book.")
libroj	books (e.g., *La bonaj libroj estas sur la tablo.* "The good books are on the table.")
librojn	books (e.g., *Vi aĉetis du bonajn librojn.* "You bought two good books.")

Adjectives end in –a, and agree with nouns (e.g., la *ruĝa aŭto* "the red car", *la belaj floroj* "the pretty flowers"), and adverbs end in –e (*rapide* "quickly"). Personal pronouns in Esperanto are very straightforward for an English speaker, as can be seen in Table 14.4. Finally, verbs are not conjugated by person, and differentiate tense and mood as follows:

Mi parolas	I speak, I am speaking
Mi parolis	I spoke, I was speaking
Mi parolos	I will speak
Mi parolus	I would speak
Parolu!	Speak!
paroli	to speak

Table 14.4
Esperanto Personal Pronouns

Esperanto Personal Pronouns			
		Singular	Plural
First Person		mi	ni
Second Person		vi	vi
Third Person	Masculine	li	ili
	Feminine	ŝi	ili
	Neuter/Epicene	ĝi	ili
Indefinite		oni	oni
Reflexive		si	si

Although the "Sixteen Rules" are certainly basic to the language, they provide an incomplete description of the grammar of the language (Nuessel, 2000, p. 24), as Janton (1993) has explained:

> Fundamental though they may be, these rules alone cannot describe the language adequately. Esperanto cannot be reduced to such a skeletal structure: like all living languages, it has its own complex autonomy. Accordingly, we must apply to it the same methods of investigation as we would use for any living language. (p. 44)

Indeed, although Esperanto has not been a major focus of contemporary linguistics, it is still the case that a great deal of quite good linguistic research has been conducted on the language, and that work continues in a number of fairly cutting-edge aspects of contemporary linguistics on Esperanto (see Dasgupta, 1989; Gledhill, 2000; Hana, 1998; Jansen, 2007, 2013, 2016; Kalocsay & Waringhien, 1985; Wells, 1978; Wennergren, 2005).

The Extralinguistic Characteristics of Esperanto

The language that Zamenhof created, although by no means succeeding in its broad objective of becoming a shared universal language, nevertheless survived and even, to some extent, thrived over the course of the twentieth century—in spite of becoming a target for suspicion and even oppression in many societies, most notably in Nazi Germany and in the USSR under Stalin.[14]

Although it is indeed difficult, if not impossible, to estimate the number of speakers of Esperanto, it is considerably easier to observe its status and use in the contemporary world. As Richardson (1988) notes,

> Taken worldwide, Esperanto movement these days is a far-flung but close-knit network of mostly independent bodies. Local, national, and international organizations, as well as specialized societies, book and magazine publishers, and even a few special-interest groups work side-by-side to further the language and its usefulness. Among these disparate bodies there is considerable cooperation, but little hegemony: rarely does one group have any real authority over another. (p. 45)

The Esperanto movement is united in part by the *Universala Esperanto-Asocio* ("Universal Esperanto Association"), as well as by various local and national organizations. There is a wide array of publications (books, journals, magazines, and newspapers) available in Esperanto, including both translated materials and original publications written in Esperanto (see Sutton, 2008). There are annual World Esperanto Congresses, as well as a voluntary travel service, the *Delegita Servo*, and speciality organizations representing religious groups, sports groups, cultural groups, and so on. In short, there is a well-established and effectively functioning international Esperanto speech community (although perhaps it may be more accurate to call it a "speech network"). Esperanto, as already noted, has been the focus of a good deal of linguistic research in recent years, and this has especially been true, not surprisingly, with respect to the growing work in the area of interlinguistics especially in the area of interlinguistics (see Blanke, 1985, 2003, 2006; Duličenko, 1988, 1989; Fettes, 2001, 2003; Fiedler, 2008; Jansen, 2007, 2008; Pool & Fettes, 1998; Schubert, 1989; Sikosek, 2006; Tonkin, 1997; Tonkin & Fettes, 1996).

The *Esperanto-movado*, a phrase that refers both to the formal and informal aspects of the Esperanto community, has at its core a commitment to and belief in the efficacy and value of Esperanto itself—called la interna ideo (the "Internal Idea;" Janton, 1993, pp. 34-37). More than this, *la iterna ideo* distinguishes between those who wish to use Esperanto for utilitarian or practical purposes, and those who are willing to work "to create a neutral foundation on which the various ethnic groups might communicate with one another in peace and brotherhood, without forcing on one another their ethnic differences" (Zamenhof, 1929, pp. 378-379).

In addition to the commitment to *la interna ideo*, there are a number of other typically shared features of the Esperanto community that are relevant here. Although it is a clearly articulated principle in the Esperanto community that the language should be politically unbiased (Auld, 1988; Foster, 1982; Janton, 1993, p. 34), at the same time the webpage of EsperantoUSA[15] notes that, "People who speak Esperanto are internationally minded, concerned about social justice and peace, and are helping to preserve linguistic diversity" (http://esperanto-usa.org/)—an accurate generalization, in my experience, but one that also suggests that the Esperanto speaker community is in general somewhat less than politically neutral on many issues.

Esperanto as the "Aggressor Language"

In the midst of the Cold War, in the 1940s, 1950s and 1960s, the U.S. Army engaged in a number of different activities to ensure military readiness. One way in which this was accomplished was in the creation and execution of extensive, realistic training exercises in which two groups of U.S. soldiers—one representing the United States, or home army, and the other identified only as the forces of the "aggressor." Such exercises were, and continue to be, known as "military training simulations" (Page & Smith, 1998). The characteristics of the aggressor army were worked out in considerable and realistic detail, and the soldiers assigned to serve in the aggressor army were required to wear special uniforms and insignia, carry appropriate false identity papers, and engage in war exercises that targeted the occupation of parts of the United States. Toward this end, the U.S. Army produced maps of "aggressor campaigns" (see Figure 14.1), as well as both manuals on the aggressor army and its strategies and on its language (FM 30-101), the "aggressor language" (FM 30-101-1; see Figures 14.2 and 14.3), and photographs were taken of aggressor soldiers (see Figure 14.4).

Figure 14.1 Map of 'Aggressor Campaigns', 1946-1949.
Licensed under Public Domain Mark 1.0

Figure 14.2 Field Manual, Aggressor: The Maneuver Enemy.
Licensed under Public Domain Mark 1.0

Figure 14.3 Field Manual, Esperanto: The Aggressor Language.
Licensed under Public Domain Mark 1.0

Figure 14.4 Field Manual of Aggressor Language.
Licensed under Public Domain Mark 1.0

The language selected by the Army to serve as the language of the aggressor army was Esperanto. In spite of its long affiliation with pacifism and neutrality, Esperanto was nevertheless an ideal choice for the Army's use: it was "a living and current media of international and oral communication" with a well-developed lexicon, it was regular and easy to learn, and, as a non-national language, it was "consistent with the neutral or international identified implied by Aggressor" (Okrent, 2013). Its use would offend no one, since (unlike Russian, French, Spanish, etc.) it had no national ties, and it had the further advantage that since it already existed, creating such a neutral language from the ground up was not necessary. In short, as Korzhenkov (2009) has explained, "After World War II, the United States Army, looking for a language to represent the enemy in military manoeuvers, settled on Esperanto, of all languages, to avoid offending anyone else. Thus, for a brief time, Esperanto became, in Army parlance, 'the aggressor language'" (p. iii).

This did not mean that there was no work to be done on Esperanto to prepare the language for military use, however. In order to ensure that the vocabulary was suitable for military means, a number of new lexical items were added (see Table 14.5).

Table 14.5
Created Esperanto Military Terminology

Created Esperanto Military Terminology	
Esperanto Neologism	**English Translation**
bombardaproksimigo	bombing run
kirasportilo	armored carrier
larma gaso	tear gas
linĉi	lynch
malabeo	insubordination
mortigi	kill
pafpovo	fire power
pikegi	stab
pikipdrato	barbed wire
pugnobati	punch
senresalta pafilo	recoilless rifle
ŝtrafi	strafe
sufoki	choke
torturi	torture
tranĉo	slash
veneni	poison

Selected both because it would offend no one, as Kozhenkov (2009) noted, and because of its relative ease of acquisition for military personnel in the field, Esperanto nevertheless ultimately failed to serve the goals of the Army. The experiment of using Esperanto as the "aggressor language" ended in the 1970s, not because of any objections from Esperantists, but for the far simpler reason that in spite of its relative ease of acquisition, it still took too long to learn to be useful in such military exercises. As Okrent noted, "the Army removed Esperanto from its field manual in the 1970s because it took too long to learn to be practical" (2013).

Conclusion

Peace education is increasingly recognized both as one of the great challenges and as a fundamental need of the twenty-first century. It is, at its heart, basically a challenge to violence, as Harris and Morrison (2003) have noted:

> Violence in our world may be seen in its various forms from domestic abuse to militarism, which has been defined as "the result of a process whereby military values, ideology and patterns of behavior achieve a dominating influence over the political, social, economic and foreign affairs of the state." Militarism comes from values, opinions and social organizations which support war and violence as legitimate ways to manage human affairs. Military traditions ... are deeply rooted in minds throughout the world and contribute to a global predicament ... where political elites use military means to protect their privileges. (pp. 9-10)

The contrast between peace education and militarism (and, by extension, the potential use of military force) is often presented as oppositional in nature, and of course this is appropriate to a significant extent. At the same time, not all military actions, undertakings or organizations are inherently or necessarily in conflict with the goals of peace education—the military often provide essential humanitarian support in response to natural disasters, for instance. The case of the use of Esperanto by the U.S. Army is an interesting one, in part because it provides us with an extremely powerful example of how what might seem on first sight to be a positive undertaking (the use of the "language of peace") can be subverted to accomplish quite different—and even contradictory—aims and goals.

References

Adams, J. N. (2003). *Bilingualism and the Latin language*. Cambridge, UK: Cambridge University Press.

Auld, W. (1988). *La fenomeno Esperanto* [The Esperanto phenomenon]. Rotterdam, Netherlands: Universala Esperanto-Asocio.

Baugh, A., & Cable, T. (2002). *A history of the English language* (5th ed.). Upper Saddle River, NJ: Prentice Hall.

Bergen, B. (2001). Nativization processes in L1 Esperanto. *Journal of Child Language, 28*(3), 575-595. https://doi.org/10.1017/S0305000901004779

Beyer, K. (1986). *The Aramaic language, its distribution and subdivisions.* Göttingen, Germany: Vandenhoeck & Ruprecht.

Blanke, D. (1985). *Internationale plansprachen. Eine einführung* [International Planned Languages. An Introduction]. Berlin, Germany: Sammlung Akademie-Verlag.

Blanke, D. (2003). *Interlinguistic und Esperantologie* [Interlinguistics and Esperantology]. (Esperanto-Dokumente 7). Bamberg, Germany: Deutscher Esperanto-Bund e.V., Geschäftsstelle.

Blanke, D. (2006). *Interlinguistische Beiträge: Zum Wesen und zur Funktion internationaler Plansprachen* [Interlinguistic contributions: On the creation and function of international planned languages]. Frankfurt am Main, Germany: Peter Lang.

Blanke, D. (2009). Causes of the relative success of Esperanto. *Language Problems and Language Planning, 33*(3), 251-266. https://doi.org/10.1075/lplp.33.3.04bla

Dasgupta, P. (1989). Degree words in Esperanto and categories in Universal Grammar. In K. Schubert (Ed.), *Interlinguistics: Aspects of the science of planned languages* (pp. 231-247). Berlin, Germany: Mouton de Gruyter.

Dillon, E. (1907). The Esperanto movement in Russia. T*he North American Review, 185(*617), 403-409.

Duličenko, A. (1988). Proyekty vseobshchikh i mezhdunarodnykh yazykov [Projects of international and universal languages]. Interlinguistica Tartuensis, *5*, 126-162.

Dulučenko, A. (1989). Interlingvstika: Snshchnost' i problemy [Interlinguistics: Essence and problems]. *Interlinguistica Tartuensis, 6*, 18-42.

Dulučenko, A. (1990). *Mezhdunarodnyye vspomogatel'nyye yazyki* [International auxiliary languages]. Tallinn, Estonia: Valgus.

Eco, U. (1994). *La serĉado de la perfekta lingvo* [The search for the perfect language]. Pisa, Italy: Edistudio.

Edwards, J. (1993). Esperanto as an international research context. In I. Richmond (Ed.), *Aspects of internationalism: Language and culture* (pp. 21-34). Lanham, MD: University Press of America.

Fettes, M. (2001). Les géostratégies de l'interlingualisme [The geostrategies of interlinguistics]. *Terminogramme, 99/100*, 35-46.

Fettes, M. (2003). Interlingualism: A world-centric approach to language policy and planning. In H. Tonkin and T. Reagan (Eds.), *Language in the twenty-first century* (pp. 47-58). Amsterdam, Netherlands: John Benjamins.

Fiedler, S. (2008) Interlingvistiko/esperantologio kiel fako en universitatuj: Spertoj el Leipzig [Interlinguistics/Esperantologies as a specialty in universities: Experiences from Leipzig]. *Informilo por Interlingvistoj, 65*, 2-25.

Fiedler, S. (2012). The Esperanto *denaskulo*: The status of the native speaker of Esperanto within and beyond the planned language community. *Language Problems and Language Planning, 36*(1), 69-84. https://doi.org/10.1075/lplp.36.1.04fie

Forster, P. (1982). *The Esperanto movement*. The Hague, Netherlands: Mouton.

Garvía, R. (2015). *Esperanto and its rivals: The struggle for an international language*. Philadelphia, PA: University of Pennsylvania Press.

Gledhill, C. (2000). *The grammar of Esperanto: A corpus-based description* (2nd ed.). Munich, Germany: Lincoln Europa.

Gold, D. (1980). Towards a study of possible Yiddish and Hebrew influence on Esperanto. In I. Szerdahelyi (Ed.), *Miscellanea interlinguistica* (pp. 300-367). Budapest, Hungary: Tankönyvkiadó.

Gold, D. (1982). Pli pri judaj aspektoj de Esperanto [More on the Jewish aspects of Esperanto]. *Planlingvistiko, 1*, 7-14.

Golden, B. (1997). Conservation of the heritage of Volapük. In H. Tonkin (Ed.), *Esperanto, interlinguistics, and planned languages* (183-189). Lanham, MD: University Press of America.

Hana, J. (1998). *Two-level morphology of Esperanto* (Unpublished master's thesis). Charles University, Prague, Czech Republic.

Harris, I., & Morrison, M. L. (2002). *Peace education* (2nd ed.). Jefferson, NC: McFarland & Co.

Hilfsbuch, A., & Linderfelt, K. (1887). *Volapuk: An easy method of acquiring the universal language constructed by Johann Martin Schleyer*. Milwaukee, WI: C. N. Casper & H. H. Zahn.

Horrocks, G. (2010). *Greek: A history of the language and its speakers* (2nd ed.). Oxford, UK: Wiley-Blackwell.

Jansen, W. (2007). *Woordvolgorde in het Esperanto* [Word-order in Esperanto]. Utrecht: Netherlands Graduate School of Linguistics.

Jansen, W. (2008). *Inleiding in de Interlinguïstiek* [Introduction to interlinguistics]. Amsterdam, Netherlands: Universiteit van Amsterdam.

Jansen, W. (2013). Esperanto parts of speech in functional discourse grammar. *Linguistics: An Interdisciplinary Journal of the Language Sciences, 51*(3), 611-652. https://doi.org/10.1515/ling-2013-0022

Jansen, W. (2016). Derivation in the lexicon: The case of Esperanto. *Linguistics: An Interdisciplinary Journal of the Language Sciences, 54*(5), 1101-1133. https://doi.org/10.1515/ling-2016-0024

Janton, P. (1993). *Esperanto: Language, literature, and community*. Edited by H. Tonnkin, trans. by H. Tonkin, J. Edwards and K. Weiner-Johnson. Albany: State University of New York.

Kalocsay, K., & Waringhien, G. (1985). *Plena analiza gramatiko de Esperanto* [Complete analytic grammar of Esperanto] (5a ed.). Rotterdam, Netherlands: Universala Esperanto-Asocio.

Kirckkoff, A. (1888). *Volapuk, or, universal language.* London, UK: Swan Sonnenschein & Co.

Knowlson, J. (1975). *Universal language schemes in England and France, 1600-1800.* Toronto, ON: University of Toronto Press.

Kolker, B. (1988). Вклад русского языка в лексику эсперанто [The contribution of the Russian language to the lexicon of Esperanto]. *Interlinguistica Tartuensis, 5,* 74-91.

Korzhenkov, A. (2009). *Zamenhof: The life, works, and ideas of the author of Esperanto.* New York, NY: Mondial.

LaFarge, P. (2000, August). Pük, memory: Why I learned a universal language no one speaks. *The Village Voice.*

Large, A. (1985). *The artificial language movement.* Oxford, UK: Basil Blackwell.

Lindstedt, J. (2006). Native Esperanto as a test case for natural language. *SKY Journal of Linguistics, 19,* 47-55.

Lins, U. (2000). *The work of the Universal Esperanto Association for a more peaceful world.* Rotterdam, Netherlands: Universala Esperanto-Asocio.

Lins, U. (2016). *Dangerous language: Esperanto under Hitler and Stalin.* Bonn, Germany: Palgrave Macmillan.

Lins, U. (2017). *Dangerous language: Esperanto and the decline of Stalinism.* Bonn, Germany: Palgrave Macmillan.

Nuessel, F. (2000). *The Esperanto language.* New York, NY: Legas.

Okrent, A. (2009). *In the land of invented languages: Esperanto rock stars, Klingon poets, Loglan lovers, and the mad dreamers who tried to build a perfect language.* New York, NY: Spiegel & Grau.

Okrent, A. (2013, March 28). How the U.S. made war with the language of peace. *The Week,* 1-10. Retrieved from http://theweek.com/articles/466135/how-made-war-language-peace

Oppenheim, A. L. (2013). *Ancient Mesopotamia: Portrait of a dead civilization.* Chicago, IL: University of Chicago Press.

Page, E., & Smith, R. (1998). Introduction to military training simulation: A guide for discrete event simulations. In D. Medeiros, E. Watson, & J. Carson (Eds.), *Winter Simulation Conference Proceedings,* vol. 1 (pp. 53-60). Washington, DC: Winter Similuation Conference Board of Directors.

Piron, C. (1984). Contribution à l'étude des apports du yidiche à l'espéranto [Contribution to the study of contributions from Yiddish to Esperanto]. *Jewish Language Review, 4,* 15-29.

Piron, C. (1989). Who are the speakers of Esperanto? In K. Schubert (Ed.), *Interlinguistics: Aspects of the science of planned languages* (pp. 157-172). Berlin, Germany: Mouton de Gruyter.

Pool, J., & Fettes, M. (1998). The challenge of interlingualism: A research initiative. *Esperantic Studies, 10*, 1-3.

Richardson, D. (1988). *Esperanto: Learning and using the international language.* Eastsound, WA: Esperanto League for North America.

Rigberg, B. (1966). The efficacy of Tsarist censorship operations, 1894—1917. *Jahrbücher für Geschichte Osteuropas, 3*, 327-346.

Rigberg, B. (1969). Tsarist censorship performance, 1894-1905. *Jahrbücher für Geschichte Osteuropas, 1*, 59-76.

Sadler, V., & Lins, U. (1972). Regardless of frontiers: A case study in linguistic persecution. In S. K. Ghosh (Ed.), *Man, language and society* (pp. 206-215). The Hague: Mouton.

Schubert, K. (Ed.). (1989). *Interlinguistics: Aspects of the science of planned language.* Berlin, Germany: Mouton de Gruyter.

Sikosek, M. (2006). *Die neutrale Sprache: Eine politische Geschiche des Esperanto-Weltbundes* [The neutral language: A political history of the Esperanto world community]. Bydgoszcz, Poland: Skonpres.

Sprague, C. (1888). *Handbook of Volapük.* London, UK: Trübner & Co.

Sutton, G. (2008). *Concise encyclopedia of the original literature of Esperanto.* New York, NY: Mondial.

Tonkin, H. (Ed.). (1997). *Esperanto, interlinguistics, and planned languages.* Lanham, MD: University Press of America.

Tonkin, H., & Fettes, M. (1996). *Esperanto studies: An overview.* (Esperanto documents 43-A). Rotterdam, Netherlands: Universala Esperanto-Asocio.

U.S. Department of the Army. (1962). *Esperanto: The aggressor language.* Washington, DC: Author.

van Oostendorp, M. (1999). Syllable structure in Esperanto as an instantiation of universal phonology. *Esperantologio/Esperanto Studies, 1*, 52-80.

Wells, J. (1978). *Lingvistikaj aspektoj de Esperanto* [Linguistic aspects of Esperanto]. Rotterdam, Netherlands: Universala Esperanto Asocio.

Wennergren, B. (2005). *Plena manlibro de Esperanta gramatiko* [Complete handbook of the Esperanto grammar]. El Cerrito, CA: ELNA.

Wood, R. (1987). The development of standard phonology in Esperanto. In M. Goninaz (Ed.), *Studfoj pri la internacia lingvo* [Studies on the international language] (pp. 58-76). Gent, Netherlands: Aimav.

Zamenhof, L. (1929). *Originala verkaro* [Original work]. Leipzig, Germany: Ferdinand Hirt.

Zamenhof, L. *Leteroj* [Correspondence] (2 vols.). (1948). Paris, France: Sennacieca Asocio tutmonda.

Zamenhof, L. (1963). *Fundamento de Esperanto*. Marmande, France: Esperantaj Francaj Eldonoj.

Zamenhof, L., & Korjenkov, A. (2006). *Mi estas homo: Originalaj verkoj de D-ro L.-L. Zamenhof* [I am a man: Original works of Dr. L. L. Zamenhof]. Kaliningrad, Russia: Sezonoj.

Notes

1. An international auxiliary language (IAL or, sometimes, auxlang or interlanguage) is a language used to facilitate communication between speakers of different languages who do not share any common language. In general, IALs are used as second languages. Although lingua francas have served as IALs, they are problematic in that they embody issues of inequity and dominance (whether economic, political, military, or whatever). In contemporary use, an IAL is intended to function as an interlanguage, while not challenging any speaker's own native language (see Eco, 1994, pp. 276-279; García, 2015, p. 169, n. 5; Janton, 1993, pp. 113-115).

2. Although estimates vary considerably and are exceptionally difficult to evaluate critically, at the start of the twenty-first century, there are very conservatively at least 120,000 fluent speakers of Esperanto in the world (including some 500 to 2,500 native speakers), and hundreds of thousands of others who have at least a passing knowledge of the language (see Nuessel, 2000, p. 24), though Glendhill (2000, p. 10) provides an even lower estimate of 40,000 truly fluent speakers).

3. The philosophical invented languages were not so much concerned with communication as with the classification of ideas (for a detailed history of these efforts, see Knowlson, 1975). As Janton noted, "they constituted coherent systems ordered around sets of fundamental concepts" (1993, pp. 2-3). A further distinction worth mentioning here is that between a *priori* and a *posteriori* languages; the former are "chacterized by largely artificial, non-ethnic word roots, schematic derivation, and fixed word categories," while the latter are simplified ethnic languages, mixed languages using ethnic and non-ethnic roots, and naturalistic languages" (Janton, 1993, pp. 6-7; see also Eco, 1994, pp. 266-267).

4. One common objection to Esperanto is that it does not have any native speakers. Although from the perspective of the *Esperanto-movado*, this would count as one of its virtues, in point of fact it is untrue. There are about 2,000 families around the world today for whom Esperanto is the daily home language (typically, where Esperanto is the only shared language of the parents), and the best estimates are that there are about 1,000 children who are indeed native speakers (*denaskuloj*) of Esperanto (see Bergen, 2001; Fiedler, 2012; Lindstedt, 2006). That said, it still remains the case that all speakers of Esperanto are functionally bilingual.

5. The structure of Volapük was extremely complex for an invented language. It had four cases (nominative, genitive, dative, and accusative), and verbs used morphemes to indicate tense, aspect, voice, person, number, and sometimes the subject's gender (see Hilfsbuch & Linderfelt, 1887; Kirckkoff, 1888; Sprague, 1888).
6. In spite of its structural challenges, the decline of Volapük has been attributed not to any linguistic factors, but rather, to the absolute refusal of Fr. Schleyer to consider any suggestions at all for the modification or improvement of the language. His dogmatism and intolerance led to multiple schisms in the Volapük community, as well as the creation of a fairly substantial number of offshoots of Volapük. It is interesting to note that in the case of Esperanto, Zamenhof took precisely the opposite position, effectively giving up 'ownership' of the language to its growing speaker community.
7. This does not mean to imply that Volapük was not an incredibly important development in the history of international auxiliary languages. Despite its ultimate failure, it demonstrated clearly the willingness of large numbers of people to invest their time and money in such a project, and large numbers of the initial supporters of Volapük ended up becoming Esperantists.
8. The use of a pseudonym by Zamenhof was, at least in part, a response to the power of the censors of the tsarist régime, which viewed "every innovation . . . with suspicion, and every new society, although, of course, it was sanctioned by the Ministry, was watched vigilantly by the police" (Dillon, 1907, p. 403). As a Jew in the Russian Empire, Zamenhof was especially vulnerable to such concerns and pressures.
9. It is interesting to note, however, that in spite of the explicitly articulated concern with matters of linguistic inequality in the Esperanto movement, there is nonetheless a comparable phenomenon within the movement itself. As Jane Edwards has observed, "The fact is, that, given the nature of the Esperanto movement, excellent Esperanto is one of the modes of establishing oneself as a person of importance in the movement . . . In fact, generally speaking, the qualifications for leadership in the Esperanto movement are good Esperanto, a willingness to work for the propagation of the language, and to have no outward signs of being certifiably insane" (1993, p. 29; see also Rigberg, 1966, 1969).
10. Although absolute regularity was intended to characterize Esperanto, over time some changes in the language have become common, and there are in fact a small number of exceptions in common speech. The accusative marker –n is often ignored in speech (except in formulaic expressions such as *Saluton*! and *Dankon* —'hello' and 'thank-you') (see Okrent, 2009, pp. 259-261).
11. In fact, the Esperanto lexicon includes words derived from Romance languages (especially French and Latin), Germanic languages (primarily German, Yiddish and English), Balto-Slavic languages (especially Russian, Serbo-Croatian, and Polish, as well as Lithuanian), Greek, and finally, small numbers of lexical items from Hebrew, Arabic, Japanese, Chinese, and other languages (see Gledhill, 2000, pp. 20-26; Janton, 1993, p. 46). Estimates of the distribution of the lexicon by source language vary somewhat, but it is reasonable to suggest that between 70%

and 75% of the lexical items in Esperanto are Romance in origin, and 10% to 20% are Germanic in origin. For studies of the effect of Jewish languages (specifically, Yiddish and Hebrew) on Esperanto, see Gold (1980, 1982) and Piron (1984); for the effects of Russian on Esperanto, see Kolker (1988).

12. The claim that Esperanto is basically an agglutinative language is argued by Wells (1978, pp. 33-34), though others have argued that this is at best an incomplete description. Gledhill, for instance, argues that Esperanto demonstrates a number of important non-agglutinating linguistic aspects, "including the freedom of word derivation and monomorphism that are reminiscent of isolating languages" (2000, p. 40).

13. 'To be drunk' here refers to a liquid that has been drunk, not to a person who has had too much alcohol (which would require the use of the adjective *ebria*).

14. Esperantists have suffered considerable oppression in a variety of societies, but the two worst cases of this have been in Nazi Germany and in the USSR under Stalin. The powerful negative reaction to Esperantists has been motivated, in large part, by two factors: anti-Semitism and populist nationalism. Zamenoff was Jewish, and a relatively high percentage of Esperantists historically have also been Jewish—thus making it, in the eyes of both the National Socialists and Stalinists a target for oppression. In addition, the very internationalist vision of the Esperanto movement was also seen in both societies as potentially problematic and characteristic of a 'cosmopolitan' outlook (see Lins, 2016, 2017; Piron, 1989; Sadler & Lins, 1972).

15. As noted in the text, in addition to the *Universala Esperanto-Asocio*, in almost every country there is also a national Esperanto organization, and often regional and local organizations. Esperanto-USA is the national organization in the U.S.

INDEX

A

action research xi, 45 61, 64, 72-76, 79-80, 82-85, 88, 93

activism xi, xiv, 45-46, 49-50, 53, 55, 58-59, 108, 288

aggression (aggressive) 73, 78-79, 82, 111-112, 115-118, 121-128, 130, 205, 207-209, 211, 220, 241, 244-245, 268

authentic x, 2-6, 19-22, 139, 197 274

B

bilingual xii, 33, 88, 90, 133, 151-161, 163-166, 168-171, 255-256, 268, 273-274, 289, 306, 311

Bourdieu xi, 23-24, 26-27, 35-39, 41, 43

C

class xii, 9, 24, 27, 31, 34, 38, 41-43, 47-56, 58, 72-77, 81-82, 86, 96, 100, 105, 108, 122, 124, 130, 154, 157, 159-160, 165-166, 168, 174-175, 179-180, 182-183, 188, 227, 249, 252-253, 261

conflict xi-xii, 7, 19-20, 54, 63, 67-69, 71-72, 74, 80-81, 83, 85-88, 90-96, 98-99, 104-105, 107, 109-111, 115-118, 122, 126, 128, 130, 155, 162, 169, 196-198, 205, 208, 211, 213, 221, 238, 241, 244-245, 248-249, 256, 265, 268, 271-278, 282-283, 285-286, 288-289, 295, 306, 329

critical media literacy 133, 135, 138, 143, 148, 150, 329

critical pedagogy 53, 70, 88, 90, 119-120, 129, 155, 159, 170, 241, 243, 245-248, 325, 328

cultural capital xi, 27, 38

culture x-xi, 1-4, 6-7, 12-14, 16, 18-

20, 25, 34, 41-42, 49, 54, 61, 64, 68, 79-80, 87, 90, 92, 109, 120, 130, 148-149, 156-158, 162, 164-166, 169-170, 181-182, 184, 188, 191-193, 212, 225, 228, 239, 242, 260, 264, 266, 307, 324-325, 329
Cummins 158, 170

D

discursive language 209, 212
dual language 151-152, 158, 160, 163, 165, 167-170, 249, 328

E

economic capital 23-24, 27
English as a Foreign Language (EFL) 63-64, 74, 85, 91, 103, 108, 111, 122
English learner 151, 165, 170
equal (equality) 23-24, 27, 34, 66-67, 81, 85, 128, 135, 137, 144, 147, 165, 248-249, 324
equity 57, 70, 117, 129, 155, 163, 165, 168-169, 171, 189, 329

F

feminist (feminism) 138, 175-176, 190, 267
Freire 49, 60, 65, 70, 87, 112-113, 119, 128-130, 135, 144, 148, 155-156, 159-161, 170, 241, 245-246, 248, 256, 267

G

Galtung 7, 20, 67-68, 85, 87, 94-95, 110, 115, 128, 131, 241, 244-245, 268
gender xii, 19-20, 24, 42, 69, 72, 77, 97, 130, 133-134, 137-139, 143-144, 147, 174-175, 180, 188, 312
Giroux 70, 87, 113-114, 117-118, 128, 130, 134, 148, 156, 160, 170, 248, 268
global x, 19, 23-26, 28, 35, 37, 39, 43, 53-54, 59, 64, 90-92, 94-99, 104-106, 108, 110, 147, 153, 167, 195, 246, 268, 272-273, 306, 324

H

habitus xi, 24, 26-28, 35-40, 43
harassment 63, 77, 119, 142-143, 146
hooks 46, 60, 173, 176, 189, 191

I

identity ix, xii, 41-43, 51, 134, 136, 151, 154, 156-159, 162-163, 168, 177-178, 180, 190, 193-194, 236, 243, 255, 257-258, 273, 302, 326, 329-331
interaction 45, 53-54, 108-109, 111, 113-117, 122, 130, 200, 203, 227

K

Kachru 24, 41, 241, 248, 268

L

language learner 27, 113
language learning x, xi, 4-7, 13, 15, 18, 20-22, 24, 26, 28, 30, 34-35, 39-40, 42-43, 46, 61, 79, 81, 157-158, 167, 247, 265, 324, 328-330
languaging 50, 61, 248, 267
lingua franca 23-24, 26, 43, 226, 291, 293

M

media x-xii, 1-2, 4-5, 7, 9, 17-18, 20, 22, 79, 133-139, 142-150, 224, 226-228, 236, 238-240, 242, 249, 254, 262-264, 266, 273, 288, 304, 325-326, 329-330
multilingual (multilingualism) xiii, 168-170, 225, 242, 247, 249, 252, 254-255, 257-262, 264-266, 289, 294, 328-331

N

negative peace 95, 115

P

peace education xii, 2, 5, 21, 46-48, 60-61, 65, 71-72, 81, 86-87, 91, 93, 109-111, 115, 117-118, 120, 155-156, 159, 163-164, 169, 171, 241-245, 247-248, 256-257, 266-269, 289, 306, 308, 329
peace studies xi, 93, 114, 117, 128, 246, 289, 324-325
peacebuilding xi, 63-65, 68-69, 71-72, 77, 80, 83, 85-87, 91-96, 98-99, 103-106, 109-110, 329-330
pedagogy xi, 48-49, 53, 60, 64, 70-71, 75, 82, 86-90, 111-120, 129-130, 136, 142, 145-146, 148-149, 155, 159, 169-171, 190, 241, 243, 245-248, 267-268, 324-326, 329
policy (policies) 5, 24-25, 28, 35, 37, 39-42, 64, 69, 81, 86-88, 90, 96, 105, 147, 151, 154, 168-170, 226, 230, 239, 242, 244-246, 252, 255-256, 258, 265-266, 307, 330
politics xiii, 86, 88, 130, 148-149, 154, 170, 190, 197, 241, 243, 248, 253, 255, 263-264, 266-268
pragmatic(s) x, xiii, 112, 124, 126-131, 195, 197-209, 211-215, 219, 228-232, 234-235, 328-329
praxis 65, 72, 130, 149, 169, 267-268

R

race 12, 16, 24, 51-52, 63, 72, 174-175, 182, 188, 193, 234, 237

S

social capital 24, 27
social justice xiii, 63-67, 69-74, 76, 80, 82-83, 85-90, 93, 109-110, 119-120, 129, 133-134, 137-138, 144-146, 150, 155, 163, 168, 246, 301, 329-330
solutions 26, 59-60, 73, 79-81, 95, 98-99, 118-120, 140, 143, 246

T

teacher candidate 156, 160
teacher training 111-112
teaching xi, 1, 3, 19-20, 22, 24-27, 31, 38, 40-42, 46-48, 54-55, 60-61, 64-66, 70-71, 74-75, 83, 85-90, 93-94, 98, 108-113, 119-120, 122, 127-131, 148-149, 156, 160-162, 191, 246, 249-250, 255, 263, 266, 324-326, 328-331

V

violence x-xi, 1-2, 5-7, 9, 14, 16-18, 20, 27, 37-38, 48, 63-71, 74, 76-77, 79-83, 85, 87, 89-90, 92, 105, 107, 115, 117-119, 123-124, 128, 138-139, 142-144, 147, 166, 183-184, 205, 221, 233, 265, 289, 306

W

war (warfare) xiii, 14, 63, 68, 72, 92, 94-95, 117-119, 128, 155, 192, 195, 197-198, 202-203, 205-213, 215-216, 218-221, 237-238, 247, 287, 291, 302, 304, 306, 309
world Englishes 20, 23, 267-268, 273, 289, 328

ABOUT THE EDITORS

Sai Bhatawadekar, Ph.D., is an Associate Professor of Hindi-Urdu at University of Hawai'i and the Director of the Center for South Asian Studies. Her cross-cultural, interdisciplinary, and creative work spans comparative philosophy and religion, film studies, creative performance based language pedagogy, theater, music, dance, and positive peace studies. On the philosophy front she works on Hegel and Schopenhauer's interpretation of Hinduism, Buddhism, and Islam. She is also currently working on a *Journal of Dharma Studies* special issue on Religion and Ritual: The Poetics and Performance of the Ineffable. In film studies, she has worked on film adaptations of literature in German cinema and also on Bollywood's global orientation. In language pedagogy and program development, after teaching German for a few years, she single-handedly created a Hindi language program and a South Asian initiative at the Ohio State University. At University of Hawai'i she innovates her Hindi-Urdu program with creative project and performance based learning, which includes poetry writing and recital, children's story books, music, theater, and documentary/short film making. These projects have contributed to the National Foreign Language Resource Center's work on Project Based Language Learning. She co-founded her Bollywood dance group—Aaja Nachle Hawaii, which, in addition to free community classes and performances, has done two full concerts of classical, folk, and Bollywood dances at the Honolulu Museum of Art. Sai is currently co-directing a cross-cultural Shakespeare adaptation—A Midsummer Night's Bollywood Dream—for Kennedy Theater Mainstage production in Honolulu. These varied aspects of Sai's work essentially embody the cross-cultural creative movement of Indian philosophy, languages, and art and are being recognized within positive peace studies as a way to build not only diversity and cultural education but also self-esteem, genuine relationships, and happy communities. To that end, she organized a conference titled Pedagogy and Community Building in 2017.

Cuhullan Tsuyoshi McGivern, M.S., is Lecturer of Health and Physical Education at Akita International University in Japan, where he teaches sport, exercise, and health education courses. He is an active member of the Japan Society for the Study of Obesity with his main expertise in exercise science and weight management. His research interests also include LGBT discrimination in amateur and professional sports, and multiracial identity and equality. He has published in the peer-reviewed journal, *Queer Studies in Media and Popular Culture*, and is co-editor of the volume entitled *Queer Voices from the Locker Room*, published by Information Age. He is currently a member of the Board of Directors of the International Society for Language Studies and co-chair of the 2018 ISLS conference in Waterloo.

Erin A. Mikulec, Ph.D., is Associate Professor in the School of Teaching and Learning at Illinois State University. Dr. Mikulec received her Ph.D. in curriculum and instruction with an emphasis in second language acquisition, foreign language education, and TESOL from Purdue University. In spring 2014, Dr. Mikulec was a Fulbright Scholar at the University of Helsinki in Finland, where she studied teacher education and taught English at schools throughout the area. Her research interests include teacher education, international education, and second language studies. She has served as Interim Director of the English Language Institute at Illinois State, and has worked as a Visiting Professor in Japan and Panama. She has been a member of the Board of Directors of the International Society for Language Studies, has served as co-chair of several ISLS conferences, and is currently President-Elect.

Paul Chamness Iida, Ph.D., is currently Professor of English for Academic Purposes in the Faculty of International Liberal Arts at Akita International University in Akita, Japan, where he teaches writing and teacher preparation courses. His research focuses on instructional methods of teaching languages, critical pedagogy and the issues of under-represented youth and teachers in the K-12 setting. He has published many books and peer-reviewed articles in such journals as *Queer Studies in Media and Popular Culture, Teaching and Teacher Education, Journal of Thought, Multicultural Perspectives*, and *Journal of Second Language Teaching and Research*, and was guest editor for a special LGBT issue of the *International Journal of Critical Pedagogy*. He recently completed a term as Immediate-Past President of the International Society for Language Studies, and is co-chair of the upcoming ISLS conference in Hong Kong in June, 2019. He is also editor of *Critical Inquiry in Language Studies*, an international journal published by Taylor & Francis and co-editor of *Research in Queer Studies, Contemporary Issues in Learning Environments*, and *Contemporary Issues in Problem-Based Learning*, three book series published by Information Age in the U.S.

ABOUT THE AUTHORS

Babatunji Adepoju, Ph.D., is a lecturer at the Department of English, University of Lagos, Nigeria. Adepoju's areas of academic interests are Systemic Functional Linguistics, English and Yoruba Phonology, Semiotics, Language Change and Variation, Grammar, Applied Linguistics and Discourse Analysis.

Tamara Anatska, Ph.D., is College Associate Professor at the Center for English Language Programs (CELP) at New Mexico State University. Dr. Anatska's teaching and research are centered around working with adult English language learners from diverse cultural and linguistic backgrounds. Her research primarily focuses on language learning and identity negotiations.

Waheed Adeyimika Bamigbade, Ph.D., is a Lecturer in the Department of English, Obafemi Awolowo University, Ile-Ife, Nigeria. Formerly a visiting Assistant Professor at YELI, Saudi Arabia, Dr Bamigbade's research interests are Systemic Functional Grammar, Pragmatics, and Cultural Linguistics.

Kamal Belmihoub, Ph.D., is a Lecturer and ESL Director in the English Department at Baruch College, City University of New York. He focuses primarily on writing studies and world Englishes in multilingual contexts.

Ana M. Hernández, Ed.D., is Associate Professor and Program Coordinator of Multilingual and Multicultural Education in the School of Education at California State University San Marcos. She is also Director and Principal

Investigator of Project ACCEPT—a US Department of Education National Professional Development grant. Dr. Hernández's research examines instructional practices and cross-cultural equity in dual language education.

Kirk Richard Johnson, M.A., is a professor at Chiba Institute of Technology in Narashino, Japan. His research interests focus on the intersections of peace education, media literacy and second language pedagogy.

Nicole King, M.Ed., is a doctoral student in the Foreign, Second, and Multilingual Language Education Program at the Ohio State University. Her research interests include digital multimodal literacy practices, critical peace education, and systemic functional linguistics in the field of teacher education for multilingual students in the K-12 context.

Chieko Mimura, Ed.D., is Professor of English at Sugino Fashion College in Tokyo, Japan. Dr. Mimura teaches general English and ESP for fashion-major students. Her research focuses primarily on language and identity, and issues related to inequality in language learning as well as in education itself.

Gerrard Mugford, Ph.D., is Senior Lecturer in the Modern Languages Department at the Universidad de Guadalajara, Guadalajara, Mexico. His research centres on second-language pragmatics, with a special focus on politeness and impoliteness, and critical pedagogy in foreign language teaching/learning.

Tim Murphey, Ph.D., has authored or co-authored 17 books: *Song and Music* (OUP 1992), *Teaching in Pursuit of Wow!* (ABEX 2012), and with Zoltan Dornyei, *Group Dynamics in the Classroom* (CUP 2003). He has taught in 17 universities and at 65 is looking for a place to take him until he is 70.

Yecid Ortega is a doctoral candidate in the program of Languages and Literacies & Comparative, International, and Development Education at OISE/University of Toronto. Mr. Ortega's research focuses on critical ethnographic and case study approaches to social justice and peacebuilding in language education (ESL/EFL/TESOL) in international contexts.

About the Authors

Timothy G. Reagan, Ph.D., is Dean of the College of Education and Human Development at the University of Maine in Orono, Maine, USA, where he is also Professor of Education.

Jackie Ridley is a doctoral student in the foreign, second, and multilingual education program at the Ohio State University. Her research focuses on the language and literacy practices of young refugees, an interest born from her experience as an EL teacher in Northeast Ohio and overseas in Thai-Burmese refugee camps.

Brian G. Rubrecht, Ph.D., is a Professor in the English Department of the School of Commerce at Meiji University in Tokyo, Japan. Dr. Rubrecht's research interests include language learning motivation, pronunciation, identity, and cultural aspects that influence the learning and use of foreign languages.

Mia Sosa-Provencio, Ph.D., is an Assistant Professor of Secondary Education in the Department of Teacher Education, Educational Leadership, and Policy at the University of New Mexico. Her research centers culturally relevant Ethics of Care, educational justice, and shaping academically rigorous, culturally rooted schooling spaces for especially marginalized youth of color.

Sabiha Sultana, M.Phil., is Lecturer of Education in the Directorate of Secondary and Higher Education in Dhaka, Bangladesh. Sultana's research interest encompasses first and second language teaching and learning; teacher education and training; developing critical media literacy for social justice; ICT and pedagogical development; and on-line and off-line course development.

Maki Taniguchi, Ph.D., is Assistant Professor in the Faculty of Human Cultures at the University of Shiga Prefecture, Japan. Dr. Taniguchi's research focuses primarily on education for conflict transformation and peacebuilding and issues related to nonviolent actions.

K-C. Nat Turner, Ph.D., is Associate Professor of Language, Literacy, and Culture in the College of Education at University of Massachusetts in

Amherst, USA. Dr. Turner's research focuses primarily on the development of multiliteracies; language and literacy practices of culturally and linguistically diverse urban adolescents; and racial justice/reparations in education.

Esther Hye-min Yoon, M.A., is a Ph.D. student studying Foreign, Second and Multilingual Education and a Graduate Teaching Associate teaching undergraduate academic ESL writing at the Ohio State University in Columbus, OH, USA. Her research interests include minority, multilingual literacies and multilingual/second language composition of underrepresented populations in the US.

Also Available from ISLS!

READINGS IN LANGUAGE STUDIES
VOLUME 1
Language Across Disciplinary Boundaries

Edited by
Miguel Mantero, University of Alabama
Paul Chamness Miller, Akita International University
John L. Watzke, University of Portland

Available at all bookstores and online vendors
ISBN-10: 0977911411
ISBN-13: 9780977911400
Publisher: International Society for Language
Publication date: 2008
Paperback Pages: 652; 35 Chapters
Average Price: $39 Paperback, $55 Hardcover

READINGS IN LANGUAGE STUDIES
VOLUME 2
Language and Power

Edited by
John L. Watzke, University of Portland
Paul Chamness Miller, Akita International University
Miguel Mantero, University of Alabama

Available at all bookstores and online vendors
ISBN-10: 097791142X
ISBN-13: 9780977911424
Publisher: International Society for Language Studies, Inc.
Publication Date: 2010
Paperback Pages: 466; 23 Chapters
Average Price: $45 Paperback, $60 Hardcover

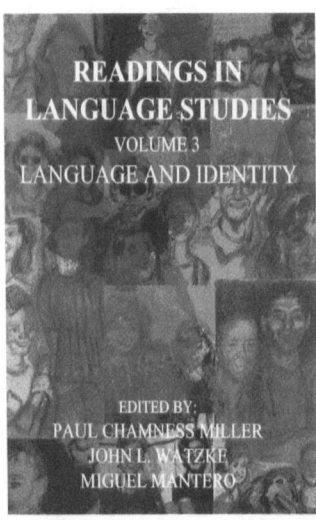

READINGS IN LANGUAGE STUDIES
VOLUME 3
Language and Identity

Edited by
Paul Chamness Miller, Akita International University
John L. Watzke, University of Portland
Miguel Mantero, University of Alabama

Available at all bookstores and online vendors
ISBN-10: 0977911446
ISBN-13: 9780977911448
Publisher: International Society for Language Studies, Inc.
Publication Date: 2012
Paperback Pages: 467; 32 Chapters
Average Price: $50 Paperback, $63 Hardcover

READINGS IN LANGUAGE STUDIES
VOLUME 4
Language and Social Justice

Edited by
Miguel Mantero, University of Alabama
John L. Watzke, University of Portland
Paul Chamness Miller, Akita International University

Available at all bookstores and online vendors
ISBN-10: 0977911462
ISBN-13: 9780977911462
Publisher: International Society for Language Studies, Inc.
Publication Date: 2014
Paperback Pages: 348; 18 Chapters
Average Price: $30 Paperback, $60 Hardcover

READINGS IN LANGUAGE STUDIES
VOLUME 5
Language and Society

Edited by

Paul Chamness Miller, Akita International University
Hidehiro Endo, Akita International University
John L. Watzke, University of Portland
Miguel Mantero, University of Alabama

Available at all bookstores and online vendors
ISBN-10: 0977911497
ISBN-13: 978-0-9779114-9-3
Publisher: International Society for Language Studies, Inc.
Publication Date: 2015
Paperback Pages: 316; 14 Chapters
Average Price: $30 Paperback, $45 Hardcover

READINGS IN LANGUAGE STUDIES
VOLUME 6
A Critical Examination of Language and Community

Edited by

Paul Chamness Miller, Akita International University
Brian Rubrecht, Meiji University
Erin A. Mikulec, Illinois State University
Cu-Hullan Tsuyoshi McGivern, Akita International University

Available at all bookstores and online vendors
ISBN-10: 0996482016
ISBN-13: 978-0-9964820-1-1
Publisher: International Society for Language Studies, Inc.
Publication Date: 2017
Paperback Pages: 326; 14 Chapters
Average Price: $35 Paperback, $50 Hardcover

A publication of the International Society for Language Studies, Inc.

To learn more about ISLS and its mission, visit their website:

HTTP://WWW.ISLS.CO

ISLS retains a low membership fee that includes:
a quarterly journal, a weekly newsletter, and a reduced conference rate

www.ingramcontent.com/pod-product-compliance
Lightning Source LLC
Chambersburg PA
CBHW030432300426
44112CB00009B/967